VIRGIL

STUDIES IN LATIN LITERATURE
AND ITS INFLUENCE

Editors

D. R. Dudley and T. A. Dorey

CICERO

Chapters by J. P. V. D. Balsdon, M. L. Clarke, T. A. Dorey, A. E. Douglas, R. G. M. Nisbet, H. H. Scullard, G. B. Townend

LUCRETIUS

Chapters by D. R. Dudley, B. Farrington, O. E. Lowenstein, W. S. Maguinness, T. J. B. Spencer, G. B. Townend, D. E. W. Wormell

ROMAN DRAMA

Chapters by W. R. Chalmers, C. D. N. Costa, G. L. Evans, J. A. Hanson, A. Steegman, T. B. L. Webster, T. L. Zinn

LATIN HISTORIANS

Chapters by E. Badian, F. W. Walbank, T. A. Dorey, G. M. Paul, P. G. Walsh, E. A. Thompson, J. Campbell

VIRGIL

Chapters by M. Ayrton, B. Otis, A. J. Gossage, J. H. Whitfield, W. F. J. Knight, R. D. Williams, A. J. McKay, D. E. W. Wormell

VIRGIL

Chapters by

Michael Ayrton	Brooks Otis
A. J. Gossage	J. H. Whitfield
W. F. Jackson Knight	R. D. Williams
A. G. McKay	D. E. W. Wormell

Edited by

D. R. DUDLEY

LONDON

ROUTLEDGE & KEGAN PAUL

First published in 1969
by Routledge & Kegan Paul Ltd
Broadway House, 68–74, Carter Lane
London, E.C.4
Printed in Great Britain
by C. Tinling & Co. Ltd
Liverpool, London and Prescot
SBN 7100 6212 5

Contents

v

List of Plates

Introduction

THIS, the sixth volume of the series, is the first to be devoted to Virgil.
It will not be the last. Virgil himself, like Shakespeare, is inexhaustible,
a definitive book on him will never be written. On literature and art, his
influence has been the strongest, the most pervasive, the most enduring,
of any Greek or Roman author. Nor is the issue one that can be kept
within the bounds of scholarship. Virgil speaks directly to the human
heart: the reaction between the poet and his readers is of peculiar
intensity. In the last resort, we write about Virgil in order to come to
terms with ourselves.

The first two essays deal with a problem that we have only recently
begun to understand—that of Virgil's originality. For the *Eclogues*,
Professor Wormell shows how Virgil's ambition to be the Roman
Theocritus implies far more than translating Greek poetry into Latin.
The careful arrangement of the *Eclogues* Book has endowed it with an
artistic unity not to be found in Theocritus. Where Theocritus describes
vividly the countryside of Sicily or Cos, Virgil's poems are set in
Arcadia, a country outside space or time, whose trance-like landscape
can take on—but only fleetingly—the aspects of something we know.
It was Virgil, too, who infused it with that nostalgic and pensive air, in
which visions are seen but never realised—*nec quid speraret habebat*.
Professor Brooks Otis—who has perhaps done more than anyone else
in our time to establish a new view of Virgil—demonstrates the contrast
between Homeric and Virgilian epic, between the heroic code that
motivated Achilles and Ajax, and the *pietas* which had first claim on
Aeneas. The *Aeneid*, as he rightly insists, is a seamless robe: unlike the
Iliad, it cannot be broken down into *aristeia*, unlike the *Odyssey*, it has a
programme that rises above personal ends. In both the *Eclogues* and the
Aeneid, Virgil has used his Greek models not for imitation, but for
creative transformation.

The next three essays explore various aspects of Virgil's influence on literature. With the Flavian epic poets, Dr Gossage shows how, as so often, *le mieux est l'ennemi du bien*. Statius, Silius Italicus, and Valerius Flaccus, regarded Virgil with uncritical awe and imitated him all too faithfully. Most of their borrowings are mechanical and unapt: thus Scipio may be endowed with the qualities of Aeneas, but his use of them is fatally restricted because, historically, he cannot be sole leader of the Roman cause. But Silius made good use of Dido's curse as the driving force of Hannibal: and it is interesting to find that Valerius Flaccus used Dido and Aeneas for his Medea and Jason, thus reversing the loan that Virgil had once taken from Apollonius Rhodius. However, these poets are most interesting when they are most original, as when Statius works over the Jupiter of epic tradition to give him the features of Domitian. Professor Whitfield, it seems to me, puts the relationship of Dante and Virgil in a new light. The *lungo studio* and the *grande amore* are still there. So is the political affinity, in devotion to the destiny of the Roman Empire. So, too, is the common rôle of both poets as *scriba Dei* and *vates*. But the Virgil who is Dante's guide to the underworld is not what he professes to be, the poet who lived in the time of Augustus and the false gods—he is Dante's mouthpiece. And, in the end, the two great poets, though bound together, look in opposite directions—Virgil backwards to destiny fulfilled, Dante forwards to hopes unrealised. Mr Williams follows the fortunes of Virgil through the fluctuations of two centuries of English literary taste from the assured but blinkered approbation of Dryden, through the disparagement of the Romantics, to the rehabilitation of Tennyson and the mid-nineteenth century. It is a curious story, in striking contrast to that told by Professor McKay in the next essay. Here we see how three great painters—Poussin, Claude, and Turner—dealt with Virgilian landscape, each faithful to the original, but each in his own way. Here it would seem that the painters showed a sureness of taste and judgement that puts the literary critics to shame.

The last two essays—beyond the Cumaean Gates—form a self-contained section, devoted to Virgil's eschatology and its interpretation. Mr Jackson Knight's paper is posthumous: I am most grateful for the kindness of his brother, Professor G. Wilson Knight, and of Mr J. D. Christie, of the University of Glasgow, in placing it at my disposal and helping to prepare it for publication. I hope that its appearance will be taken as an act of *pietas* from my fellow-editor and myself towards a personal friend and a man who, in character and learning, might fairly be termed *homo Virgilianissimus*. Mr Michael Ayrton gives what is all too rare—a creative artist's account of the sources of his inspiration. He came to the myth of Daedalus by many paths, through the opera of Berlioz, through the numinous quality of the acropolis of Cumae, and through the encouragement of Jackson Knight. He has spent ten years on the interpretation, and indeed, the elaborations, of the myth. The results—powerful, sombre, enigmatic, startlingly relevant to our own situation—may be seen in the illustrations which follow his essay. They will surely stimulate many readers to see the originals for themselves.

Bibliographical references are given in the notes at the end of each article. Two general surveys must be mentioned here: G. E. Duckworth, *Classical World*, li (1957-8), 89 ff, and lvii (1963-4), 193 ff; R. G. Austin, *A Bibliography of Virgil* J.A.C.T. Paper No 1. (1963), and supplement, (1965). Since the excellent survey by R. D. Williams (*Virgil*, Greece and Rome, New Surveys in the Classics, No. 1, 1967) has appeared, it would be otiose to say anything here about recent trends in Virgilian scholarship.

D. R. DUDLEY

I

The Originality of the Eclogues
sic paruis componere magna solebam

D. E. W. WORMELL

PASTORAL had its roots in a Mediterranean tradition of folk-song, orally transmitted, and in peasant contests in singing such as are frequently encountered in simple agricultural communities. But 'a constant element in the pastoral as known to literature is the recognition of a contrast, implicit or expressed, between pastoral life and some more complex type of civilization.'[1] It is in fact the poetry of escape into a world where the strains and burdens of life are eased, and existence is closer to mother earth, simpler, less bewildering or frightening, more spontaneous, more natural. Homer in his description of Achilles' shield, the prototype of so many later ἐκφράσεις of real or imaginary works of art, presents a vision of human life in microcosm, based on balancing pictures of city and country in peace and war. The pastoral element is significantly introduced at the point of maximum contrast. The city at war, where the two herdsmen playing their pipes are cut down in the ambush, is balanced by the country at its most peaceful, seedtime and harvest lead on to the vintage, when the harvest-home is celebrated by a boy playing the lyre and singing the Linos-song (a dirge for the death of the shepherd-god Linos, symbolizing the passing of summer—dirges being integral to the pastoral). Even more moving is the scene where Hector despairingly nerves himself to face Achilles, and there floats into his mind the idyllic picture 'now it is not the time to dally with him from oak or rock, like lad and lass, as lad and lass hold dalliance with each other'. Hesiod too is in the pastoral tradition, as Virgil (or Cornelius Gallus) well knew, when he describes how the Muses appeared to him as he tended his flocks at the foot of

Helicon, gave him the rhapsode's staff, and breathed their inspiration into him.[2]

As a distinct literary form pastoral emerges in an environment where the pressure and tempo of life in a big city, the rigours of court or palace etiquette, the impact of private unhappiness and public indifference in a highly artificial social milieu drive men to seek relief, relaxation, and refreshment in flight into a simpler and less complicated existence, whether this has any real being or is wholly or in part a creature of fantasy. In classical Greece few writers or thinkers were in any doubt that the good life is lived in a city. Even Plato and Aristotle in planning the reform of the body politic, which clearly was critically ill in their day, do not dream of departing from the framework of the polis—γινομένη μὲν οὖν τοῦ ζῆν ἔνεκεν, οὖσα δὲ τοῦ εὖ ζῆν in the familiar formulation. But the foundation of Alexandria (corresponding to the rise of the hellenistic nation-state) meant a change in scale; the emergence of the cosmopolitan capital with its huge polyglot population, its colourful and jostling crowds, its complex of noble public buildings and mean slums, dwarfed the individual and brought the neuroses which have afflicted city-dwellers ever since and are still very much in evidence. And the legacy of Alexandria fell to Rome. Civilized man in the hellenistic age still lived in cities; but in his leisure moments he also sought to recapture the peace and serenity of mind which life in megalopolis inevitably destroyed. Some (like Lucretius) sought refuge in philosophy; others (like Propertius) in art. But the Romans were originally a race of peasant farmers and felt the pull of the land, whether it was the real countryside (and every Roman who could afford it had a country villa) or a countryside of the imagination. Many city-dwellers having escaped into rusticity began immediately to long for the town again; indeed the city-country tension characteristic of pastoral is built into the Roman way of life. Horace, as one would expect, found a middle way, residing by preference in the country, but not too far from Rome. His invitation to Maecenas is typical: *omitte mirari beatae/fumum et opes strepitumque Romae.* Rome is too dirty, too wealthy, too noisy, especially in the summer heat. But she is still *beata Roma.*[3]

In general pastoral is anchored in a timeless present, in a long summer day which may be interminable, and depicts a world populated by shepherds with their flocks and herds and by the familiar deities of the countryside, an idyllic landscape unmarred by war or violence or struggle, clouded only by the unhappinesses which human relationships bring, by the lover's jealousy of his rival, and by the distant darkness of death (Virgil chooses to end half of his Eclogues with the falling shades of night). At the same time this rustic paradise is displayed for the delectation of an urban reading public who half-patronizingly look to find in the treatment a polish to match their own and in the characterization a boorishness or ingenuousness to contrast with it. There is an obvious danger of losing contact with reality: art can lapse into artifice, artifice into artificiality. Sentimentality and pretentiousness are only one remove away; the château with a formalized village on its roof, the world of patched and powdered shepherdesses in hoop skirts, of bewigged courtiers masquerading as country swains, is perilously near. If the masters of pastoral escape these risks and successfully hold a balance between city sophistication and rural realism this is partly because they are helped by the form of pastoral itself. It is a kind of dramatic poetry, and as such invites with special force 'that willing suspension of disbelief for the moment, which constitutes poetic faith'. Yet the shepherds must be credible as shepherds if they are to hold the reader's attention. The world of pastoral is a masculine world. Even Amaryllis' incantations, degraded by Virgil to comprise only half an Eclogue, are put into the mouth of Alphesiboeus. (Theocritus ii is admittedly different, but it is hardly pastoral, the setting being apparently urban.) And the pastoral poem is normally quite short. The two longest Eclogues barely exceed a hundred lines each, the rest are briefer. The range of subject matter is, then, limited, and the reader's attention must be immediately captured and held. All this makes for the most complete dramatic realization of the characters possible. At the same time the city reading public was unlikely to be interested for long in shepherds as such; they wanted something more in accord with their own cultured sensibility. And pastoral is from the beginning a milieu in which the personal world of the poet obtrudes on the dramatic world of the characters, and the outside world obtrudes on the personal world of the poet. There is thus a strong tendency to be allusive, to suggest more than is immediately stated, and to invite allegorical interpretation. Theocritus and Virgil refused to move far in this direction, and it is misguided to interpret their

3

poems as *mascarades bucoliques* (though too many critics ancient and modern have fallen into this trap for the unwary), but their successors were not in general such disciplined artists, and the tradition became established that allegory is integral to pastoral. Given the circumstances in which he found himself, one can sympathize with Johnson's conviction that pastoral was played out in his day, that it 'wants that exaltation above common life which in tragic or heroic writings reconciles us to bold flights and daring figures', that it 'has nothing peculiar but its confinement to rural imagery, without which it ceases to be pastoral'.[4] Yet he should surely have thought again. The vitality of the pastoral tradition speaks against him, and the fact that Virgil, Spenser, and Milton chose this medium for the expression of their unfolding poetic genius, before venturing on epic. He might also have reflected on the imagery of the twenty-third psalm, so deeply rooted in the consciousness of the Jewish and Christian worlds; and have recognized how much its pastoral setting contributes to the gospel story, and especially to its beginning which tells of a Divine Child born in a stable in the presence of oxen, while shepherds abiding in the field keeping watch over their flock by night were given an angelic prophecy of peace on earth and good will toward men. For all Johnson's destructive criticism the pastoral lived on in English literature, gaining new life from Shelley and Arnold, and chosen by Yeats for his *Shepherd and Goatherd,* a poem in memory of Robert Gregory. Nor can one fail to see the influence of pastoral on the novels of George Eliot and Thomas Hardy. No doubt this vitality owes something to the close observation of nature and mystical communion with its powers which characterized the poets of the Lake School. But pastoral itself is inspired and ultimately sustained by one of the deepest and most satisfying of human emotions, the sense of man's age-old kinship and harmony with the soil he tills and the beasts he tends.

Theocritus, two hundred years Virgil's senior, is much the strongest literary influence on the Eclogues. His career reflects many characteristic features of life in the hellenistic age. Born at Syracuse, he emigrated to the eastern Mediterranean, and there is no evidence that he ever revisited his native land (though he would clearly have liked to do so, and tried to secure the support of Hiero II). He was familiar with Alexandria and with Cos, and was almost certainly patronized by the court of Ptolemy Philadelphus, perhaps by Ptolemy himself. His art derives in part from folk-song and in part from the literary tradition of his native Sicily extending from Stesichorus to Sophron; but he owes most to contemporary literature—to new comedy, mime, the epyllion, and the epigram. His poems were designated Idylls (meaning probably 'vignettes'); only one of his four greatest works is in fact a pastoral. He realized that the hexameter could be used as the medium for an art which is essentially dramatic and lyric. He has the born dramatist's ear for the cadence and idiom of the spoken word, and brings his characters vividly to life through their dialogue. It seems likely that he deliberately chooses to write an artificial Doric to add a touch of rusticity to a medium which was in danger of appearing too accomplished and sophisticated. Certainly his realism is always tempered by good taste and avoids the coarseness of mime almost completely.

The pastoral poems are probably early and may well have made his reputation. The shepherds and goatherds with their abundant leisure, their singing-contests, their loves, their rustic banter and laughter, together with the archetypal pastoral shepherd, Daphnis, and the grotesque Polyphemus (both perhaps recalled by Theocritus from Sicilian traditions he had learnt in his youth) are set in a hilly countryside, sunlit, well-watered, with verdant trees and meadows, observed with a precision and recaptured with a feeling for the scents and sounds and sights of the landscape unparalleled in Greek literature. Plants, cattle, sheep, goats, dogs, even insects come intensely to life, and although the form is dramatic the setting is realized no less sharply than the human actors who occupy the foreground. It is precisely in this blend of dramatic and descriptive poetry that the secret of Theocritus' art is to be found.[5]

Servius informs us that Virgil had before him a collection of ten bucolic poems by Theocritus, and it is not unreasonable to suppose that this is why Virgil wrote neither more nor less than ten eclogues. The poems concerned were pretty certainly Idylls i and iii–xi. It is quite likely that this is the edition alluded to in the extant epigram by Artemidorus, an approximate contemporary of Virgil; but the evidence is inconclusive. To the source of Suidas' life of Theocritus, these were the only Theocritean poems of undisputed authenticity. In fact ix is certainly, and viii is probably not by Theocritus. This, however, merely goes to show that his poetry won an immediate success and that more or less able imitators early attempted the genre. Virgil quite clearly knew other Idylls of Theocritus (notably ii, xviii, and xxiv); but apart from his close study of ii, which inspired the second part of the eighth Eclogue, the vast bulk of his echoes and adaptations comes from the pastoral poems.[6]

Virgil's debt to Theocritus is almost incalculable. It has been said with justification that 'the Eclogues are in form and even in substance a closer reproduction of a Greek original than any other branch of Latin literature with the exception of the comedy of Terence'.[7] Virgil's Muses are Sicilian, his verse Syracusan. His shepherds have Greek (mostly Theocritean) names. Even in Eclogue 7, set beside the Mincius, it is Meliboeus who listens to the contest between the Arcadians, Thyrsis and Corydon, adjudicated by Daphnis. The dramatic form, the metre, the slanging- and singing-matches of the shepherds and goatherds, with their amoebean balance and refrains, many of their themes and much of their emotional range find their source and inspiration in Theocritus. Equally profound is Virgil's debt in style and treatment; his blend of naiveté and subtlety, of realism and romanticism owes much to the Idylls. In the four most Theocritean Eclogues (2, 3, 7, 8) there is a borrowing or echo, conscious or unconscious, literal or ironic, from Theocritus on average once every five lines. There is no doubt at all that Virgil regarded himself, and wished others to regard him as the Roman Theocritus. At the same time the Eclogues avoid the effect of pastiche. Virgil in fact creates a new artistic unity, and contrives to write with a most attractive spontaneity, freshness, and lyricism. How is this achieved?

One of the lessons Virgil may have learnt from Theocritus is that a book of poetry should add up to more than the sum of the individual poems. Theocritus of course far transcended the range of pastoral (two of his masterpieces are beautifully realized portraits of women viewed in their tragic and comic aspects). He contrives to present an impressionistic but brilliant picture of a cross-section of city and country life in the hellenistic age. His book of poetry was appropriately designated as Idylls (it is in fact doubtful if ἐιδύλλιον can be used in the singular). But there is no evidence that the arrangement of his collected poems was other than haphazard and arbitrary. The Eclogues on the other hand are not only the assembled works of the youthful Virgil, but also his unified vision of life, already tinged with melancholy, and conditioned of course by the conventions and limitations of pastoral, but with a power to delight and move the reader which is enhanced because the individual poems were placed in their present order by the poet himself.

It seems likely that the chronological order of composition was 2, 3, 5, 9, 1, 6, 4, 8, 7, 10. In assembling the Eclogues into their present order Virgil no doubt put 1 first because it directly honours Octavian, and placed, and indeed composed 10 last, as directly honouring Gallus. 4, 5, 6, would be grouped centrally; 4 and 6 as dedicated to Pollio, and to Varus and Gallus, respectively, and as fitted by a certain shared dignity of style (witness the similarity of their opening lines) to occupy the centre of gravity of the book, being separated, for *variatio*, by 5 which honours Daphnis-Caesar. For the rest Virgil seems to have aimed at formal *variatio*, dramatic Eclogues with dialogue (1, 3, 5, 7, 9) alternating with narrative Eclogues, in which the poet speaks in person (2, 4, 6, 8, 10). He will also have felt that the early Theocritean Eclogues 2 and 3, should be balanced by the late exercises in the manner of Theocritus, Eclogues 7 and 8; while 1, 5, 9, which are chronologically close to each other and have affinities in theme are spaced at equal intervals through the book. One can continue this analysis further, and argue that Virgil composed the later Eclogues to round off a pattern which had shaped or was shaping itself in his mind. But apart from 10, clearly designed to stand last and composed last, there is no supporting evidence. Whatever may have underlain the design of the Aeneid, it is most unlikely that Virgil composed the Eclogues in accordance with a blue print, real or imaginary. Serious-minded critics are in some danger of taking the Virgil of the Eclogues too earnestly. Twice in the Eclogues and once in the Georgics he uses *ludere* to describe his youthful achievement as a poet.[8] Quite apart from the possibility of self-depreciation, Virgil is no doubt contrasting his petty poetizing with the impressive military and political achievements of Octavian and others who were winning and consolidating an empire. But the idea of 'playfulness' is not wholly absent. Horace surveying the style of the Eclogues can say

molle atque facetum
Vergilio adnuerunt gaudentes rure Camenae.

7

The critical terminology is not precisely defined, but the probable meaning of *molle atque facetum* is 'delicacy and humour'. Though direct imitation of Idyll vii is infrequent in the Eclogues, their tone derives largely from it, and one may fairly apply to Virgil Theocritus' description of Lycidas:

$$καί\ μ'\ ἀτρέμας\ σεσαρώς\ ἔιπε$$
$$ὄμματι\ μειδιόωντι,\ γέλας\ δέ\ οἱ\ εἴχετο\ χείλευς.$$

There is a great deal of quiet comedy in these poems; the comic vision of life balances and complements the tragic vision. Virgil's poetic imagination and sensibility reconcile and harmonize the two into a deeply satisfying unity.

It is natural to begin a closer study of the Eclogues with the four most Theocritean poems, 2 and 3, which are the earliest in the book, and 8 and 7, which, apart from 10, are the latest. 2 and 3 are in a sense programme pieces. Each includes a tactful (only half-explicit) defence of the poet for essaying (*audax iuuenta*) the pastoral mode. It is quite likely that the two were separately circulated by Virgil amongst his circle of friends and criticized by them. But the group of four pieces belongs closely together. 2 and 7 are set in the timeless pastoral world, in 3 and 8 the contemporary scene obtrudes in the person of Pollio. Formally 2 balances 8, both being cast in narrative form, Virgil himself being the narrator. 3 is linked to 7, both being amoebean contests, but whereas 3 plunges *in medias res*, 7 has a graceful introduction put into the mouth of Meliboeus, who witnesses the contest and gives the verdict of the judge Daphnis; the form is in fact very close to dramatic narrative. In 8 the form *is* dramatic narrative, though the poem largely consists in the balancing songs of Damon and Alphesiboeus; a technique owing something to 2, which after the stage has been set in the opening five lines is in fact an agonized soliloquy. The amoebean unit in 3 is of two lines, in 7 of four; in 8 Alphesiboeus answers Damon in balancing poems of forty-six lines. The contest in 3 ends as a draw, in 7 with Corydon being declared victor, in 8 with silence. All this is typical Virgilian patterning and *variatio*. But for all their homogeneity, and although the gap in time between the composition of the earliest and the latest of these poems cannot be more than three years, it is clear that there is an evolution, away from the dramatic towards the narrative, a growing complexity and subtlety of structure, a more conscious and more disciplined control over the medium, but bought at the cost of some sacrifice of spontaneity and lyricism.

Virgil's earliest Eclogue is a portrayal of hopeless love, cast in the form of a dramatic monologue. Corydon roams restlessly abroad in the heat of an Italian summer day and voices his passion and despair. For all its naturalness (*incondita*) the poem is carefully constructed. The stage is set in the opening five lines. Corydon's lament leads directly into a new attempt to win Alexis, which is the core of the poem, and when he realizes that this is in vain he relapses again into lamentation. The two plaints (6–18, 56–68) balance exactly. The second with its symbolism of the setting sun, as contrasted with the high noon of the first, brings the moment of truth with the words *a Corydon Corydon quae te dementia cepit*, and in the final five lines (balancing the opening) Corydon finds the beginnings of a peace which is not wholly that of exhaustion. The central section may well have inspired Marlowe's 'Come live with me and be my love, and we will all the pleasures prove, that hills and valleys, dale and field, and all the craggy mountains yield.' The fabric of the whole is knit together most skilfully of elements deriving from Theocritus, from Idylls xi and iii in particular. Yet even formally Virgil is poles apart from anything in his Theocritean models. The Cyclops and the rather boorish shepherd of iii cannot discipline their thoughts which ramble endlessly on. Corydon's plea moves to a controlled climax describing with almost Keatsian sensuousness the colour, texture, and fragrance of his rustic presents. Moreover the Cyclops and the shepherd-lover are both grotesque; their approaches rouse our amusement but there is too much of Caliban in the one, and too much of the Yahoo in the other, for us to feel emotional involvement, let alone sympathy. They are observed with ironic detachment. But Corydon's sensibility is almost as great as Virgil's, and his suffering (*nec quid speraret habebat*) is realized from within. In this sense, but in no other, the ancient commentators were right when they said that Corydon *is* Virgil.[9]

Eclogue 3 seems designed as a distillation of the quintessence of Theocritus' amoebean contests. It is modelled on Idylls iv, v, and viii, with some echoes of i and vii. In the opening encounter between the shepherds Menalcas and Damoetas, which sets the scene, Virgil draws freely on Theocritus, while avoiding the cut and thrust of the stichomythia of iv and the rather protracted bickering of v. He also hints at, rather than reproduces, the coarseness of Theocritus' herds, though beginning with the calculated rusticity of *cuium pecus*. Everything is dramatic, crisp, and vigorous, with Virgil gaining in point and attack from his economy, and with his characters expressing themselves with enough wit and bite to enlist the interest of Milton and Dryden. Virgil avoids formal patterning here, since spontaneity is aimed at and achieved, and the amoebean contest will impose its own pattern on the second half of the poem. The effect on the reader is to convey something of the exhilaration of the spring day evoked as the background of the contest by the adjudicator Palaemon (*nunc formosissimus annus*). The themes in the singing match range over love, literature, and life in the country, ending with a pair of riddles, but the unifying theme is *amor*. It is Pollio's love of the rustic muse which motivates the mention of his name; it is love in the final section that causes the bull to waste away. Part of the fascination of this poem is the way in which Virgil hints at themes which are to be important in his later development. Thus Pollio's name evokes a mention of the Golden Age anticipating Eclogue 4, where they are eternally linked; the chill snake lurking in the grass reminds us of Eurydice; the yoking of foxes and mating of he-goats looks forward to Eclogue 8. And the wooden cups described in the middle of the first half of the poem, may, as we shall see, have special significance. At the end Palaemon announces that he cannot judge between the competitors, and implies that he is himself distracted by love. In fact the thoughts that have been flitting through his mind during the contest must have been in tune with the rival songs, but he has not been listening. 'What is encountered here is that characteristic blend of naturalism and artificiality, of ingenuousness and sophistication, which gives the Eclogues their peculiar flavour and special charm.'[10]

Eclogue 8 faces squarely the challenge of adapting to a Latin medium Theocritus' two supreme masterpieces in the tragic mode, Thyrsis' song of Daphnis from Idyll i, and Simaetha's incantation from Idyll ii. Virgil recasts these poems in the form of an amoebean singing match with almost exactly balancing songs of equal length, each held together by a refrain. The burden, going back to the beginnings of Mediterranean song was acclimatized in bucolic poetry by Theocritus. Its effect was partly to suggest in hexameters the structure of sung verse, but chiefly to give a ritualistic undertone suitable for an invocation of the Muses, or for introducing a magically binding spell.[11] There was an obvious danger that diptych composition, with the juxtaposition of two highly dramatic, even melodramatic episodes, allied to Virgil's power imaginatively to identify himself with his characters would destroy the unity of the poem. In fact he goes out of his way to reduce the dramatic impact. He dedicates the Eclogue to Pollio by whom, he hints, its theme was suggested. He makes it clear that this is a *certamen* (though there is no judge) and stresses the correspondences between the two songs, and their common theme of love's jealousy. Above all he casts it in the form of a narrative, so that the singers do not plunge *in medias res*, and are not called upon in turn by an adjudicator, but Damon is introduced by the poet, and it is the Muses who are summoned to rehearse Alphesiboeus' song. Conington's comment 'Damon need not be supposed to be singing of his own despair, but merely to be performing in character, as Alphesiboeus evidently is' seems fully justified. The poem in fact gives Virgil's report of Damon's account of his passion. Nor should the opening lines of the Eclogue be forgotten with its Orphic and unrealistic setting, and its hint that the power of song is Virgil's theme, a theme also stressed in the second paragraph.

Each of the narrative songs moves rapidly and with great economy to a mounting climax. In the first the progress of the affair from its idyllic beginning to final self-destruction is vividly and impressionistically conveyed. Damon's emotional disturbance finds a counterpart in natural anarchy and in Medea's unnatural jealousy, and culminates in suicide. The balancing song shows Amaryllis deserted by her lover trying to win him back through magical binding spells. Nature's sympathy is again made manifest in the simile of the heifer restless for her mate. Amaryllis' growing desperation drives her to think of murder, but her spells work and restore her lover just as she is thinking of having recourse to poison. In both poems the Theocritean original is very freely remodelled. Throughout it is *carmen* and *carmina* which are the emotive words; it is well to remember that they never quite lose their meaning of 'magical formulas' in Latin, and Virgil introduces the jingles, characteristic of ancient *carmina*, with great skill into his poem. It is Virgil's early narrative style at its best, lyrical, disciplined, supple.

Eclogue 7 is Virgil's final treatment of the amoebean contest. The stage is set in strong subtle strokes with Meliboeus introduced as narrator of the contest between Corydon and Thyrsis, adjudicated by Daphnis. The subsequent contest has been described as a bucolic *ars poetica*; it does in fact contain a model of Virgil's ideal of what pastoral should be (Corydon), and examples, amounting on occasion to parody, of what it should not be (Thyrsis). 'Every quatrain of Thyrsis contains one or more weaknesses. Weaknesses of character, which are all that many editors admit, may be irrelevant; weaknesses of versification and weaknesses of sense are not.' Thyrsis, however, is deficient not only in versification and in sense, but also in sensibility. Disrespectful towards gods and men, arrogantly complacent, with a boorish vulgarity capable of broad indecency, he sings verses that are a tasteless caricaturist's coarsening of Corydon's fine and delicate art. Here, as often in the Eclogues, there is change and development of character as the poem proceeds. Thyrsis is learning from Corydon's example as the contest draws to its close. Even his uncouthness is softened by love: Virgil was soon to write *omnia uincit amor*.[12]

It is unlikely that more than three years had elapsed between the writing of 3, 4, and 8, 7,; but it is not wholly fanciful to see a growth and development, a turning from the dramatic towards the narrative, an enhanced ability to control a more complicated and more subtly articulated composition. Virgil had suffered a good deal in these years. He had also deepened and matured as an artist. In the first part of Eclogue 3 there is the ἔκφρασις of the beech cups, which Menalcas is prepared to stake on the outcome of the contest, and of the balancing pair owned by Damoetas. It is freely modelled on the famous description of a wooden cup in Theocritus' first Idyll. Theocritus in the Alexandrine manner imitates on a small scale Homer's description of the shield of Achilles, and makes the figures on his cup an allegory of life. The woman with the two lovers, balancing the boy with the two sly foxes represent city and country at play; while the aged fisherman centrally placed symbolizes the world at work. Virgil's cups are treated impressionistically (otherwise the balance of the poem would be disturbed) but they characteristically illustrate subjectively his own personal and poetic world rather than objectively symbolize

the world outside. The figures—Conon and the unnamed astrono-
mer, and Orpheus with the spellbound trees, are not chosen at
random. Virgil's range of subjects in the Theocritean Eclogues is
very much that covered by Corydon and Thyrsis in Eclogue 7:
poetry, the countryside, love. But he is already raising his eyes to
the heavens, and is already conscious that as a poet he has been
endowed with more than human powers and has especial responsibilities. He has come to realize also that his genius lies in descriptive and narrative rather than in dramatic poetry. He is already
looking forward not only to the other Eclogues, but also to the
Georgics and even the Aeneid.

The action of all four of these Eclogues takes place on a long
summer day in the pastoral present. The sun may as we have seen
decline in the heavens as the poem proceeds, but otherwise this is
a timeless world, and this is true even of the songs within a song
of Eclogue 8. What of the landscape? Theocritus idealized a
realistically observed Sicilian or Coan countryside as the background to his pastoral idylls. Virgil in his early Eclogues seems to
be merely recreating the Theocritean scene. Corydon's lambs in
Eclogue 2 wander *Siculis in montibus,* Virgil's Muses like his verse are
Sicilian and Syracusan. Yet in the later Eclogues he translates
ἄρχετε βουκολικᾶς ἀοιδᾶς by *incipe* Maenalios *uersus,* his shepherds are *Arcades,* and Eclogue 10 is actually situated at the foot
of Maenalus and Lycaeus. All the more bewildering to find in 7 an
allusion to the Mincius in an Arcadian landscape. In 5 we encounter lions (there being no lions in Sicily, as Conington observes),
in 8 we encounter lynxes (but this is in a semi-magical landscape).
We are in fact outside space as well as time, in Arcady rather than
Arcadia, and Eclogue 10 describes Gallus' adventures in wonderland. Virgil's landscape exists only in his poetic imagination, but
this is sufficiently vivid to bring the whole to autonomous life.
No doubt his picture derives from memories of childhood happiness, the golden moments which linger in most men's recollection,
random and arbitrary, and, no doubt idealised, yet evoked with
extraordinary sharpness and clarity.

> There was a time when meadow, grove, and stream,
> The earth, and every common sight,
> To me did seem
> Apparelled in celestial light,
> The glory and the freshness of a dream.

Part of the charm of the Eclogues lies precisely in their ability to recapture the child's vision—Virgil's unforgettable picture of a boy falling in love is seen through the eyes of an adolescent not yet in his teens. Scenes are vividly realized, but only for a moment, the light tends to shimmer, shift and waver, and they dissolve mysteriously or melt into something else. Walking in the hills on a day of tenuous sunlit cloud one moves in a radiant mist that obscures all but the foreground though that is bathed in light. From time to time the veil parts revealing distant views of astonishing brilliance and luminosity; but soon the curtain of mist closes again dazzling but unfathomable. In this trance-like landscape most worldly values become meaningless or irrelevant, even the human characters become such stuff as dreams are made on. In Eclogue 10 Gallus is at the same moment a soldier and a shepherd, Virgil speaks in person but also as a goatherd, the gods associate readily with the human characters, and Gallus laments his lot in a cento of his own poetry. There is an obvious danger that such a setting will result in a picture that is wholly blurred. But though this may be a child's vision, it is described by a poet of exquisite sensibility and extreme accomplishment, whose instinct for orderly composition and for clarity never fails.[13]

From Hesiod onwards the ancients had been familiar with the idealized picture of a remote age of peace, plenty, and rustic simplicity, when the gods mingled freely with men, who did not need the protection of walled cities. The similarity between this picture and Virgil's idyllic pastoral world leaps to the eye; it may seem natural to merge and blend the two, as Virgil did. Each derives strength from the other, and joined together they were to catch the imagination of Augustan poets in general, and of Tibullus in particular. It is a part of Virgil's achievement here that he is giving new life to myths which had withered under the impact of Greek rationalism. His vision owes something to Lucretius, as indeed does his whole picture of idyllic carefree country life. But it is essentially his own. He creates a world in which all living creatures, divine or human, animal or vegetable, live together in mutual sympathy and harmony. Nor is this limited to the animate world. Mountains and rocks weep for Gallus' sufferings; forest-clad hills and crags rejoice that Daphnis has been deified. Project the pastoral world into the past and it readily fuses with traditional accounts of the golden age. Viewed in its tragic aspect it becomes a vision of innocence betrayed and paradise lost, and could be symbolically represented in the deaths of Daphnis or Adonis, cut off in the flower of their youth. Project the pastoral world into the future and it becomes a prophecy of the return of Saturn's reign. Viewed in its tragic aspect it shows a cycle of disaster following inevitably on renewal in accordance with laws the gods themselves cannot modify. But in general Virgil's vision of the golden age is assimilated to the timeless present of his pastoral world. Viewed in its tragic aspect it now becomes a representation of the unhappiness which men or gods bring on themselves (mostly through ill-starred love). *Floribus Austrum perditus et liquidis immisi fontibus apros.* But great events in the outside world may cast shadows so long that they reach even into the summer sunshine of pastoral. And the city-country tension integral to pastoral (*Pallas quas condidit arces ipsa colat; nobis placeant ante omnia siluae*) may culminate in the outside world bursting violently into the world of the countryside and shattering its peace.

In Eclogue 5 Menalcas and Mopsus meet and interchange compliments in a charmingly drawn Theocritean setting. It is as if the poet were at pains to balance the gathering confusion ensuing on the murder of Julius Caesar by his own clarity and lucidity. Virgil must have been acutely aware of the storm clouds massing on the horizon even of the pastoral world. He finds a symbol for chaos in the death of Daphnis, freely modelled on Theocritus Idyll i, and for the promise which the future still holds in the picture of the deified Daphnis, which seems to be largely original in concept, although there are, as usual, brief echoes of Theocritus from time to time. The poem closes with an exchange of presents and compliments, and a broad hint that Menalcas is to be identified with Virgil. The core of the poem lies in the two exactly balancing songs of Daphnis' death and of Daphnis' deification. All nature joins to mourn his passing; the nymphs weep, Pales and Apollo desert the fields; the harvests fail; finally a mound is raised above him with the epitaph which with narcissistic sensibility he had devised in praise of his own beauty. In the answering song all nature joins in rejoicing at his apotheosis; Pan, the Dryads, the shepherds dance for joy; the golden age returns; the worship of Daphnis is integrated with the cult of the nymphs (from one of whom traditionally he was born) and with the *Ambarvalia*. There is no doubt that Caesar is here largely equated with Daphnis, just as Virgil is with Menalcas. This is very much in the pastoral convention. Difficulties arise only if the reader is over-literal and presses the equation too far. The Eclogue is then Virgil's announcement of political allegiance to Caesar dead, and, by implication, to Caesar's living heir. It is, however, still set in the timeless world of pastoral, and as such is somewhat lacking in immediacy and urgency. But events were soon to break in upon the idyllic peace here represented and destroy it for ever.[14]

Behind Eclogues 9 and 1 there lies an intensely painful personal experience. It is plain that after the Perusine war Cremona was punished by the confiscation of much of her territory, and that Mantua also suffered when Cremona's resources proved insufficient. The distasteful task of land allocation was entrusted by Octavian to Alfenus Varus. Cornelius Gallus was made responsible for taxing such of the Transpadane towns as were not punished by confiscation. It is clear that Virgil's farm was threatened. He appealed to Octavian (the case may well have been argued against Varus by Gallus). The outcome seems to have been to leave a three-mile strip around Mantua (in which Virgil's farm fell) undisturbed, while the rest of the confiscations were confirmed. The earlier stages of the crisis are reflected in Eclogue 9—Moeris and Menalcas had come near to losing their lives at the violent hands of the new settlers on their land. In Eclogue 1 Virgil records his emotions after he had met with at least a partial success, and had been confirmed in possession of his land.[15]

Eclogue 9 has clear links with 5, as the verbal echoes show. Moreover the new courtesy and gentleness in the relationship between the actors in the bucolic drama already manifest in 5 (and attributable partly to the identification more or less complete of Virgil with Menalcas—much as Theocritus shows country-life at its most sympathetic in Idyll vii, where he is identified with Simichidas), continues in 9, largely concerned as it is with Menalcas' poetry and experiences, though here the whole is tinged with Virgilian melancholy. The theme of the two discouraged countrymen going on their way to the town together, and finding some solace in each other's company and in Menalcas' songs doubtless shows that Virgil, shaken by the events which have befallen him, is stressing that friendship and poetry are among the things he can cling to even in his darkest hours. The landscape is imaginary, blended of elements drawn from personal memory and from literature; but the Italian names *Mantua uae miserae nimium uicina Cremonae* are wrung from Virgil like a cry of pain. Of the quotations from Menalcas' poems the first is a close translation of Theocritus, the second (for which a preference is indicated) is part of an appeal to Varus on behalf of Mantua—as urgent and immediate a reaction to the real world as is possible in pastoral, the third is a free adaptation of Theocritus in Virgil's later manner, the fourth addressed to Daphnis as the typical shepherd, describes him as watching the heavens and observing Caesar's star—a conscious variant of 5, but surely a specific allusion to it. It is clear that we have here an outline of Virgil's poetic development, with the key themes of the heavens and the Muses very much in evidence. Caesar's death had been followed by his apotheosis, and Caesar could be worshipped in 5 as a beneficent power. The symbol of his deification was his star, and at its appearance the cornfields and vineyards flourished. What was wanted, however, was an avatar, a divine saviour manifest on earth. Virgil is already half-conscious that his mission is to announce Caesar's heir as the divine youth who is to bring again the age of peace. The poet is no longer merely a poet, he is a prophet. Even in 5 he is still *diuinus poeta*; here in 9 he is described by implication as *uates*, the prophet of the greatness and grandeur of Rome, whose destiny is linked with that of Caesar's house.

Eclogue 1 is a break-through into a new dimension transcending the previous limits of pastoral. The poem is most carefully constructed moving to a climax thematically and poetically with the mention of the *iuuenis* who is worshipped by Tityrus as a god, who gave him his freedom and secured for him the possession of his land.[16] It is Virgil's manifesto of allegiance to the new régime and with the introduction of the divine youth centrally placed in the poem a glimpse is afforded of the historical mission and the majestic scale of the Empire. The only liberty that meant anything to Virgil was the liberty to write his poetry, and what Tityrus is implying here is surely that Octavian offered Virgil his protection and patronage. To say this is not of course to suggest that Virgil is fully identified with Tityrus (any more than he is with Menalcas); but it remains true that Tityrus represents the small farmers who were Virgil's neighbours and on occasion Virgil himself. The greatness of Rome, not so much a city as The City, is set against the simplicity and peace of the countryside, and the two are to some extent reconciled in the reconciliation between Tityrus and the *iuuenis*. So too the happiness of Tityrus secure on his small farm in its idyllically realized setting is balanced by the misery of Meliboeus, whose fate is exile and whose beloved flock is suffering along with him. The melancholy opening, most skilfully constructed and with glimpses of the familiar landscape which Meliboeus is leaving for ever yields to a mood of gratitude and rejoicing in which Meliboeus himself joins (the praises of the countryside secured to Tityrus with its barren soil but blessed climate, its soothing shade and sounds, are indeed spoken by him). But this gives place to gathering depression, following immediately on the mention of the divine youth, and motivated by the realization that the extent of Rome's dominion is also the extent over which the hapless exile may have to wander. Here the tone changes to asperity, and in the bitter echo of Eclogue 9 momentarily verges on satire. Tityrus' human sympathy and kindness bring mitigation as evening falls. Virgil shows a new constructive power, a subtler control of the ebb and flow of emotion in a poem which has far outdistanced the traditional limits of pastoral. The scenery indeed is still blended into unity only by the power of his imagination; but the outside world is now fully admitted into the private world of the poet, modifying and enlarging it. The characters are still shepherds, and their dialogue, idealized but with glimpses of rusticity, is skilfully contrived. But by linking together Rome's imperial destiny, the young and divine ruler who is to contribute to its fulfilment, and the fate of the countryside of Italy in a single poetic vision, Virgil grows to his full stature as a *uates*. The prophet, however, is one who sees not only what is, but also what was and is to come. *Paulo maiora canamus.*

In the opening of Eclogue 6 Virgil pays tribute to Varus in a delicate *recusatio*. He had meant to write of epic themes in praise of his patron's exploits, but Apollo plucked him by the ear and told him that his sheep should be fat but his poem thin. Yet he writes at his patron's prompting and honours his name in simple bucolic verse. The dedication has been brushed on one side as perfunctory, but it is no more so than the equally graceful words addressed to Pollio in Eclogue 8. Virgil now launches into the story of Silenus surprised in a drunken slumber by the shepherds Chromis and Mnasyllus, aided and abetted by the nymph Aigle, and made their prisoner. To win his freedom he has to sing, and his song, magical in its divine beauty, Orphic in its power to enchant the listeners, fills the rest of the poem. His choice of themes is fascinating and obviously significant. He opens in Lucretian vein with the beginnings of the world and traverses the themes of the Golden Age, Prometheus, Pyrrha, Hylas, and a series of *Amores,* before digressing to describe how Gallus received from Linus in the presence of the Muses the pipes once played by Hesiod. There followed the stories of Scylla, Tereus, and Philomela, all the songs in short that Apollo sang by the Eurotas, until evening stills Silenus' voice. There is a clear similarity between the first sequence of themes and the opening of Ovid's *Metamorphoses.* How are we to explain the apparently arbitrary selection of subjects? The theory that Virgil is here summarizing the contents of a series of epyllia by his friend Cornelius Gallus has been much criticized, not least because it implies that Gallus, who was still young, had a very large output of poetry considering his busy public career. It is, however, to be noted that according to Servius, Gallus translated Euphorion into Latin (the Grynean grove being specifically mentioned in this context). Now amongst Euphorion's poems were two entitled *Hesiodus* and *Hyacinthus.* This does fit in remarkably well with 6, 70 and 6, 82–83. And if Euphorion's *Hesiodus* was modelled on Hesiod's *Catalogus* this would help to explain why so many of the myths of the sixth Eclogue are mentioned in the fragments of Hesiod. It would not be unreasonable to suppose that Gallus found time to translate Euphorion; and Ovid could well have taken Euphorion's *Hesiodus* or Gallus' version as his source in the opening of the *Metamorphoses.* Such a theory does presuppose that Gallus, Varus, and Virgil were close friends, but this is perfectly possible. Although the songs sung show humanity slipping into gathering chaos, the genial personality of Silenus dominates the poem. In so far as the Eclogue gives a tragic vision of human destiny, it is not to be taken too seriously.[17]

At first blush Eclogue 4 has little obvious connection with the other Eclogues. Here more than anywhere else Virgil is a prophet foretelling the future. And he uses the language of prophecy consciously breaking with his normal bucolic style. But in fact the prophecy is of the return of the Golden Age, which is precisely the idealized world of pastoral. And his style on closer scrutiny reveals itself as a sublimation of Virgil's style in the other Eclogues; no doubt because 'oracles derive from a remote past . . . and draw much of their inspiration from early folk poetry. . . . It is a literary genre close to the earth, rough and coarse in tone, yet vigorous and with an underlying sanity and even wisdom'. All this has of course been refined and purified by Virgil, but his poem remains oracular. The setting is the consulship of Pollio, and this is the one Eclogue that can be dated with some precision. If, as is likely, Pollio had asked for a poem on his consulship, he must have been surprised at the response. Virgil is inspired by a Sibylline oracle foretelling that now

> The world's great age begins anew,
> The golden years return.

This is to be associated with the birth of a miraculous and divine child in whose lifetime the process will be consummated, and history will have retraced its course to its beginnings: *redeunt Saturnia regna*. A cardinal characteristic of the oracular style is ambiguity. Virgil is at pains to conceal the identity of the boy's parents; but it is plain that in some sense he comes from heaven. It is foretold that he is to rule over a world at peace, but it has been pacified *patriis uirtutibus*. Indeed it is far from clear what actions on his part Virgil hopes to celebrate. The world is returning to primeval simplicity because it is fated to do so. As he grows to manhood wars and their causes will die away, and universal peace, unlimited leisure, and general happiness will ensue, with gods and men freely associating together. As *Saturnus rediuiuus* the young ruler would in fact face an existence not unlike that of the Epicurean gods. In one aspect he symbolizes the aspirations of humanity for peace and plenty in a war-weary world.

It was natural for the Christians to take this poem as a prophecy of the coming of Christ. Virgil foretells the birth of a divine saviour, who on growing to manhood shall have dominion over all peoples in a pacified world. His stress on the child's mother, and suggestion of a divine father is also significant. And much of his imagery echoes that of the Old Testament. But Virgil anchors his poem firmly in the year of Pollio's consulship, and announces that the child is to be born in that year. If we consider the sequence of Eclogues 5, 9, and 1, with its evolving consciousness of Caesar as the divine saviour of the Roman world, the miraculous child must be connected with the house of Caesar. This is true even if the child is to be interpreted symbolically. But the imagery is surely too concrete to make it possible to sustain such an interpretation; Virgil has a very human (though also divine) child in mind. Beyond this he was not prepared to go. If a son had been born to Octavian and Scribonia, and if he had proved an enlightened prince, no doubt Virgil would have regarded this as the fulfilment of his prophecy. If Octavia had borne a son after her marriage to Antony, he too might have been regarded as the divine saviour, though this is less likely.[18]

This is in many ways the most eclectic of Virgil's poems. Epicurean, Stoic, Platonic, and neo-Pythagorean elements are blended together, and there are echoes of Homer, Hesiod, Catullus and Lucretius. Yet the whole is fused together by the enthusiasm and apocalyptic intensity of what is clearly a moment of insight, an emotional and spiritual experience in which the hopes and fears of a disturbed and revolutionary age inspire a lyrical and ecstatic vision of the promise still latent in the future. The music of Virgil's pastoral style, with its slow-moving and simply-linked sentences, its subtle echoes, and its patterning of assonance, alliteration, and rhyme, here becomes so compelling as to be almost hypnotic in its impact on the reader—we join Virgil in a trance-like world, though our dreams are soothing. It is the world of the inspired Prophet, the *uates*. It is significant that Horace in his contemporary sixteenth Epode advocating an escape to the Golden Age in the Islands of the Blest ends with the words *piis secunda* uate me *datur fuga*.

In Eclogue 6 Virgil had given, however cursorily and with whatever literary undertones a vision of the past, of poetic history; in 4 he gives a vision of the future, of poetic prophecy. There was still a partially unpaid debt to his friend Gallus, and he chose to end the Eclogues with a tribute making clear that he owed most to him after Octavian. It is a return to the pastoral present and to Arcady. The Golden Age is here and now; as Gallus laments his unfaithful Lycoris in tones borrowed initially from Daphnis' lamentation in Theocritus, he is comforted by shepherds and rustic gods. Virgil (Menalcas) also comes to console his friend. The first half of the poem, Theocritean in colour and full of echoes and reminiscences, culminates in Gallus contemplating his early death from a broken heart, with a melancholy which affords him aesthetic satisfaction if only it provides a theme for song;

alternatively he wishes to find happiness as a shepherd in Arcady. The second half breaks new ground. It seems most likely to be a skilfully contrived cento from Gallus' erotic poetry, recast by Virgil in hexameters, poetry which had been written under the inspiration of Euphorion. Gallus in wonderland is complemented by Gallus through the looking-glass. This is the perfect evocation of Virgil's world of the poetic imagination, with time all but suspended, though night begins to fall at the close, with scene melting into scene, and theme into theme. It is the ideal medium for depicting the thoughts and feelings of a man of sensibility in the grip of unrequited love. *Omnia uincit Amor; et nos cedamus Amori.* The dramatic element integral to pastoral is here almost swallowed up in introspective narrative; this is the art not so much of the theatre as of the cinema.[19]

This analysis has tended to stress the differences in subject, treatment, and emphasis between the individual Eclogues. Reading them consecutively, however, and in the order in which Virgil placed them it is impossible not to be struck by their uniformity of style; there is an *unus color* which pervades the whole book. So far as we can judge it is something new in Latin. One would expect Virgil in his youth to be under strong neoteric influence. And it is only necessary to cast an eye down his pages studded with Greek personal and place names and epithets to realize that he is introducing into Latin in the simplest and most direct way the sound and music of Greek. His versification too owes a good deal to Catullus (though he fights shy of the affectation of spondaic endings); lines like

> *Amphion Dircaeus in Actaeo Aracyntho*
> or *Orphei Calliopea Lino formosus Apollo*
> or *Nerine Galatea thymo mihi dulcior Hyblae*

could easily have been written by one of the *poetae novi* of the previous generation. Virgil's lines are in general slow-moving; the sentence structure deliberately simple, with key words picked up and echoed, linking phrase with phrase and line with line, the paragraphs being marshalled paratactically. Virgil's feeling for assonance, alliteration, and rhyme, and his ear for the music of Latin is constantly creating ravishing effects of sound, and for all his indebtedness to his predecessors and the artificiality of the genre he achieves a limpid and unforced lyricism.

22

Virgil invites, almost challenges, comparison with Theocritus, and it is easy, as many critics have done, to dismiss the Eclogues as derivative, and as inferior in brightness of colouring, sharpness of outline, and lightness of touch to the Idylls. Alternatively the Eclogues are brushed aside as the first daring but insecure flights of a genius whose true bent lay in other directions, in didactic (or more accurately in descriptive) poetry, and in epic. It is true that part of the interest in studying the Eclogues lies in observing the increasing freedom with which Virgil reshapes Theocritean material and his increasing independence as his art matures. It is also instructive to watch for anticipations of the Georgics and the Aeneid in the Eclogues. But the book of Eclogues merits assessment as a work of art complete in itself.

The wavering outlines, the shifting shapes and colours, the vivid pictures which melt and dissolve into each other, do not reflect youthful immaturity or lack of control, but something quite different. Part of Virgil's poetic endowment is a genuine simplicity, an open-eyed childlike innocence, an extreme vulnerability in the face of human inhumanity, of adult cruelty, of inexplicable suffering. He can recapture, as no other ancient writer does, the child's time-scale, in which a summer day can stretch almost without end. Virgilian pastoral in some respects is close to the world of fairy-tale or ballet. But this is only a part of Virgil's extremely rich and complex poetic personality. He is also a mature and immensely subtle and sophisticated artist, as far removed from the genuinely primitive as he well can be. The interplay between these two factors gives the Eclogues much of their variety and appeal.

From a chaotic, violent, and dangerous world Virgil escaped into an idyllically beautiful dream-world of pastoral peace and serenity. He gave it a new extension in space by equating it not with any identifiable Mediterranean setting but with the autonomous world of his own poetic imagination, and by designating it as Arcady. He gave it a new extension in time by equating it with the Golden Age, which might be set in the past, or in the present, or in the future. Dreams, however, may turn into nightmares; and in any case the sleeper wakes. When the outside world intruded in all its naked ugliness Virgil found a focus of sanity and hope in the house of Caesar. In identifying himself with Octavian as the principle of order in a disordered world Virgil came to realize that

the artist has, or should have, obligations to the society in which
he lives, that he cannot withdraw for ever into a poetic or philosophical ivory tower; and that he himself is more than an aesthete
in the neoteric tradition exploring his own exquisite sensibility,
more too than an Epicurean whose flight from harsh reality is
ultimately motivated by selfishness. Virgil becomes a prophet with
a vision of the future's potentiality and of Rome's imperial destiny. His new realism makes possible the writing of the Georgics.
His new ideal, whereby the society of which he is a part is to merge
in a wider entity, the greatness of Rome is to be absorbed into a
Roman world order, elevates Octavian from a *iuuenis* into a world-
ruler, and ultimately into a more than human symbol of the unity
of mankind, and makes possible the writing of the Aeneid. Virgil
in fact transcends the limits of pastoral while still keeping within
the pastoral form and convention; and as his horizons broaden so
his artistic control grows and matures. He is a more assured and
more accomplished artist in the later Eclogues. There were, as he
well knew, losses as well as gains in being thus committed to a
man and a programme, but Virgil had weighed the cost; and in the
outcome his choice was abundantly justified.[20] In the Aeneid he
speaks for the aspirations of Rome with such authority that they
become identified with the aspirations of humanity.

> What though the radiance which was once so bright
> Be now for ever taken from my sight,
> Though nothing can bring back the hour
> Of splendour in the grass, of glory in the flower;
> We will grieve not, rather find
> Strength in what remains behind;
> In the primal sympathy
> Which having been must ever be;
> In the soothing thoughts that spring
> Out of human suffering;
> In the faith that looks through death,
> In years that bring the philosophic mind.

NOTES

I owe most to the following: W. Y. Sellar, *The Roman Poets of the Augustan Age*.[3]
Virgil (Oxford, 1897). F. Skutsch, *Aus Vergils Frühzeit* (Leipzig, 1901); *Gallus und
Vergil* (Leipzig and Berlin, 1906). H. J. Rose, *The Eclogues of Vergil* (Sather Classical

Lectures 16. Berkeley and Los Angeles, 1942). B. Snell, *The Discovery of the Mind* (translated by T. G. Rosenmeyer. Oxford: Blackwell, 1953). K. Büchner, P.-W. R.E. ii. xv. 1180 *s.v.* P. Vergilius Maro (1955). F. Klingner, *Römische Geisteswelt*[4] (Munich, 1961). Brooks Otis, *Virgil, A Study in Civilised Poetry* (Oxford, 1963). V. Pöschl, *Die Hirtendichtung Virgils* (Heidelberg, 1964).

[1] The quotation is from W. W. Greg, *Pastoral Poetry and Pastoral Drama* (London: A. H. Bullen, 1906) p. 4.

[2] *Iliad* 18. 523 ff., 569 ff. The lyre does not belong in the pastoral tradition, but the rest of the picture fits perfectly. *Iliad* 22, 126 ff. Hesiod, *Theogony* 22 ff. Hesiod catches the authentic pastoral note here. His lines (as often with Virgil) are linked by assonantal rhyme; see especially 32–35, (and cp. the opening of *Works and Days*, cast in rhyme couplets, perhaps suggesting a magical incantation constraining the Muses to inspire the poet. It is interesting that two of the most pastoral passages in early Greek poetry contain varieties of the same semi-proverbial and emotive phrase οὐδ᾽ ἀπὸ δρυὸς οὐδ᾽ ἀπὸ πέτρης; a symbol as it were of the unspoiled countryside. The only other occurrence (*Odyssey* 19. 163) is as a description of a simple country fellow. Part of the compelling power of the words may be due to the fact that Oak and Rock do oddly suggest the two great religious centres Dodona and Delphi. The difference between the world of the countryside seen realistically, and the pastoral vision, is well illustrated by the description of Eumaeus in Odyssey 14, compared with the scenes on Achilles' shield.

[3] Horace, *Odes* 3. 29. 11–12.

[4] Cp. *The Adventurer* No. 92; *The Rambler* No. 36; *The Rambler* No. 37, from which these quotations are taken.

[5] See U. von Wilamowitz-Moellendorff, *Hellenistische Dichtung* (Berlin, 1924) 1. pp. 189 ff.

[6] Cp. A. S. F. Gow, *Theocritus* (Cambridge, 1952) 1. p. lxi.

[7] W. Y. Sellar, *op. cit.* p. 159.

[8] See Eclogues 1. 10; 6. 1; Georgics 4. 565.

[9] On Eclogue 2 see F. Klingner, *Gnomon* 3 (1927) pp. 576 ff.

[10] For Milton and Dryden in this context, see Conington's note on line 27. Virgil modulates with much finesse from the deliberate disorder of the opening to the very strictly observed correspondence of the amoebean contest—he is already moving towards disciplined formal balance in lines 49–54, where Damoetas echoes Menalcas' words: *ecce Palaemon* eliciting *uicine Palaemon*, and *uoce lacessas* being answered by *parua reponas;* the metrical pattern of the two groups of three lines is also very similar and *effugies* provokes *si quid habes*. The amoebean contest falls into a satisfying shape if it is divided into eight-line paragraphs. The first three such paragraphs deal with *amor*, and each is rounded off by a mention of Amyntas. The fourth deals with literature, the fifth and sixth with 'life in the country,' though the final riddle has surely literary undertones. It is difficult to resist the conclusion that Virgil's words bear more than their surface meaning. He depicts the dangers of incautiously going too far. Has he been under pressure from his friends and patrons to celebrate their achievements in more exalted strain (cp. the opening of Eclogue 6)? The quotation is from an article in *C.Q.* 54 (1960) pp. 29 ff., in which I proposed a solution of the riddles.

[11] The repetition wholly or in part of an emphatic word within the line, ideally in hexameters a self-contained dactyl in the first and fifth foot, is characteristic of the refrain. I list some representative lines:

ἄρχετε βουκολικᾶς Μοῖσαι φίλαι ἄρχετ᾽ ἀοιδᾶς.
αἰάζω τὸν Ἄδωνιν· ἐπαιάζουσιν Ἔρωτες.

Currite ducentes subtegmina currite fusi.
Ducite ab urbe domum mea carmina ducite Daphnim.
Cras amet qui numquam amauit quique amauit cras amet.

In a highly inflected language the effect of such repetition is close to that of rhyme. And rhyme was of course associated with magic from primitive times. Set in this context the metrical structure of Eclogue 6. 25 *carmina quae uoltis cognoscite; carmina uobis* . . . may be significant; cp. Horace, *Epistles* 2. 1. 138 *carmine di superi placantur, carmine Manes,* in a passage celebrating the supernatural power of poetry.

[12] There is a full and sensitive treatment of the seventh Eclogue by Pöschl, *op. cit.* pp. 93 ff. The quotation is from F. H. Sandbach, *C. R.* 47 (1933) p. 219—an article apparently missed by Pöschl. See too the remarks of O. Skutsch in *Gnomon* 37 (1965) pp. 162 ff.

[13] See Snell *op. cit.* Chapter 13, pp. 281 ff. *Arcadia: the discovery of a spiritual landscape.*

[14] Virgil's development in Eclogues 5, 9, and 1 has been studied by Klingner in *Hermes* 62 (1927) pp. 129 ff., reprinted in abbreviated form in *Römische Geisteswelt*[4] pp. 312 ff. *Das erste Hirtengedicht Virgils.* The description of Octavian as *deus* is partly derived from Theocritus vii 93.

[15] The most recent account of what happened to Virgil is also the simplest and most convincing: see L. P. Wilkinson, *Hermes* 94 (1966) pp. 320 ff.

[16] The poem falls into the following groups of lines: 5, 5; 8, 8; 13, 6, 13; 5, 15, 5. This kind of patterning may well be instinctive on Virgil's part, but it does suggest that the articulation of the Eclogue has been long and carefully considered.

[17] See Skutsch, *Aus Vergils Frühzeit,* pp. 28 ff. Servius on Eclogue 6. 72 after discussing the story of the *Gryneum nemus* continues: *hoc autem Euphorionis continent carmina, quae Gallus transtulit in sermonem latinum.* Cp his comment on Eclogue 10. For Hesiodic themes echoed by Virgil see Skutsch, *op. cit.* p. 43. The few extant fragments of the *Hesiodus* and *Hyacinthus* are to be found in J. U. Powell, *Collectanea Alexandrina.* One could imagine the *Hesiodus* describing the beginnings of our world, and the *Hyacinthus* dealing with metamorphoses including that of Hyacinthus himself; but this is pure speculation.

[18] For the oracular style see Parke and Wormell, *The Delphic Oracle* 2. xxi ff. It is just feasible to imagine the poem as being fulfilled in the birth and subsequent career of Pollio's son, Asinius Gallus, consul in 8 B.C. and regarded as a possible successor to Augustus. This however is very farfetched, and disregards the need for the child to be in some sense a child of Caesar.

[19] See Skutsch, *op. cit.,* pp. 2 ff.

[20] In his noblest lines on Rome's imperial mission, Aeneid 6. 847 ff., he carefully counts the cost; and Book 6 of the Aeneid ends with the evocation of the young Marcellus. By now the Golden Age is to be hoped for only in Elysium.

II

The Originality of the Aeneid

BROOKS OTIS

THE shortest way, perhaps, of characterizing the *Aeneid* is to call it a Roman *Odyssey-Iliad*. This somewhat clumsy label at least has the advantage of distinguishing at once the originality of Virgil's enterprise. We can be fairly certain (though certainty in such matters is rare indeed) that no previous epic could be so described. There had been plenty of Roman epics—either *Annales* (like those of Ennius, Volusius, et al) or *Bella* (from Naevius on to the *Bellum Actiacum* that some think Virgil intended to write) and behind these an indeterminate quantity of Greek historical epics; some, like those of Archias, on Roman themes. There had also been a number of mythological or homerically-styled epics on the general 'cycle' of Homeric-Mycenean saga or myth: of Virgil's contemporaries, for instance, Ponticus, Propertius' friend, wrote a latin *Thebais*, Varro of Atax a latin *Argonautica*. Behind these was also a long tradition of similar Greek epics running back to Apollonius of Rhodes (*Argonautica*) to Antimachus (*Thebais*) and behind him to the so-called Cyclics who seemingly originated the idea of completing Homer by dealing with all the saga that the *Odyssey* and *Iliad* left out. The important point is that though they imitated Homer's style and employed a similar content (the saga of the Heroic Age: the deeds of heroes who consorted with gods), they deliberately dealt with themes other than the *Odyssey* or *Iliad* themselves.[1]

Yet this in a sense is just what Virgil did. It is worthwhile once again to ask *why*? Or more concretely to ask how a sensitive, extremely well-read and apparently not over-conceited Augustan could attempt to 'rival' the acknowledged summit and paragon of all known poetry.

Here, of course, it is easy to answer that the *Aeneid* is also
Roman, that its subject is after all Aeneas, his travels and battles,
and that Homer is really not reproduced or at best reproduced in a
very oblique and indirect way. This is certainly a partial truth but
it evades, I think, the real problem. For it is clear, I think, that
Virgil did after all set out to write an *Odyssey-Iliad*. Though his
hero was Aeneas, not Odysseus or Achilles, and the Homeric
motifs were in large part given new labels and settings, Virgil was
still reproducing the actual *Iliad* and *Odyssey* and not some other
heroic story. His Roman legend, in other words, did not determine his plot but merely the filling of his plot. The pre-Virgilian
Aeneas, unlike Theseus or Oedipus, was largely 'plot-less'. This
has quite recently been pointed out by Professor Georg Knauer in
his extremely interesting *Die Aeneis und Homer*.[2] However one may
disagree with him (and I myself disagree with many of his points,
especially with some of his conclusions), I think he is largely right
in saying that Virgil attempted to reproduce the content of Homer
(or at least a huge portion of Homer: e.g. *Odyssey* V–XII in *Aeneid*
I–VI) not just partially but completely (vollständig) or in its
entirety. There are of course many other borrowings in the
Aeneid (Apollonius of Rhodes especially, Euripides, Lucretius,
Ennius, Naevius, etc.) as Macrobius and so many others have
insisted, and there is also the rather amorphous Aenean legend
itself, not to mention Rome and Augustus, but the Homeric plan
and content is certainly primary. It is there. Those, like Paratore,
who have tried to minimize it, have not, it seems to me, been
particularly successful.

But it is also plain—and here I think Knauer's book can mislead
us if we do not constantly bear its special emphasis and limits in
mind—that Virgil would never in the world have attempted a
simple imitation of Homer. Others imitated: he reproduced. In
other words, he deliberately used Homer for a reason and not at
all out of a sense of rivalry or competitiveness. And that reason
can, I think, be best seen if we turn briefly to his actual rivals (if
one may so call them)—the more or less contemporary writers of
historical and mythological epics to whom I have just referred.
Their trouble was quite simply that they were out-of-date—that
the old gods and heroes were dead, and that the Homeric content
and style were glaring anachronisms. Homer could handle all the
wonders of the *Odyssey* or embattled gods of the *Iliad*: later writers

lacked Homer's credulity and command of his material. This remained true whether they rewrote mythology or dressed up contemporary events in an epic-mythological garb.

I have elsewhere attempted to show this at some length. But for present purposes I am only concerned to show that the *Aeneid* is *of itself* a sufficient witness. Some think that Virgil in the proem of *Georgics* III (written shortly before 30 B.C. in all probability) was declaring his intention of writing a *Bellum Actiacum,* an epic on the battles (pugnae) of the Actian war. I doubt this, but the main point I am concerned with is that the *Aeneid* is in fact nothing of the sort. Virgil, instead, chose for his epic's subject a legend of ostensibly Homeric date—the one legend that would permit him to connect Rome and Italy with the Trojan war and by this means to reproduce Homer. Only so could he avoid what he probably thought of as an absurd and preposterous thing—the direct rivalry of Homer or what amounts to the same thing, the attempt to imitate Homer. For in reproducing Homer in the most obvious possible way—even more obvious to an ancient than to us—he in effect proclaimed a very different aim. While one aspect of his programme was negative and revealed his shrewd sense of contemporaneity, his feeling that Homer was Homer and could be taken or left but not in his day and age, imitated—another aspect was positive and came out of his insight that Homer, though impossible to imitate, was supreme—indeed indispensable—as a source of symbols, a means of giving heroic connotation to contemporary reality.

The danger—and the danger was terrible indeed—lay in the very necessity of inventing at least something, enough certainly to put the Homeric motifs where he wanted them, in the proper Roman light so to speak. From this point of view the 'success' of Virgil meant also the limiting of invention to an absolute minimum, the subordinating, so far as possible, of the 'imitation' of Homer to the very different 'reproduction' of Homer. Virgil had to reduce the non-Homeric element, the element that had to do the job of putting Homer in a Roman context, to the least possible compass. Only so could he avoid the absurdity of 'rivalry' and give the Homeric motifs a chance to act and react. Any suggestion that he was 'inventing' them would have been fatal. A knight in arms may under proper circumstances be a good symbol of a modern soldier or statesman but only on the understanding that the knight cannot talk or act like one: he belongs in the legend with which we associate him. The legend is a powerful thing but it is hard indeed to release its power or to make it do original symbolic work for us. The job of mixing the ages is not easy but it may, for all that, pay enormous poetical dividends. I think it is fruitful to look at Virgil from this particular angle.

In *Aeneid* I–VI it is at once apparent that Virgil made the greatest effort to repeat both the plot of the *Odyssey* and a considerable amount of its specific content. *Aeneid* I–VI repeats the main plot of *Odyssey* V–XII: the hero's *nostos* or voyage to his home overseas; the divine machinery (with opposing and helping gods under the general authority of Zeus-Jupiter); the original 'detention' of the hero by a powerful female figure; his release by divine intervention; his narrative of the preceding part of the *nostos* (essentially a series of sea adventures); and his extraordinary visit to the underworld. The only *non-Odyssean* book in this sense is Aeneid V (the games and ship-burning) though even here the games have at least a partially Odyssean source. Then there are the various specific motifs: the initial storm, the divine planning of the hero's salvation from it and hospitality received after it, some at least of the sea-adventures (storm, Cyclopes, Scylla-Charybdis, part of the episode of the Cattle of the Sun), most of the specific individuals encountered in Book VI (at least the Elpenor-Palinurus, Ajax-Dido, Agamemnon-Deiphobus and Anticleia-Tiresias-Anchises parallels are intended). Nor is this all: specific similes (e.g. Dido-Diana), specific speeches (e.g. the two initial speeches of Aeneas in Book I), specific phrases and turns of language are all obvious reminiscences of the *Odyssey*.

Yet it is clear that the whole context is also quite radically non-Odyssean. The Odyssey is a typical *nostos*: Odysseus quite simply wants to go home, to restore his former authority in Ithaca. He is detained by a congeries of forces—human and divine—but none of them affect his determination though all of them serve to demonstrate his cleverness and courage. He is in short the ideal hero of the *nostos*, the foil, for example, of the others—Ajax, Agamemnon especially—who lacked both his canniness and his piety. Aeneas, on the contrary, had lost his home: Troy was dead and gone. Nor did he have a specific intelligible task such as the Golden Fleece was for Jason. Instead, a divine mission was imposed upon him and one moreover that was originally covered with obscurity, even though it was also associated with the most ominous hints of danger and difficulty. The very start of his exodus from Troy began with the loss of his *Penelope* (Creusa); it continued with the loss of his *Laertes* (Anchises). When he encountered the central detaining element—his *Calypso*—he still had his Trojan companions and heir (Ascanius)—he was not physically isolated like Odysseus—but these really only enhanced his sense of loss—of disparity between all that he wanted to live for and that for which he now had to live. Every Odyssean parallel only accentuated the non-Odyssean reality.

Furthermore, Aeneas did not even encounter the obstacles of the *Odyssey*. His retreat from Troy was carefully safeguarded (his own actions mainly hindered it). None of the adventures of Book III really endangered him: Polydorus, the Harpies, the Cyclopes were just terrible sights whose effect was psychological: they were not physical threats like those of the *Odyssey*. As for Dido, she was certainly no physical menace. The conflagration of the ships was stopped by Jove's rainstorm before Aeneas could even grasp what had happened. As for the underworld, the whole thing was foreordained even to his securing of the bough that gave him invulnerability. Here, again, nothing could well be more un-Odyssean. There are prophets and aiding gods in the *Odyssey*—Athena in particular and, in one crucial instance, Zeus—but these do not in the least remove the necessity for the most intense action, courage and initiative. In the *Aeneid* I–VI, it is the gods who seem to take *all* the initiative.

Virgil thus seems to be at vast pains to repeat or suggest the *Odyssey* at every point while he is at equal pains to undercut and undermine the essential motivation and spirit of the *Odyssey*. Our problem is not just to see this 'undermining' of the *Odyssey* (which is relatively easy, though I think that some new things are yet to be said) but much rather to understand why the *Odyssey* should have been used in this very curious way—that is both copied, reproduced in a really 'bare-faced' manner, and at the same time turned inside out or against its very self. But we must consider the 'undermining' first.

I

Here the essential 'keys' to understanding lie in the following facts:

31

1. The Odyssean sequence of *Calypso-storm-reception by Alcinous in Phaeacia—Odysseus' narrative (including nekuia or journey to the underworld)—arrival in Ithaca* is changed to: *storm-reception by Dido-Aeneas' narrative—funeral games and shipburning-nekuia.* In other words 'Alcinous' is omitted (or the roles of Calypso and Alcinous are merged) with a consequent changed emphasis of the storm and a re-setting of the first-personal narrative. On the other hand, the *nekuia* is taken out of the first personal narrative and related in the third person at the very end (the last book) of the Odyssean *Aeneid* as an integral part of the main plot. The non-Odyssean games and shipburning (*Aeneid* V) thus separate the Dido complex (I–IV) from the *nekuia*.

2. Of the two books of first-personal narrative (Aeneid II–III) only one (III) reproduced the Odyssean material. The other (II) is an innovation. The fall of Troy is only incidentally alluded to in the *Odyssey* (e.g. the discussion of the horse in *Odyssey* IV) and forms no part of Odysseus' narrative.

3. The Dido episode combines some features of Calypso (the detention of the hero, his release by the intervention of Zeus-Hermes = Jupiter-Mercury) but is mainly based on Apollonius' *Argonautica* Books III–IV (Medea) with the addition of elements drawn from tragedy. But Virgil uses Apollonius very differently from the way he uses Homer. Here we can truly speak of 'imitation' rather than of 'reproduction'.

4. The Homeric plan of the Hermes scene (*Od.* V) is reversed: in the *Odyssey* Hermes warns Calypso (who heeds the warning but does not even inform Odysseus of it); in *Aeneid* IV Mercury warns Aeneas only (who, however, does later report it to Dido).

5. The additional games-ship-burning (*Aeneid* V) is based on Iliadic, not Odyssean material and is therefore a radical innovation. It is the only *Iliadic* part (*Iliad* XV, XXIII) of the *Odyssean Aeneid* (I–VI).

6. Because of the entirely changed *nostos*, the family of Aeneas accompany him on his journey (even though Creusa, his wife, dies at its very inception and the father, Anchises, dies before the storm and arrival at Carthage). On the other hand, Aeneas' Trojan *socii* (the future ancestors of Rome) remain with him throughout while all of Odysseus' men are lost by the time he (alone) reaches Ogygia and Calypso. Thus, broadly speaking, Aeneas loses what Odysseus retains (home, family) and Odysseus loses what Aeneas

32

retains (his men). The roles of wife (Penelope-Creusa) and father (Laertes-Anchises) are thus completely different. So too with the mothers: where Odysseus meets his mother in the underworld, Aeneas meets only his father. Venus, of course, is immortal. But it is noteworthy that Virgil combines the underworld roles of Anticleia and Tiresias (the Homeric reminiscences are clear) in the single role of Anchises.

All of these changes (and some others of lesser importance) are readily explicable in terms of Virgil's Roman purpose. Unlike Odysseus, Aeneas is confronted with a programme, so to speak, a 'divine plan'. This programme is, in a quite definite sense (though not an absolute one), self-acting or automatic: Aeneas is the instrument of the gods (all is, as it were, fated) whereas Odysseus is really only their beneficiary. Or in other words: Aeneas is not called upon to take the initiative, to depend on his own resources, in the way that Odysseus is. Yet the whole programme would be quite impossible without Aeneas' active co-operation. To a certain extent, this is another version of the old predestination-freedom paradox but the point of resolution (the factor that reconciles the programme to Aeneas' own freedom of choice) is the Virgilian conception of *pietas*. Aeneas is called to account when and if he disobeys or wavers but it is only through his disobedience and lack of resolution (free will in the negative sense of 'sin') that he learns to obey in freedom: this and only this is true *pietas*. The conception is really quite like the Augustinian progression from an original *posse peccare* to a final *non posse peccare* that is yet free because the intention of sinning has been freely relinquished. But the Christian analogy can also mislead: we stay closer to Virgil's thought if we think of *pietas* as a free response to fate, free because it is ultimately based on an understanding experience of it.

A brief survey of the Odyssean *Aeneid* (I–VI) will make this clear. The poem begins (à la Horace) *in mediis rebus*: unlike the *Odyssey* (where Odysseus' wretched sojourn in Ogygia is repeatedly alluded to in the *Telemachia—Od.* I–IV—before Odysseus himself is introduced in the fifth Book), we start with a very minimum of preparation. We are given (in the Venus-Jupiter colloquy of lines 223–296) a brief survey of the 'programme' (the divine plan for Aeneas) but Aeneas is of course quite unaware of this celestial conversation: for aught he seems to know he has undertaken a thankless task only to be miserably drowned when he

33

might so much better have died with his friends and kindred at Troy. On the other hand, Venus is also deceived: though she is now reassured as to the long-run, she is wholly ignorant of the short-run, and hence can proceed, with flippant assurance, to cooperate with Juno in an enterprise that all but wrecks the whole programme and certainly would have wrecked it, had not Jupiter himself intervened in the very nick of time.

Here, of course, Virgil was combining the Homeric schema of the hostile divinity (Juno, à la Poseidon, sends the storm) with the Apollonian schema of the erotic plot (Hera, Athena, Aphrodite and Eros in league to gain Medea's help for Jason by making her fall in love with him: this is of course reproduced in the *Aeneid* as the league of Juno, Venus and Cupid *vis à vis* Dido and Aeneas) and the result was not wholly satisfactory. But the point of importance for Virgil and for us is not the plotting of the lesser divinities (the existence of a gap, a gap of both knowledge and power, between Jupiter and the other gods is a fundamental premise of the *Aeneid*) but the response of Aeneas. Actually, Virgil had no need for any divine motivation of the amour. Aeneas' emotional involvement with his 'Calypso' was the decisive thing. But obviously this could not be the real or Homeric 'Calypso': the 'detention' of Aeneas had to be a self-detention, a real 'culpa' to be overcome, a real inner engagement, if the final goal of free commitment to *pietas* were ever to be reached. In other words: freedom for sin was the prerequisite of freedom for *pietas*. Thus only a real love affair—not certainly the dreary imprisonment in Ogygia—could do, and here of course Apollonius was the inevitable resource: he alone was responsible for the tremendous innovation of introducing a Euripidean *amoureuse* into an Homeric epic.

But Apollonius also required drastic rehandling: his Medea was certainly no 'test' for Jason; Hera was quite right in seeing that her magic was indispensable to him. And while he had considerable trouble in keeping her when Apsyrtus and his army were bent on getting her back, he managed, after considerable tergiversation, to do it in a way that also saved his own skin. Though the awakening passion of Medea is beautifully described, the subsequent events seem to fly in the face of all psychology or consistency of characterization: I at least find it all but impossible to understand how the passionate but fresh and attractive Medea of *Arg*. III

34

could in Book IV so unhappily combine the roles of virgin and murderess until finally the curious legalism of Alcinous necessitated the hasty cave marriage in Phaeacia.

In any event, Virgil by combining the roles of Medea, Alcinous and Calypso and of course by adapting all of them to the legend of the Carthaginian queen (who did not love Aeneas at all)[3] obtained exactly the situation he wanted: a fusion of the hospitality (Alcinous) and amatory (Medea) motifs and at the same time a remarkable parallelism of Dido with Aeneas—so that his 'Medea' became also an 'Aeneas' in her own right, a woman with her own mission, *pietas* and fate. This was indeed an obstacle, and a test for which he was quite unprepared. The man that we see in Book I and that Dido also sees there, is the Trojan hero who has not yet overcome the loss of his Trojan identity. It is Dido's respect for his Trojan heroism (he had already divined this from the Iliadic frieze of the Juno temple: the *lacrimae rerum* are really Dido's tears; the temple and frieze were obviously her own doing) and Aeneas' inevitable appreciation of her respect—Dido's hospitality, sympathy, admiration are all, as it were, incipiently amatory—that motivate the awakening passion and explain its mutual character. (The Apollonian Venus-Cupid motif is, humanly speaking, quite supererogatory.) All this leads inevitably to Aeneas' narrative: the hero's revelation of his heroism is of course the best of all courtships (especially with a Dido) but neither Aeneas nor Dido yet understand that *this* Aeneas (the Aeneas of ruined Troy) can never be resuscitated, and that his new commitments envisage a world in which neither Troy nor Dido can have any place. This is the tragic irony that Virgil deliberately produced by rearranging the Odyssean sequence. The narrative that is an implicit courtship is also an explanation of why that courtship must lead to tragedy.

The function of the 'Fall of Troy' (*Aeneid* II) has often been missed or curiously underestimated. In a sense, there is truth in calling the Aeneas of Books III, IV and V (and indeed a good deal of Book VI), a Jason-type, a hero without initiative and without the spur of real danger, a hero guaranteed, so to speak, by divine assistance. But this truth is limited and redefined by the content of Book II. For the Aeneas of this book is the Aeneas of the Juno-frieze, the Trojan Aeneas, the true Homeric hero, an utterly different figure from the one we see later. Consider the sequence of events: once he wakens from his dream of Hector, and surveys the terrible panorama of dying Troy, he begins to act with reckless initiative and courage. He is the fighter, the leader, the embodiment of ferocious energy. And for a moment he carries all before him: the Greeks even begin to retreat into the wooden horse. This was *furor, dolor*—Venus and the ghost of Creusa alike reprehended it—but it was precisely what anyone would expect an Homeric hero to be and do at such a time. There is no hesitation and wavering here, no problem of motivation: the case is desperate but the response is immediate and the duty is clear. Not even the experience of overwhelming defeat, the sorry sight of Priam's murder with its obvious lesson for himself (Anchises was also a helpless old man) can mitigate his heroic fury. Only when Venus shows him the gods destroying Troy—when he finally sees the absolute futility of his and all human effort—will he consent to return to and save his family.

All this Virgil had to show. Without it the *Aeneid* simply could not stand. We have to comprehend what Aeneas originally was if his subsequent story is to make any sense at all. Otherwise, the whole problem of Aeneas' *pietas* would be quite unintelligible. For we have to see how the loss of the heroic code by which he acted in Book II is replaced by another code, the code of Roman *pietas*. But the transition could not be immediate: there had to be an interim, a period in which all bearings were lost and despair replaced initiative. And this stage begins with the end of Book II and continues through Book III. Here Aeneas lives in a world that makes no sense, provides no credible or emotionally valid motive for living. His aged father's natural reluctance to leave Troy (why indeed should he have wanted to outlive the meaning of an existence that was anyway approaching its end?) had triggered a rapid succession of incredible events: the omens, the unexpected appearance of a sizable band of refugees, the death and ghostly reappearance of Creusa, strange talk of a new Troy far overseas, of a new wife there, a new destiny. It is out of such experience that the harassed, uncertain, dependent Aeneas of Book III emerges. Nothing here seems definite: even the gods speak in the most obscure and terrifying language. Even Helenus' 'favourable' prophecy is deliberately elliptical and ambiguous. Only Anchises, the strange revitalized *senex*, shows real initiative. And this too is withdrawn: Anchises dies and leaves him spiritually alone with an

36

unwanted, meaningless responsibility—the Roman programme.

This then is the Aeneas that Dido entertains. His narrative reveals not only the hero he once was (Book II) but the dependent son he had also so recently been (Book III). It is not perhaps over-clear why Anchises should at once (after the omens of Book II) have taken charge, as it were, of Aeneas' new destiny or, more exactly, why he should have been converted to it so much more readily and profoundly than Aeneas himself. He had a special relation to the gods (both Jupiter and Venus) and was obviously much more experienced in omens: yet there is a residuum of mystery here. At any rate, the fact of his conversion is one of the pivots on which the whole epic turns. For it is only by Aeneas' *pietas* toward Anchises that his *pietas* toward Rome is developed. Virgil's intention was obviously to make of Anchises a double figure, a peculiar sort of link between two worlds: the converted *senex* whose life was prolonged just enough to establish his initiative over Aeneas; and the supernatural authority (the divine ghost) through whom the final and independent *pietas* of Aeneas could be assured. In the last analysis, Anchises was the only possible mediator between Aeneas and the gods.

But Anchises' death is first and foremost the harbinger of near disaster: without him Aeneas quickly forgets his mission and succumbs to Dido; he is not yet at all independent; his *pietas* is still very fragile. We see this, indeed, in the very way in which Dido dominates the action of the fourth Book. But Dido is no Calypso: she detains Aeneas only because Aeneas detains himself. The proof of this is the fact that Mercury (unlike Homer's Hermes) comes to Aeneas, not Dido. Aeneas can leave when he will but he does not want to leave; he has forgotten Rome. He has let Dido take the place of Troy. It requires a great deal to change him. Anchises haunts his dreams; his own conscience troubles him (there are his waiting *socii* and Ascanius); but finally Jupiter has to intervene. Mercury's harsh words, however, do find a voluntary response. Aeneas, once warned, is the firm oak against which all the winds beat in vain. Yet it would, I think, be a great misrep-resentation of Virgil's design to attribute any particular finality to the break with Dido. The famous recovery of *pietas* (IV, 393) really conceals the precariousness of the whole situation. Aeneas was to Dido the Trojan hero, not the prospective Roman, and Aeneas himself had confirmed her in this estimate. Even his final speech to her is full of it: had he had his wish, he would have rebuilt Troy, not followed the Roman programme. Now he can have neither Troy nor Dido. He recognizes his duty, but only under supernatural prodding and with a heavy heart. There is no emotional commitment at all: *Italiam non sponte sequor.*

This is a view that, I think, the fifth book (the games and ship-burning) amply confirms. It is, at first sight, doubly curious. It consists in large part of funeral games for the dead Anchises and we naturally wonder why they should have been so long deferred. Virgil, of course, gives us an explanation; it is the first 'anniversary' of Anchises' death—an anniversary very opportunely coinciding with the unexpected 'diversion' of their course to Sicily. But this excuse is hardly a convincing reason for the strange 'displacement' of the games. In the second place, the book's content is odd: both the games and the ship-burning that follows them are clearly not Odyssean but Iliadic. The games are very obviously modelled after those for Patroclus in *Iliad* XXIII and the ship-burning, of course, recalls that of *Iliad* XV. Yet Book V is obviously part of the Odyssean *Aeneid*. For it is followed by the clearly Odyssean VI, the *nekuia*. But why should the *nekuia* also be transposed, that is, taken out of its Odyssean position in Odysseus' narrative as well as separated from the Dido episode by the intervening fifth book?

There is only one satisfactory explanation of these apparent anomalies. Anchises' 'death' (at the end of III) is not really final: Aeneas still needs him, requires at least one final confrontation with him. Book IV is, as it were, bracketed by Anchises: the deferred games of V complete the unfinished funeral of III. But the games themselves are premature: Anchises is not just the benevolent snake, the genius of a tomb, who can be honoured like any other dead man, but also the august messenger of Jupiter who after the ship-burning appears to Aeneas as such, his role fully analogous to that of Mercury in the Dido book.

Here he first of all reinforces and explains the advice that Nautes had already given Aeneas. The ship-burning demanded a reconcentration of forces (four ships were lost before Jupiter's saving downpour) but this, as Anchises now reveals, was necessary anyway for the successful conduct of the impending war in Latium. Furthermore we can, on looking back, see that the whole book has been leading up to this: the games are Iliadic because they antici-

pate the Iliadic *Aeneid* (VII–XII) to come; they either look ahead
to the corresponding episodes of Book IX (Mnestheus, Nisus-
Euryalus) or (in the case of the Sicilians, Entellus and Acestes)
look ahead to the ship-burning itself or more exactly to the
Sicilian founding of Acesta that the ship-burning necessitates
since a home must be secured for the weaker Trojans who must
now be left behind.

Yet the real cause of Anchises' solemn reappearance is not
merely the necessity of the impending Latin war but an obvious
failure of nerve on the part of Aeneas. He forgets the fates
(*fatorum oblitus*) and even entertains the thought of abandoning his
Roman mission. It is evident that he is anything but ready for the
final and decisive test ahead—the last and supreme effort of Juno
to thwart him (Allecto episode in VII). What V really shows,
therefore, is that Aeneas still needs Anchises if he is to meet the
crisis of war. But the relative positions of III, IV and V also
indicate that the crisis of IV had not been fully resolved. Aeneas,
on leaving Dido, encounters a windstorm that makes him change
his course and make for Sicily instead of Italy. It is clear then that
he is no more ready for Italy at the end of IV than he was at the
end of III or beginning of I (the storm that blows him off course
to Africa). The two storms (I and beginning of V) both delay or
interrupt his course toward Italy: but in the one case (Book I) the
delay is due to his enemy, Juno; in the other, it is due to Jupiter
himself or at least the *numen* that connects Aeneas with Anchises
(V, 56–7). And just as there are two storms, there are two crises
(Books IV and V) and two reappearances of Juno (storm at cave,
ship-burning). So the two interventions of Jupiter (*via* Mercury in
IV, *via* Anchises in V) really fuse into one message in two parts,
the latter of which (the one *via* Achises) is the clinching and
decisive part. At the close of Book IV there is yet more to be said:
the secret is not yet out.

This secret is finally disclosed when Anchises, after confirming
the advice of Nautes, demands that Aeneas meet him in the underworld as a necessary preliminary to his landing in Latium:

730   gens dura atque aspera cultu
         debellanda tibi Latio est. Ditis tamen ante
         infernas accede domos et Averna per alta
         congressus pete, nate, meos.

Aeneas, in short, must see the future of Rome under Anchises' guidance: only thus can an effective transference of his *pietas*—from Anchises to Rome—be brought about. Aeneas had indeed obeyed the god in Book IV but only with fear, after long and guilty neglect of his duty, without having achieved the independent and inward, the convinced *pietas*, that his future Roman destiny required. Book V shows the same thing in quite another context. But all this is also fate: Jupiter had sent Aeneas back to Sicily and Anchises; had prepared Anchises' role in II, III and V; had woven the Dido story and the ship-burning, the machinations of Juno and the misdirected plotting of Venus, above all the death and the return of Anchises, into a linear pattern that required the completion of the *nekuia*.

Book VI is thus meant to be the definitive encounter of Aeneas with Anchises where Aeneas, by seeing the Roman future that Anchises stands for, can now 'transfer' his *pietas* from Anchises to Rome. Henceforth, he will no longer be 'dependent' on Anchises and thus also no longer subject to failure when thrown on his own. Roman *pietas* at last replaces Trojan; the Trojan becomes a Roman hero. Thus the sixth *Aeneid* is designed (in contrast to the Odyssean *nekuia*) to come to a climax in the triple confrontation of Anchises, Aeneas and the future heroes of Rome. This is really quite obvious. What is not so obvious is the reason for the long preliminary section that so explicitly reproduces its Odyssean counterpart: just as Odysseus encounters Elpenor, Ajax and Agamemnon, so Aeneas encounters Palinurus, Dido and Deiphobus. The explicit parallelism of these three pairs is obvious and meant to seem so. Yet the differences are even more striking. In Homer there is a thronging mass of shades clamouring for the momentary revitalization of the blood that Odysseus defends with his drawn sword: Elpenor, Ajax and Agamemnon are only three out of many. Tiresias, the real object of Odysseus' visit, has already been interviewed; the others are simply there to arouse Odysseus' and the audience's curiosity. Virgil, however, concentrates on his three figures and makes everything else into background. The Styx, the gloomy sights, all the wonderful atmosphere of the place, are only there to give setting to Palinurus, Dido and Deiphobus. And even Palinurus is obviously peripheral as the very topography indicates: the main encounters are beyond the Styx; the main emphasis is on Dido and Deiphobus. Nor can there be any real doubt as to why Virgil concentrates on these: they stand clearly for the two great 'moments' or crises of Aeneas' past: the grand passion of IV; the fall of Troy in II.

Aeneas, in other words, recapitulates his past before encountering his future. I have tried elsewhere to show that this same recapitulatory technique is employed in the last book, XII. There Turnus also recapitulates his past, his two great sins or failures: his breaking of the treaty (*foedus*) and his withdrawal from the heat of battle while his allies suffered in consequence. It is the recapitulation, however, that finally forces him to face his failure, to discard his protecting divinity (Juturna) and meet Aeneas and his fate. This provides, I think, the key also to Aeneas' recapitulation of his great crises in Book VI. Aeneas cannot rid himself of his old self and its motives (Troy, Dido) until he re-encounters them and realizes that there can be no going back, no reluctance to advance. Dido, as it were, refuses to admit his present existence; Deiphobus is a pathetic relic of the ghostly past who, in a supremely symbolic gesture, even turns his back on Aeneas. There is now nothing left in the past to hold Aeneas. So then the boundary of the past (mythological Hades) is reached. When Aeneas moves from the *ultima arva* where Deiphobus is, he crosses the line (the two ways) that separates the past from the future. The Sibyl hurries him on to Anchises and the Show of Heroes.[4]

II

I have tried so far to explain why and how Virgil 'undermined' the *Odyssey*, for what purpose he, so to speak, turned it inside out. To sum it all up in a sentence: he transformed a simple narrative of adventure into a complex narrative of motivation. No such summary, of course, does justice to the integrity of any epic (Homer's or Virgil's) but it does I think touch the main points at issue. One can, certainly, dispute details and perhaps essentials of my analysis above. I cannot, of course, go into alternative interpretations here (such as e.g. those of Paratore and the Italian school) but I think it is useful to discuss the major problem that my own interpretation (which is after all not so different from others) involves, especially since I did not discuss it in my recent book—at best I only alluded to it and even then very elliptically— and since it has recently been called to our attention by Knauer's imposing monograph. This is the problem mentioned on p. 31. Why, indeed, did Virgil try to 'reproduce' Homer so carefully when he in fact 'undermined' him, turned him inside out?

Here, first of all, we must I think discard the usual 'imitation' theory. I have briefly discussed this above (pp. 27–29). Former imitators of Homer did not (so far as we can tell and I think we *can* here tell) copy Homer as Virgil did. From the Cyclics on they either treated themes on the Mycenean or heroic-age periphery of Homer (but not Homer's own themes) or they 'Homerized', so to speak, later 'historical' events (i.e., treated them in the Homeric manner to at least some degree). But they did not 'reproduce' Homer as Virgil did—that is, they did not deliberately compose another *Odyssey* and *Iliad* with intended 'correspondences' at almost every point. We cannot, of course, hope to read Virgil's mind here. All we can do is to describe, as best we can, what is the effect, the meaning (so far as we can see it), the aesthetic and philosophic significance, of Virgil's 'reproduction' of Homer. Even if this only leads to a statement of what Virgil *means to us,* what his 'Homerizing' does to us, it will I think be worthwhile.

Virgil, as we have just seen, fitted Homer into a quite different or unhomeric context. The important thing about this context, for our present discussion, is that it was *subjectively* conceived: a narrative of motivation or motive-development must obviously penetrate the *psyche* (the mental-emotional *ego,* so to speak) to a far greater degree than a relatively 'physical' or 'external' narrative such as Homer's—a narrative of adventure wherein the motives are obvious and constant. Hence, what I have called the 'subjective style' of Virgil. This can be characterized by its *empathy*—the author's reading of the characters' minds, his easy penetration of their feelings, and his *partizanship*—his sympathy with or censure of his characters, his covert and often overt bias, his *parti pris.* A character is not, in such a style, left to make his own impression on the reader or audience through a relatively objective recital of his acts and by quoted remarks or speeches that are clearly meant to belong to him and not the author. Quotation in such a style tends to be indirect or only vaguely differentiated from the main narrative and even direct quotation is not set off from the narrative with the sharpness of a more objective style. There is, of course, a rather dim boundary between complete objectivity and complete subjectivity of style (and no objectivity or subjectivity is really complete) but the distinction is I think clear and is particularly evident when we set the 'subjective' Virgil beside the 'objective' Homer.

Let us consider, for example, the way in which both poets introduce the first-personal narratives of their heroes (Odysseus and Aeneas). In the *Odyssey* (VII) Odysseus arrives in Phaeacia, is clothed and fed by Nausikaa and entertained by Alcinous and Arete: yet he conceals his home and his identity to the utmost extent, only telling Arete (in answer to her leading question) about the storm and Calypso. He is nonetheless promised all he could possibly desire: either Nausikaa for a wife or a safe voyage to his home, however remote it may be.

On the second day (Book VIII) he partakes of refreshment and hears the bard Demodocus sing of his own quarrel with Achilles. He weeps and hides his face: no one notices but the king Alcinous. The latter, therefore, interrupts the singing and, in an obvious effort to cheer his guest, proposes that they all go outdoors and engage in contests of wrestling, jumping and running. Odysseus at first does not participate: he tells the young men that he is too sore at heart, too tired for such sport. At this, one of them, Euryalus, indulges in a bitter jest: Odysseus has the mind of a merchant, not a sportsman. The remark angers Odysseus and he proceeds to show what he can do by throwing a huge weight far beyond all the other marks. He then recounts his other athletic skills: he acknowledges inferiority in archery to Philoctetes or such ancients as Heracles. But he is unsurpassed with the javelin and can run faster than anyone, though, tired as he is, he cannot yet expect to be at his best. This hint of past prowess, revealed only because of his resentment of Euryalus, is another step in the 'revelation' of his identity. But this is obviously not a good moment for Alcinous to express his curiosity.

So he again suggests a diversion (he is indeed the very soul of courtesy) and summons the dancers. Demodocus supplies the music: it is the jolly tale of Aphrodite, Ares and Hephaestus. Odysseus is delighted and praises the Phaeacian dancers to the great pleasure of Alcinous: he responds by suggesting that the company each and all present Odysseus with appropriate gifts. The donation (it is described in considerable detail even to the coffer that Arete gives him to keep the gifts in) is followed by a bath and supper: after it, Odysseus 'treats' the bard, Demodocus, to a particularly choice piece of meat and asks him to sing of the Wooden Horse. Again Odysseus weeps: this time his tears are described in a fine simile (a wife weeping for her dying husband) though again he hides them from all but Alcinous.

Now, however, Alcinous does not try to divert his guest (after all Odysseus has asked for it!) but openly requests his name and that of his country (they must know where his home is if the marvellous ship is to take him there). The coyness of Odysseus is thus at last unmasked, though with exquisite politeness, and Alcinous proceeds:

Od. VIII, 572

ἀλλ' ἄγε μοι τόδε εἰπὲ καὶ ἀτρεκέως κατάλεξον,
ὅπῃ ἀπεπλάγχθης τε καὶ ἅς τινας ἵκεο χώρας
ἀνθρώπων, αὐτούς τε πόλιάς τ' εὖ ναιεταούσας,
ἠμὲν ὅσοι χαλεποί τε καὶ ἄγριοι οὐδὲ δίκαιοι,   575
οἵ τε φιλόξεινοι καί σφιν νόος ἐστὶ θεουδής.
εἰπὲ δ' ὅ τι κλαίεις καὶ ὀδύρεαι ἔνδοθι θυμῷ
Ἀργείων Δαναῶν ἠδ' Ἰλίου οἶτον ἀκούων.
τὸν δὲ θεοὶ μὲν τεῦξαν, ἐπεκλώσαντο δ' ὄλεθρον
ἀνθρώποις', ἵνα ᾖσι καὶ ἐσσομένοισιν ἀοιδή.   580
ἦ τίς τοι καὶ πηὸς ἀπέφθιτο Ἰλιόθι πρό,
ἐσθλὸς ἐών, γαμβρὸς ἢ πενθερός οἵ τε μάλιστα
κήδιστοι τελέθουσι μεθ' αἷμά τε καὶ γένος αὐτῶν.
ἦ τίς που καὶ ἑταῖρος ἀνὴρ κεχαρισμένα εἰδώς,
ἐσθλός ἐπεὶ οὐ μέν τι κασιγνήτοιο χερείων   585
γίνεται, ὅς κεν ἑταῖρος ἐὼν πεπνυμένα εἰδῇ.

9. ΟΔΥΣΣΕΙΑΣ Ι

Τὸν δ' ἀπαμειβόμενος προσέφη πολύμητις Ὀδυσσεύς·
Ἀλκίνοε κρεῖον, πάντων ἀριδείκετε λαῶν,
ἦ τοι μὲν τόδε καλὸν ἀκουέμεν ἐστὶν ἀοιδοῦ
τοιοῦδ', οἷος ὅδ' ἐστι, θεοῖσ' ἐναλίγκιος αὐδήν.   5
οὐ γὰρ ἐγώ γέ τί φημι τέλος χαριέστερον εἶναι
ἢ ὅτ' ἐυφροσύνη μὲν ἔχῃ κατὰ δῆμον ἅπαντα,
δαιτυμόνες δ' ἀνὰ δώματ' ἀκουάζωνται ἀοιδοῦ
ἥμενοι ἐξείης, παρὰ δὲ πλήθωσι τράπεζαι
σίτου καὶ κρειῶν, μέθυ δ' ἐκ κρητῆρος ἀφύσσων   10
οἰνοχόος φορέῃσι καὶ ἐγχείη δεπάεσσι·
τοῦτό τί μοι κάλλιστον ἐνὶ φρεσὶν εἴδεται εἶναι.
σοὶ δ' ἐμὰ κήδεα θυμὸς ἐπετράπετο στονόεντα
εἴρεσθ', ὄφρ' ἔτι μᾶλλον ὀδυρόμενος στεναχίζω.
τί πρῶτόν τοι ἔπειτα, τί δ' ὑστάτιον καταλέξω;   15
κήδε' ἐπεί μοι πολλὰ δόσαν θεοὶ Οὐρανίωνες.

'But come, tell me this and speak frankly: where you have been in
your wanderings, what countries you came to, the people and the
cities, the cruel, wild and uncivilized as well as the hospitable and
god-fearing. And tell me why you weep and sorrow within your
heart when you hear of the fate of the Argive Danaans and of
Ilium. This the gods devised, and spun an evil doom for men that
there might be a song for generations to come. Or did a connection
of yours die before Ilium, a good man, brother-in-law or father-in-
law perhaps? They are the dearest to us after our own kin and
blood. Or was it a comrade, a dear, true friend? For he is not at all
worse than a brother, a comrade who understands.'

Then in answer spoke the clever Odysseus: 'Noble Alcinous,
famous among all peoples, it is indeed good to hear a bard such as
this one is, god-like of voice. Nothing, I say, is more pleasurable
than the occasion when joy seizes all the people, and the guests at
dinner hear the bard in the hall, as they all sit in a row, with the
tables full of bread and meat and the cup-bearer pouring the wine
from the pitcher into the cups. This seems to me the best thing
there is. But your heart is inclined to ask me about my bitter
troubles, so that I may groan and weep yet again. What first, then,
what last, shall I tell? For of woes the gods in heaven have given
me many.'

Virgil obviously had this scene in mind when he described
Aeneas' reception by Dido in Book I. But the circumstances are
strangely altered: Aeneas' identity is known from the very
moment that the divine mist suddenly leaves him and he stands
revealed to Dido, in the fresh beauty with which Venus invests him:

1.595   coram quem quaeritis adsum Troius Aeneas

he at once proclaims. Dido, of course, is stunned at the sight of
this famous hero!

613   obstipuit primo aspectu Sidonia Dido
            casu deinde viri tanto

But the whole book has led up to their encounter: Venus had
told Aeneas of Dido's past and prepared him to see in Carthage the
visible evidence of her remarkable character; moreover, we have
had a clue to Dido's probable feelings for Aeneas in the temple-
frieze that celebrated the heroes of the Trojan War and not least
himself. All is ready for the intervention of Venus and Cupid, as
we have noted above. The official reception of Aeneas and his
Trojans is thus both an historical event (all the characters are

historically 'placed' before it begins) and an emotional one: Dido
has already embraced the false Cupid, already begun to give her
heart to Aeneas. When the time for libation comes, she shows that
she fully recognizes the historicity of the occasion. She prays to
Jupiter as the god of hospitality:

1.732   hunc laetum Tyriisque diem Troiaque profectis
          esse velis, nostrosque huius meminisse minores.

Then they all drink in due order of precedence. The time for the
bard (Iopas) has come. He sings not of Troy (like Demodocus) but
what amounts to part of a didactic epic on astronomical phenomena: why winter days are short and winter nights are long, on
the phases of the moon, etc. Here Virgil follows not Homer but
Apollonius (song of Orpheus, *Arg.* I 496 f): he is saving the
Trojan theme for the climax of the scene and he does not need,
like Homer, to whet the curiosity of Dido by exhibiting the
Trojan sensibility of Aeneas. Dido knows too well who Aeneas is.
Dido herself must show the emotion, originate the curiosity. We
come therefore to the following conclusion of the episode:

I. 748   Nec non et vario noctem sermone trahebat
          infelix Dido, longumque bibebat amorem,
          multa super Priamo rogitans, super Hectore multa,
          nunc, quibus Aurorae venisset filius armis,
          nunc, quales Diomedis equi, nunc, quantus Achilles.
          'Immo age, et a prima dic, hospes, origine nobis
          insidias' inquit 'Danaum, casusque tuorum,
          erroresque tuos. Nam te iam septima portat
          omnibus errantem terris et fluctibus aestas.'

II. 1   Conticuere omnes intentique ora tenebant.
          Inde toro pater Aeneas sic orsus ab alto:
          'Infandum, regina, iubes renovare dolorem,
          Troianas ut opes et lamentabile regnum
          eruerint Danai; quaeque ipse miserrima vidi
          et quorum pars magna fui. Quis talia fando
          Myrmidonum Dolopumve aut duri miles Ulixi
          temperet a lacrimis? et iam nox umida caelo
          praecipitat suadentque cadentia sidera somnos.
          Sed si tantus amor casus cognoscere nostros
          et breviter Troiae supremum audire laborem,
          quamquam animus meminisse horret luctuque refugit,
II. 13   incipiam.

If we compare the two quoted passages, it is easy to see that wholly different techniques of narration are employed. Since Alcinous does not know Odysseus' identity, he asks only the most general questions. In lines 572–6 he wants what we might almost call geographical and ethnological information: the places, cities, men, kinds of society that Odysseus must have seen in his obviously extensive wanderings. Then in lines 577–86 he alludes specifically to Odysseus' evident sensitivity to the Trojan-war songs. They are the woes out of which the gods have made a song for posterity. Only a participant or the relative or close friend of a participant could have been really touched by them. All this, it is easy to see, is politely modulated inquisitiveness. The generalizations—almost the platitudes—amount to a social gambit—a nice way of breaking the ice. Obviously, this is not Homer speaking: this is the courteous Alcinous who has so admirably restrained his curiosity for a whole day.

But Virgil (in describing Dido's curiosity) avoids long direct quotations and empathetically seizes the inner feelings of Dido: *noctem . . . trahebat, longum . . . bibebat amorem* show us the love-sick queen (the imperfects indicate the process at work, the strategy of delay, the reiterated gulping of the long draughts of love); the present participle *rogitans* and its objects (multa super . . . super, quibus armis, quales equi, quantus Achilles, etc.) are decidedly empathetic; Virgil here penetrates Dido's mind and above all her feelings. She does not want so much to know about Troy *per se* as to hold her lover before her, hear his voice, hear his own story (it is not the *insidias Danaum* but *erroresque tuos* on which she concludes her request). Nor does Virgil restrain his sympathy or conceal his own point of view: *infelix Dido* expresses a feeling, a prophecy and a judgement. And Aeneas' feelings also come through: he is not like Odysseus relating a generality of troubles (ἐμὰ κήδεα *Od.* IX. 12) but the one specific *dolor*, the Fall of Troy —the terrible event of which he was, alas, so great a part.

We may perhaps say that the difference of the passages is due to the different settings, as of course is at least partly the case. Odysseus is not Aeneas; Alcinous is not Dido. But the two settings are also parts of the two styles. The elaborate by-play between Alcinous and Odysseus (we have already touched on the salient points of it) is in its way a masterpiece of objective characterization: the careful repetition of the same situation (Odysseus'

47

grieving response to the bard's songs), the coyness of Odysseus and the courtesy of Alcinous, the introduction of the games and the dance (the consequent variation of Demodocus' repertoire) as polite stratagems of Alcinous, the effect of Euryalus' rudeness on the whole situation—all this and much more (for Nausikaa, Arete, Athene and the other Phaeacians also count) is a work of finished art. Its objectivity is manifest: the speeches belong to the characters; the actions are described without comment; adjectives, verbs, syntax are the simplest that will serve the immediate narrative purpose. (In the narrative, for example, the simple aorist or past prevails: there are few imperfects, no historical presents. There are stock epithets but no 'fingerpointing' adjectives.)

In the long Virgil passage, the precise tense variations (note the sequence: bibebat, rogitans . . . venisset, inquit, conticuere, tenebant, iubes, vidi, praecipitat, suadent, etc.), the sympathetic adjectives (infelix, infandum, lamentabile, etc.), the historical presents, the indirect questions, the syntax and metric, the emotional rhetoric (especially the anaphora), and much, much else, break through the barrier between author and characters, between narrative and quotation, between bare event and editorial judgement, so that all objectivity seems almost wholly relinquished. But it is quite clear that Virgil could never have done this if the setting of the passage had not permitted it. Thus we have already been shown how Dido had begun to succumb to love and Aeneas, how Aeneas reacted to Troy, how the sequence of events has brought Dido and Aeneas together and also prepared them for each other. We know the general parallelism of Trojan and Tyrian history, of Aeneas and Dido. At no point has an *i* been left undotted or a *t* left uncrossed. We anticipate Dido's inner emotion because we have already begun to penetrate her motivation, her *psyche*. The passage is subjective because the setting is. The poem is a seamless whole.

If I had space, I could expand this comparison to a great many other passages, such as, for example, the *Nisus-Euryalus* (*Aeneid* IX, 367–99) and *Doloneia* (*Iliad* X. 354 ff.) or the *Pallas-Turnus* (X, 439 ff.) and *Sarpedon* (*Iliad* XVI, 419 ff.) episodes. I have in my book compared the games of *Aeneid* V and *Iliad* XXIII. There is, I think, much to be done in this area of analysis—the stylistic in the broadest sense—but I hope I have at least suggested the main points with which I am here concerned.[5]

I am not of course making a comparative judgement here. There is much to be said for and against each style. What is important for the understanding of Virgil is what he did with his subjective style. We can define this, in very general terms, as the erection of an inclusive frame of reference that enabled him to correlate the principal elements of his epic material, as Homer and all objectively styled epic could not. Because he empathetically and sympathetically reproduces his divine and human characters' motives, they can be co-ordinated with one another.

This principle holds for all levels of the plot. There is Jupiter and the Roman programme, the divine plan, of which he alone has full cognizance and full command. Then there are the lesser deities—Juno and Venus most of all—who either thwart or aid the hero and his mission but who in fact negate each other or contradict their own basic intentions. (Venus and Juno, for example, combine to set a trap for Dido—Venus in order to get her on Aeneas' side; Juno in order to keep Aeneas from Rome and so defer or stop Rome's prophesied conquest of Carthage—but both effect the exact opposite of what they propose: Aeneas' whole enterprise is threatened until Jupiter intervenes; Dido's death preludes and in a sense motivates the Punic wars.) Below the deities, are the semi-divine or supernatural figures: the ghostly Anchises, Eros, Polydorus, Harpies, Cyclopes, Fama, the Sibyl Charon, the Shades of the underworld. Finally, the human beings: Dido, Aeneas, Anchises before his death, Creusa, Trojans and Tyrians, etc. Each of these levels of being, so to speak, is carefully co-ordinated. Human and divine, natural and supernatural, physical and psychic are not arbitrarily mingled but logically connected so that a free human act, a plainly human motive or feeling, is at the same time an event on two or more divine levels and has also other repercussions.

Homer's gods are not so divided (Zeus is more powerful and more omniscient than the other gods but there is no definite and consistent system of subordination) and they for the most part enter or leave the action on the same objective basis as the human characters. The monsters—Polyphemus, Scylla, the self-acting Phaeacian ships and so on—physically obtrude on Odysseus and are taken with the same matter-of-factness as the purely natural phenomena. There is a vague programme or divine plan (as the divine Councils bring out) but for the most part the human

49

characters are on their own with the exception of specific divine interventions. It seems curious for example that the 'good' and pious Odysseus is allowed to go to sleep (and just after a solemn act of prayer) at the very time his men so disastrously slaughter the cattle of the Sun-God. There is no real organization of the gods: Zeus may countermand Poseidon and Calypso or encourage Athene but he certainly does not weave destiny out of the complex of their acts. There is really no idea of a fully contrived equilibrium between freedom and fate.

But Virgil of course could neither copy nor accept the 'natural piety' or 'credulity' of Homer. He was the poet of a much more sophisticated age and he himself was unusually conscious of anachronism. Though Aeneas is given a 'revelation' (he could not possibly have invented by natural human means the divine plan of Rome) he is not forced to take it. The very assurance of divine aid and supervision, his relative immunity to the kind of danger that besets Odysseus (especially in *Aeneid* III vs. *Odyssey* IX–XII) only make his own inner acceptance of fate, his Roman and divine motivation, so much the more important. *Pietas* can never be imposed: otherwise, it would lose all its meaning. Hence the primary significance of his attitude, his emotional responses, his motives, his psyche. The gods and supernatural powers never override him any more than Aeneas overrides them. The rule is correlation, coincidence, the simultaneous action of earth and heaven.

We can see this all along the line. To take a relatively trivial example first: Venus at a pivotal moment of Book I dispels the mist with which she has enveloped Aeneas. This is an obvious reproduction of Homer (though Apollonius has it too): Athene dispels the mist around Odysseus at the exact moment he reaches Arete in Alcinous' great hall. He is thus protected against any unpleasant curiosity until he can actually carry out Nausikaa's instructions (that he speak to her mother first). The result is the mild surprise of Arete and the Phaeacians; the incident only slightly enhances the importance of Odysseus' entry. But in *Aeneid* I (unlike *Odyssey* VII) the dissolution of the mist comes at a carefully prepared psychological moment: we have seen and empathetically followed the growth of Aeneas' conception of Dido (from the time when Venus told him about her through his gradual exploration of her city) and we have seen how Dido is 'softened' toward him, so to speak, by the immediately prior encounter with Ilioneus, by the parallelism of their previous experiences, etc. The sudden clearing of the mist is obviously a very dramatic way of giving éclat to an emotional encounter.

But this is just as true of the more important acts of divine intervention: the Venus-Cupid scene, for instance, is in Apollonius (from whom it is taken) made to precede the Medea narrative at the very beginning of the Medea Book (*Arg.* III). Thus, though Medea's love is natural and human enough (its origin and growth is actually told with great psychological finesse), its human reality is definitely not correlated with its supernatural origin and motivation: we are obviously meant to think of Eros as the actual agent of the emotion; he really does shoot his arrow at Medea. In *Aeneid* I, on the other hand, the Cupid episode (in itself I think decidedly awkward) comes only at the psychological moment when Dido and Aeneas have been prepared for each other, have met in the most dramatic of meetings and are obviously predisposed to love. Even so Virgil is careful to leave out the business of the arrow: Cupid only starts a gradual process—paulatim abolere Sychaeum incipit et vivo temptat praevertere amore. And we can *mutatis mutandis* say the same thing of the storm by which Juno forces the lovers into the cave, of the publicity that Dido's infatuated pretence of *coniugium* excites (Fama) and, much more significantly, of Jupiter's (Mercury's) intervention: everything leads up to the moment when Aeneas' sense of guilt, of dereliction from duty, must come out. *Fatum* and *pietas*, the outer and the inner, the divine and the human here coincide. But this coincidence is of course very different from the two coincidences (the Cupid-Dido and Juno-Storm-Cave) just mentioned: Jupiter and fate stood on a higher level than Venus and Juno. The divine here punctuates as it were a psychological and human drama: but the divine is no mere 'reflection' of the human any more than fate or predestination is a mere reflection of freedom. There is no 'projection' of the human on to the divine. Instead, the two go together. They coincide, they meet, they merge. The divine plan works at all levels.

It is in this way that Virgil 'modernized' Homer or converted Homeric facts into Roman symbols. Jupiter's divine plan is a Roman divine plan just as Aeneas' *pietas* (as ultimately established) is Roman *pietas* and just as Juno and Venus are in part Carthage and Rome at a lower-sub-fatal level. We can therefore now see one sense in which Homer was necessary to Virgil. Homer has real heroes, a basic morality, at least an embryonic sense of divine plan. The suitors, Aegistheus and in a sense Ajax and Agamemnon get what they deserve: and so, in reverse, do Odysseus and Penelope. In contrast Apollonius, though so much more modern, is curiously unhomeric at just this point. There is at least a prima facie case for those who would credit him with the deliberate creation of an 'anti-hero'—a hero who gets by, so to speak, with crime and trickery, who can only take the initiative by a diplomacy that finally sheds all moral principle.[6] Actually, I am more inclined to think that the *Argonautica* is a deliberate blending of incompatibles and designed shock-effects: I cannot believe that the curious beginning with a catalogue, the strange perversity of some of the Argonauts (particularly Heracles and Idas), the constantly obtruded antiquarianism and geography, the passionate Medea set so oddly beside the prudential Jason, the *amour* that proceeds from Euripidean passion to the legalistic cave marriage, the occasional apathy of the whole company and of Jason especially—above all the extraordinary blend of Homer and Callimachus in the theology —I cannot believe that all these are either accidental or resolvable into some hidden, ultimate unity. The *Argonautica* is not, I think, a piece of brilliant modernism like some of Callimachus' Hymns. Nor is it, I also think, concerned with any larger morality or any new synthesis. Apollonius could not do for Virgil what Homer in fact did. The *Odyssey*, for Virgil at least, was a moral unity.

Yet this only takes us a very little way toward the true problem of Virgil's 'inverted' use of Homer. Homer was more usable than Apollonius but Virgil's 'frame of reference', or the system of multiple correlations and coincidences to which we have referred, was what made him usable at all. The result was, it seems to me, a magnification or 'depth' effect that, on the one hand, enormously amplified the Homeric tone but, on the other, gave Homeric or epic-heroic meaning to Augustan Rome and, even more significantly, to Virgil's own Augustan sensibility. This is, I think, the secret of the effectiveness of some of the most striking Virgilian episodes.

Homer, for example, describes Odysseus as he encourages his disheartened company while they sail between Scylla and Charybdis (he knows about Scylla but they do not):

1. *Od.* XII. 208–216

> ὦ φίλοι, οὐ γάρ πώ τι κακῶν ἀδαήμονές εἰμεν.
> οὐ μὲν δὴ τόδε μεῖζον ἔπι κακόν, ἢ ὅτε Κύκλωψ
> εἴλει ἐνὶ σπῆϊ γλαφυρῷ κρατερῆφι βίηφιν·   210
> ἀλλὰ καὶ ἔνθεν ἐμῇ ἀρετῇ βουλῇ τε νόῳ τε
> ἐκφύγομεν, καί που τῶνδε μνήσεσθαι ὀΐω.
> νῦν δ' ἄγεθ', ὡς ἂν ἐγὼ εἴπω, πειθώμεθα πάντες.
> ὑμεῖς μὲν κώπῃσιν ἁλὸς ῥηγμῖνα βαθεῖαν
> τύπτετε κληΐδεσσιν ἐφήμενοι, αἴ κέ ποθι Ζεὺς   215
> δώῃ τόνδε γ' ὄλεθρον ὑπεκφυγέειν καὶ ἀλύξαι.

My friends, we have had a long experience of troubles. This is no greater evil than when the Cyclops kept us by force in his hollow cave. But we escaped from there by my courage and advice and intelligence. And I think that this too you will live to remember. Now then, come, as I urge, obey me all of you: strike the deep breakers with your oars, staying in your rowing seats—and perhaps Zeus may allow us to escape the destruction that threatens us.

and again, Odysseus, after the landing near Circe's palace, luckily kills a stag and brings it back to his famished crew with the words:

2. *Od.* X. 174–177

> ὦ φίλοι, οὐ γάρ πω καταδυσόμεθ', ἀχνύμενόι περ,
> εἰς Ἀΐδαο δόμους, πρὶν μόρσιμον ἦμαρ ἐπέλθῃ·   175
> ἀλλ' ἄγετ', ὄφρ' ἐν νηΐ θοῇ βρῶσίς τε πόσις τε,
> μνησόμεθα βρώμης μηδὲ τρυχώμεθα λιμῷ.

'My friends, not yet shall we go down to the house of Hades, troubled though we are, until the appointed day arrives. But come now, as long as there is food and drink in the swift ship, let us think of food and not succumb to hunger.'

Finally, Homer describes the disguised Odysseus (the night before his attack on the suitors) as he lies in the forecourt of his own house and debates whether or not to deal at once with the passing maid-servants who have disgraced themselves with the suitors. But he steels himself to a final act of patience:

3. *Od.* XX. 18–21

> τέτλαθι δή, κραδίη· καὶ κύντερον ἄλλο ποτ' ἔτλης,
> ἤματι τῷ, ὅτε μοι μένος ἄσχετος ἤσθιε Κύκλωψ
> ἰφθίμους ἑτάρους· σὺ δ' ἐτόλμας, ὄφρα σε μῆτις   20
> ἐξάγαγ' ἐξ ἄντροιο ὀϊόμενον θανέεσθαι.

'Endure, my heart; you once endured worse,—on that day when

the unconscionable Cyclops ate your good companions. You bore
it then until your cleverness got you out of his cave, though you
thought you would die.'

And now Virgil. Aeneas just landed after the terrible storm,
kills seven huge stags. He divides this booty with his men and
shares among them the wine that is left:

> (*Aeneid* I.197)
> et dictis maerentia pectora mulcet;
> 'O socii (neque enim ignari sumus ante malorum),
> o passi graviora, dabit deus his quoque finem.
> Vos et Scyllaeam rabiem penitusque sonantes
> accestis scopulos, vos et Cyclopea saxa
> experti: revocate animos, maestumque timorem
> mittite; forsan et haec olim meminisse iuvabit.
> Per varios casus, per tot discrimina rerum
> tendimus in Latium, sedes ubi fata quietas
> ostendunt; illic fas regna resurgere Troiae.
> Durate, et vosmet rebus servate secundis.'

The first of these Homeric passages is obviously Virgil's main
source for the words of Aeneas; the second provides the setting
(the stag and meal); the third is probably the model of the phrases
passi graviora and the actual imperatives, *revocate animos, durate*. The
chief divergences of Virgil from Homer are the following:

1. Virgil takes his setting from one Homer passage (Passage 2)
but obviously makes a vastly different use of it. In Homer the
killing of the stag merely leads to an exhortation to eat: 'We shall
not go to Hades before our time comes. Look! Food!' is the gist
of Odysseus' speech on this occasion. Here, as in the preceding
storm speech of Aeneas (1.94–101 o terque quaterque beati, etc.)
Virgil makes a specific piece of Homeric narrative into the context
for a profound and generalized reflection on the total meaning and
plan of the epic. Aeneas thus ignores food: it is but the tacit
excuse, so to speak, for a spiritual restoration and recovery (as
the storm before was an excuse for an equally 'spiritualized'
despair). Homer, of course, keeps strictly to his concrete narrative
context.

2. Thus another Homeric passage (1) was more suitable for
Aeneas' words (as distinct from their setting). Yet Odysseus'
words are here also in context as Aeneas' are not. It is a moment of
high danger: they must get by Scylla as quickly as possible, yet the

men are stunned at the roar and surf of the Πλαγκτὰι (Wandering Rocks) and let their oars go. The time has indeed come for honeyed words of encouragement (μειλιχίοις ἐπέεσι). Odysseus says in effect: 'Friends, we've had plenty of experience of trouble already. The Cyclops' cave was worse. Yet my courage and skill got us out of that. It will be the same here: this too will become just a memory.' Odysseus calms his own wrath against the suitors' mistresses with just the same specificity: 'Bear it! You bore worse before. Remember the day when the Cyclops ate your good companions. You bore that until my cleverness got you out of the cave, near to death as you were.' But Virgil generalizes: the very fact that the recollected dangers are doubled (Scylla and the rocks *and* also the Cyclops); and the very way the specific Homeric things (the Cyclops and his cave) are translated into abstracts or inanimate objects: *Scyllaeam rabiem, sonantis scopulos, Cyclopia saxa* with the personal agents (Scylla, Cyclops) made into adjectives; the obviously rhetorical anaphora (vos et . . . vos et) along with the quite different metric[7]—all these lift the Homeric content and language to a lofty plane of generalization which embraces past, present and future—the whole Roman programme: *per tot discrimina rerum tendimus in Latium, sedes ubi fata quietas ostendunt.*

3. Then the *additions* to Homer are of the utmost significance: to the Homeric *passi graviora* is added *dabit deus his quoque finem.* All one sees is part and parcel of the divine plan, as the later additions of Latium, the rebirth of Troy, the fates—all show. The idea of present trouble reduced to the status of mere memory (καί που τῶνδε μνήσεθαι ὀΐω) is changed to the idea of present trouble as *joyful* memory: here Virgil may have used the quite differently placed words of Eumaeus to Odysseus:

Od. XV. 398-401
νῶι δ' ἐνὶ κλισίῃ πίνοντε τε δαινυμένω τε
κήδεσιν ἀλλήλων τερπώμεθα λευγαλέοισι
μνωομένω. μετὰ γάρ τε καὶ ἄλγεσι τέρπεται ἀνήρ,
ὅς τις δὴ μάλα πολλὰ πάθῃ καὶ πόλλ' ἐπαληθῇ.

But now, as we eat and drink in the hut, let us rejoice in the bitter sorrows of one another, as we bring them to mind. For a man rejoices in his woes, after they are over—a man who has suffered much and wandered far.

But Eumaeus is merely uttering a soothing platitude, much like the

Euripidean fragment (131): ὡς ἡδὺ τοι σωθέντα μεμνῆσαι πόνων
In Virgil, the *memory* is to be joyful because the great Roman plan
will be fulfilled: *per varios casus,* etc., immediately follows. The joy,
the hope, is of an utterly different character.

4. But Virgil is deliberately *recalling* as well as *changing* Homer.
The moment is Heroic, Odyssean, epic: the Roman achievement
makes it such. Rome and its great men (Aeneas prefigures Augustus of course) have the right to make the comparison, to set themselves in this gallery. Horace makes (possibly in recollection of
Virgil) the same point in his Teucer ode:

Od. I. VII. 30

O fortes peioraque passi
mecum saepe viri. nunc vino pellite curas
cras ingens iterabimus aequor

Plancus is also raised to an heroic, Homeric level. He is another
Teucer.

5. Yet the 'heroic moment' of Aeneas' speech to his men is an
infinitely amplified version of Homer. The heroic changes its
character. First of all, the inherent egoism of Odysseus is dis-
carded. The idea of the Odyssean speeches is always: 'my *arete,* my
metis carried *me* (and hence *you*) through'. The Homeric hero is an
individual whose social context is not significant except by way of
contrast: in fact, all Odysseus' men are lost before he reaches
Calypso and this does not really matter very much to the *nostos*.
It is only by the last minute intervention of Athene that Odysseus
in Book XXIV is prevented from making a clean sweep of most
of his countrymen (in addition to the suitors and all the others
killed in the battle before Athene intervenes). Odysseus clearly
has the thoroughly individualistic *arete* of the Homeric hero—his
egocentric pride—even though he is, comparatively, about the
least anti-social of Homer's heroes. In Aeneas' words, the second
person (*vos*) prevails and the first person is plural (tendimus in
Latium). Aeneas without his men would have no mission, no real
reason for his survival of Troy. And the social emphasis of Virgil
obviously goes with his sense of history: he is concerned with
Rome, and its future and only because of Rome with Troy and
Aeneas: illic fas regna resurgere Troiae. The heroic moment is
historical because it is social: it is the moment of a people symbolized by a man.

The Homeric motifs are thus set in the frame of reference, the system of correlations (of divine-human coincidences) which we have already tried to describe. But it is relatively easy to see the Virgilian amplification of Homer: it is somewhat harder to see the Homeric 'amplification' of Rome, if I can, somewhat paradoxically, so put it. The point is that Virgil's idea of Rome—the programme or divine plan, the 'system' of the *Aeneid*—is homerically worked out, largely because there was no Roman system or mythology, no Roman 'heroic age' that was at all usable. There were no gods and heroes but Homer's gods and heroes. Neither Roman history—even in its 'Augustanized' Livian form—nor hellenistic philosophy (such as, e.g., the Stoic εἱμαρμένη or λόγος) could be made into poetry because they wholly lacked the poetical images, the poetical cosmos without which, at that time, no poet could function. Virgil's problem was to apply the Homeric motifs to Roman themes in such a way that each would 'amplify', would give poetical validity, to the other. But it is easy to say this: much harder to show what it really means.

Perhaps the best way to bring out the fundamental problem here is to take once more the example of Dido. Apollonius had already, as we have seen, taken the great step of putting a hellenistic (Euripidean) *amour* in a homerically-styled epic. But, whether deliberately or inadvertently, he simply did not fit her into his gallery of heroes or his generally epic milieu. This perhaps does not matter so much because the heroes themselves (especially Jason) are 'modernized' and they too conflict with their originals in Homer or for that matter in Cyclic epic, choral lyric and most tragedy before Euripides. But Virgil obviously was determined to avoid this kind of conflict. Unlike Apollonius he 'reproduced' Homer. Dido could not therefore be a Medea—that is, a woman whose eroticism would detract from or cancel the dignity of his hero or his epic. So we have also Dido the queen. But the important thing, of course, is not her rank but her heroic and thus tragic quality. Her tragedy is that of shamed *arete*: in this sense her suicide is Sophoclean; she is, from this point of view, an Ajax. She violates her duty to Sychaeus (whatever we may think of her duty, Virgil certainly intended it to be there) and her duty to Carthage also, but, even more, she violates her self-respect, her heroic identity. That, therefore, she becomes the counterpart of the Homeric Ajax, when Aeneas sees her in the underworld, is marvellously apposite. And we can, I think, without any difficulty, see in the Dido-Ajax 'transference' a tragic as well as an Homeric reminiscence. Ajax's pride insists on its tragic validation and cannot endure the pity or explanation that would quickly dissipate this: neither can Dido's. The use of the Homeric motif thus gives a poetical resonance, a linking and multiplication of epic and tragical connotations, that no invention, no merely Roman image, could possibly have given. We are once more in the world of epic and tragic heroism.

But just because these connotations have been secured, because they have been fixed in the Homeric substratum of the poem, Virgil can 'invert' them, can employ the amplification effect we have just considered. Hence the Roman reformulation of the episode—the ideas that tragic pride of this sort cannot be appeased but only accepted and transcended, that Aeneas must face and take the fact that there are things for which there is no forgiveness, and that this lesson too is one that a Roman hero must learn before he can do his full duty—would of course be inconceivable without the initial motif to be reformulated. We must add also that since Virgil's primary concern with motivation is shown in or expresses itself in his empathy or his 'subjective style', the sudden cessation of empathy, the deliberate cutting off of communication, must produce a peculiarly tragic and pathetic effect. Neither we nor Aeneas can 'reach' Dido, can establish any rapport or empathy. The unhomeric subjective style here takes extraordinary advantage of the Homeric motif.

I have of course only suggested an approach to the problem of Virgil as an inverted Homer, not attempted to supply an adequate analysis of it. It is I think dangerous to generalize about it, since generalization can so often miss the concrete poetry altogether. Thus Knauer's thesis[8] that Virgil uses Homer 'typologically' as the New Testament uses the Old, seems to me to be a generalization whose actual utility for literary criticism is quite limited and probably also misleading. Nor is it helpful to compare Virgil with T. S. Eliot because Eliot also 'inverts' motifs from the classics of earlier times or at any rate recalls them in modern contexts to produce a special kind of irony, a shock or recoil effect. Virgil saw —I think was even consciously aware—that Homer and the whole epic ensemble of heroes, demigods, ghosts and monsters were so indissolubly tied together that no author of his time or of post-

Homeric times could really succeed in dissociating them—that is, in 'inventing' a new epic of heroic life that could in some sense be set beside or *added to* Homer's epics.

The possible thing—possible that is for post-Homeric and certainly for Hellenistic and Roman poets who also aspired to be original poets—was not to invent but to reproduce the richest and most evocative motifs that could be found—and most of all to reproduce the Homeric ensemble of motifs. In this sense Rome could be raised to heroic dimensions while on the other hand, the heroism of Homer could be amplified to Roman dimensions. But this is only a very preliminary expression of a much more complex reality, for Virgil did more than 'amplify': he also inverted, shifted, 'shook up' the motifs so that all sorts of new connotations could emerge—especially those that expressed the tragic contrast between primitive and civilized man and perhaps even more fundamentally the contrast between egoistic passion and its humane renunciation.

But how does this help us to understand Virgil's specific 'reproduction' of the whole plot of the *Odyssey* as well as his specific 'inversion' of it? He could not, it is clear, 'create' another archetypal myth and indeed Homer himself did not 'create' in this sense. The fact that myth—and *in concreto* the myth of the Greek heroic age—was the traditional subject of poetry, that the two indeed were indissolubly united, was a *datum* that Virgil took from Greek literature and could not alter. But Greek and Latin poets before Virgil generally interpreted this *datum* as a limit rather than as a positive source of ideas. Poets were confined to a certain material that necessarily contracted as it was poetically 'used up'. How could they 're-do' the *Odyssey* when it had already been definitively done?

Moreover, the turn from poetry to prose in the fourth century obviously went with a turn from myth to science or *logos*: oratory, history, philosophy were the great *genres* after 400 B.C. The third-century Alexandrians—Callimachus, Theocritus, Philetas, etc.—saw very well that epic in the grand manner was no longer possible or poetically viable. What they did not see—what no one before Virgil really saw at all clearly—was that the old myth still possessed an archetypal or basic validity if it could somehow be released from its age and specific historical content. In terms of the *Odyssey*, the *nostos*, the gods, the detaining elements (especially

Calypso), the *nekuia*, etc., all had to be transformed into symbols with modern referents. This was assuredly a task of the utmost difficulty: yet it was also a necessary task (if large-scale poetry were still to be) for there was in fact no other equivalent source of available symbols.

The problem was thus to retain the evocative or poetical power of the Homeric motifs while wholly changing their literal meaning or application. Doubtless this could have been done in a number of ways; at least there is no reason to suppose that Virgil's way was the only one. At any rate what he did in Books I–VI (the Odyssean *Aeneid*) was in effect to cut the motifs off from their original base and at the same time set them up on a new base of an altogether different character. Thus the *nostos* was inverted (Odysseus goes home: Aeneas abandons home and both emotionally and literally leaves it further and further behind him); the 'detaining woman' was really converted into the hero's own detaining passion; the *nekuia* was shifted from a sort of extraneous *finis* to the hero's labours into an 'initiation' for the hero's real and decisive labour to come.

But all this was made possible by the 'innovation' of the non-Homeric second book of the *Aeneid*. Virgil in other words took the amorphous legend of Aeneas as the mythical founder of Rome (or its progenitors) and made it into the story of an Homeric hero's abandonment of his Homeric milieu and acceptance of a Roman milieu, and more specifically (as we have already seen) into a motivational story—the story of the conversion of a Homeric into a Roman psyche. So what really dominates the Odyssean *Aeneid*—until at least the final Show of Heroes—is the nostalgia for Troy, the *infandus dolor*. When Aeneas saw that all his Trojan heroism must go for nothing, that the gods had abandoned Troy, that all he really prized had perished, his approach to what followed was inevitably determined. This is the context in which his relations to Anchises and to Dido are set. Yet it is clear that this context derives all its meaning as well as its pathos, its poetical depth, from the constant parallelism of Odysseus and the *Odyssey*. There is always the pathetic similarity in difference. The gods are in one sense Odyssean but they are also part of a tight, omniscient, omnipotent fate of which the hero is only an instrument (even if it is essential that he be also a willing instrument). Aeneas himself is shorn of all that really motivates Odysseus. Dido is an amazing inversion of Calypso. So alike, so diverse are the two poems: yet assuredly it is this paradox of similarity in difference that made it possible for Virgil to use Homer, to recapture the poetical power of his images.

This is why, it seems to me, that Knauer's analogy of the Old and New Testaments is on the whole misleading. Homer is not so much an old 'history' that is being eschatologically completed by a new dispensation as an old (outmoded) myth that is being replaced by new history. Precisely because there could be no poetry without the myth, the myth was necessary. Yet the history is really new and there is no 'old' history in the Old Testament sense. The Homeric hero, and more largely the mythological hero (of tragedy as well as epic), lived and died in a relatively constant environment: the idea of relinquishing it and going beyond it was a radical Virgilian innovation. Yet the innovation was, as it were, bounded and limited by the necessity of repeating—even if 'inversely' repeating—the old myth. But the real continuity of the Old and New Testaments, in terms of which the one can be a 'type', a decisive reenactment, of the other, is quite lacking. The God of the Old Testament is the God of the New Testament (so orthodoxy, at least, against Marcion) but the gods of Homer are to Virgil only mythical symbols of the Stoic Fate or *logos* in which, for the purpose of his epic at least, he really believed. In short he had no Old Testament, no old faith to set against the new.

Yet Virgil could not do with the *Iliad* what he did so successfully with the *Odyssey*. For here (in the Iliadic *Aeneid*, Books VII–XII) he necessarily lost the guiding and pivotal idea of the reversed *nostos*, and with it his most adequate vehicle for *symbolization*, for the reformulation and 'inversion' of the Homeric motifs. The Aeneas of Books VII–XII is necessarily far more like a Homeric hero than the Aeneas of Books I–VI. Only with the greatest difficulty could his Homeric heroism be kept in successful tension with his new Roman motivation.

Let us here take a pivotal instance. The death of Hektor (*Iliad* XXII. 289–366) is the obvious model of the death of Turnus *Aeneid* XII. 887–952, the absolute conclusion of the whole epic). Here the dooms of Hektor and Turnus are divinely decreed and Achilles and Aeneas carry them out. Even so it is the *Dirae* that Jupiter sends in the *Aeneid* or the intervention of Athene in the *Iliad* that really determine the outcomes. Both Achilles and Aeneas, however, have an option: Hektor begs for the ransom of his corpse; Turnus goes further and begs for his life; Achilles and Aeneas of course can grant or refuse the requests. But we already know that Achilles will refuse: his reply to Hektor is ferocious

XXII. 346

ἀι γὰρ πως αὐτόν με μένος καὶ θυμὸς ἀνείη
ὤμ' ἀποταμνόμενον κρέα ἔδμεναι διά μ' ἔοργας.

Would that my raging spirit would impel me to cut off and eat your raw flesh, such things have you done to me!

The fact that Hektor still wears Patroclus' armour makes no real difference: Achilles is determined, anyway, to avenge his dead comrade. Yet Turnus (whose wound is lighter and not fatal: in the thigh, not through the neck) asks for his life on the ground that he too has a father, a living Anchises: fuit et tibi talis/Anchises genitor. And Aeneas hesitates, almost agrees: iam iamque magis cunctantem flectere sermo/coeperat. It is of course the sight of Pallas' belt—the symbol of Turnus' merciless arrogance toward the dead youth—that makes Aeneas once more change his mind: tune hinc spoliis indute meorum eripiare mihi? Pallas te hoc vulnere Pallas immolat.

It is clear that Virgil has to explain, to defend Aeneas' action. And this explanation is not, as in the *Iliad*, the mere desire to avenge the killing of a friend: the killing of Pallas was after all part of the chances of war; he had killed many himself. Rather it is Turnus' unnecessary blood lust (caedis cupido) and its particularly unnecessary manifestation in his disdain for the dead that cuts off the possibility of mercy. All this, of course, refers back to the dramatic contrast of deaths in *Aeneid* X: Turnus' killing of Pallas; Aeneas' of Lausus. The behaviours of the two heroes are very different. Turnus, in Virgil's eyes at least, shows *violentia* and 'hybristic' cruelty where Aeneas, when he can, shows *humanitas*.

I think there is no doubt that this is what Virgil intended. The *pietas* that had been so carefully instilled in Aeneas (in Books I–VI) had to show in battle, for battle was after all the main feature of the Iliadic *Aeneid* (VII–XII). This meant that Aeneas had to act for the Roman programme, for the destined *foedus* and peace, even for the ultimate Augustan *parcere subiectis, debellare superbos* or *pacis mos*—had to *be* in some sense what he had all along been trained or groomed for by fate and Jupiter. Yet his giving up of Troy and

Dido, his reconciliation with the Romanized Anchises, his acceptance of a reversed *nostos* and the reversal of motives this implied—were all poetically effective as his successful conduct of a war was not. Aeneas' love for Dido and his relinquishment of her are intensely pathetic: they have rightly moved the world. His devotion to Pallas, his grief at Pallas' death, his avenging of Pallas are meant to be equally pathetic, indeed climactically so: in fact they are not. Pallas is not the emotional equivalent of Patroclus: and this is why Aeneas' devotion to him does not quite excuse his killing of Turnus. Virgil at this point is at once too like and too unlike Homer: Aeneas' motive in the final Turnus scene is diluted, too Homeric to fit the 'Augustan' hero he is supposed to be and too Augustan to justify his Homeric violence.

In general the last six books are unequal to the first six. The tenth *Aeneid* is decidedly inferior to the fourth, though each is meant to mark an equally high point in the epic. The twelfth book is certainly much more effective than the tenth but it is the dramatic change in Turnus (his decision to fight Aeneas and save his honour), not Aeneas himself, that makes it so. In the sixth book Aeneas himself shows much of the pathos and heroism (the recapitulation of the past that forces a movement beyond it) which Turnus shows in the twelfth. But the twelfth is after all the end—the climax—of the epic as the sixth, in the nature of things, cannot be.

It is largely on such grounds that some critics have tried to maintain that Virgil did not intend to glorify Aeneas in Books VII–XII and that Turnus indeed must be looked upon as the true hero of the Iliadic *Aeneid*. Or, at a somewhat lower level of paradox, they have maintained that Virgil intended the fighting Aeneas of the later books to be a truly Homeric hero very much like Achilles, in which case all the 'remotivation' of *Aeneid* VI would go for nothing. Certainly we cannot say that Aeneas was uniformly humane. Yet it is I think clear that Virgil really did wish to represent Aeneas as a Roman hero, an Augustus who waged war in the interest of peace and a higher order of civilization. But I also think that he fully intended to do justice to Aeneas' opponents: no one can doubt this in the case of Camilla; and I fail to see how one can doubt it in the case of Turnus; his decision to stand and fight, to accept his doom, to reject the protection of Juturna, is and is meant to be heroic. The defect of the last six books really consists in the fact that Virgil succeeded in the second intention and, on the whole, failed in the first. Or putting it a little differently, Virgil, I think, meant to show that though the opponents of civilization are heroic, tragic, in a sense admirable, its champions are heroes of a higher order. They and they alone can make war without being corrupted by it; they only can escape tragedy because they do not succumb to *hybris* and the passions which perpetuate violence. Unfortunately, he did not succeed equally in both aims: the champions do not come off as well as the opponents.

Thus the 'inversion' of Homer does not work in Books IX–XII as it worked in Books IV–VI. The real difficulty was that the *Odyssey* was much easier to 'invert' than the *Iliad* or the *Odyssey* at least could be much more strikingly and poetically inverted. In Books VII–XII Virgil had to invent more, to work harder to adapt the Iliadic motifs to his Roman theme. It is of course possible that he could have done much in the three years which he had set apart for the *Aeneid's* revision. The greater finish of the earlier books shows I think that the major changes would have come in the later books. Yet the central difficulty would almost certainly have remained. The *Odyssey* fitted a developing hero, a narrative of motivation: the sea voyage, Calypso, the *nekuia*, above all the *nostos* theme, were capable of profound and effective transformation while yet retaining their essential Homeric identity; this was not true of the battle-pieces, the Achilles-Patroclus-Hektor trilogy, the Doloneia, or the arms-making.

Yet it is, for all that, the case that Virgil was able to express his central meaning in the whole poem and to no inconsiderable degree in the last six books of it. The Iliadic *Aeneid* may perhaps be looked upon as an outline—a roughly worked ensemble—with supremely evocative vignettes that at least suggest the main burden and message, the deeper reverberation of Virgil's Homer in Rome. I think here particularly of the shield episode (awkward as it also is), of the *Nisus-Euryalus* and *Camilla* and of the muster of the Latin tribes in Book VII. What is so striking in these last three episodes is the sympathy that Virgil lavishes on the young and particularly on the young who are also primitive. There is no minimizing of the violence, no wish to mitigate the inevitable tragedy to which it leads, but rather a sense of its greatness, its noble intensity of spirit, which is also joined to a sense of the civilization with which such noble violence is of necessity incompatible. The mission of Rome is peace: the driving spirit of Turnus, Camilla, Nisus, Mezentius, Amata, as well as of Dido, is passion, and through passion, violence. Only the civilized man— who has already put down the violence—can afford to admire it, to take the romantic view of it. This Virgil does, but he also knows that civilization has to be won and if necessary re-won. The Latins are noble, virtuous primitives: yet they are fighting fate, *pietas* and civilization. This is why some at least of the Homeric ferocity of *Aeneid* IX–XII is, as it were, pathetically or tragically 'inverted' and in this sense made to express both the disapproval and the admiration of civilized society.

We can now finally ask whether Virgil is 'original', or more exactly whether his peculiar reproduction and inversion of Homer has a right to be included among such 'creative' or 'original' achievements as those of Dante, Shakespeare, Goethe or the classical Greeks. The answer is not easy to give. The fact is that no author creates out of nothing like God. Some have the luck to inherit, at the right time, a mature *but not yet outmoded* body of ideas, motifs, patterns and, not least, a poetical language. It made, for example, a great difference whether a Greek poet wrote before or after the intellectual climacteric that is often known as the Sophistic enlightenment. Virgil, however, like T. S. Eliot and most contemporary poets, came into no such 'mature' inheritance as that of pre-Sophistic Greece. This is why I think that Eliot's famous identification of Virgil's classicism[9] with his maturity is somewhat misleading. The fact is that the contemporary epic available to Virgil was not so much mature as dead. Dead also was the mythology of Homer and the Greeks. The only available source of poetical imagery had seemingly dried up. Nor could Virgil make a new mythology of his own: no man, whatever his genius, could do that. He therefore did the next best thing: he inverted, he transformed, the old epic tradition, the old saga— Homer in short—and restored them to a new Roman existence. This was the original, the unique achievement of Virgil.

NOTES

[1] cf. on pre-Virgilian epic, my book *Virgil, A Study in Civilised Poetry* (Oxford, 1964) pp. 5–40.
[2] Göttingen, 1964 =*Hypomnemata*, Heft 7.
[3] cf. Macrobius, *Sat.* 5, 17, 4–5. There seems to be no doubt that Virgil alone was

responsible for Dido's *culpa* and liaison with Aeneas and that the original Dido of pre-Virgilian legend killed herself to escape marriage and keep faith with Sychaeus.

[4] Readers of my Virgil book (*op. cit.* above) will note that the résumé of Aeneid I–VI given in the text diverges at some points from that of the book (especially Chapter VI). I have now given a new emphasis to *Aeneid* II and have adduced some new points anent *Aeneid* V and its relation to III and IV. But there is not, I think, any essential change of view.

[5] cf. my *Virgil* ch. III and my remarks in *Phoenix*, vol. 20 (1966) pp. 59–75.

[6] See here the recent article of Gilbert Lawall, 'Apollonius' *Argonautica:* Jason as Anti-Hero,' *Yale Classical Studies* XIX, 1966 (pp. 121–69). Hermann Fränkel, 'Ein Don Quijote unter den Argonauten des Apollonius' (*Museum Helveticum*, 17, 1960, pp. 1–20) gives a much more moderate view of Apollonius' intent in creating a 'weak' hero. I am myself rather sceptical of the 'anti-heroic' conception of Jason.

[7] The passage falls into three parts (198–199, 200–203, 204–206) of which the second repeats, expands and intensifies the first and the third draws the conclusion: l. 207 applies the conclusion to the present situation.

Ll. 198 and 199 open with an exclamatory O (O socii, O passi graviora) and end with a rhetorically clinching conclusion: *dabit deus*, etc., where the metrical emphasis (diaeresis, caesura) is on *his quoque*. This part is followed by the four-line third part (*vos et . . . iuvabit*) where, after the anaphora (*vos et . . . vos et*), comes the relatively weak first conclusion (revocate animos—maestumque timorem mittite) that starts from a caesura (experti: revocate) and the clinching second conclusion which is metrically very emphatic

> mittite: forsan et haec olim meminisse iuvabit.

Note the (indicated) diaereses and caesurae as well as the third foot spondee. In the third part (ll. 204–206) note the anaphora (per . . .per) and the initial conclusion (tendimus in Latium) that is, as it were, bolstered and made climactic by the *ubi* clause introducing the clinching line, 206:

> ostendunt. illic fas regna resurgere Troiae

where the caesurae, spondees, and the accents that conflict with the ictus (ostendunt illic, fas), all slow up and give weight to the fate-laden words. The single sentence and line (207) that concludes gives the passage an almost lapidary finality.

The clashing *s* and *c* sounds of ll. 201–202 (Scyllaeam, accestis, scopulos, Cyclopia) contrast with the smooth conclusion of l. 203 (where *m* and *s* predominate; the ictus and accent coincide in *forsan* and *haec*). Virgil's 'melancholy' and yet solemnly hopeful tone is conveyed also by the pivotally placed long vowels and dipthongs (revocāte, maestum, haec, iuvābit). The metric enhances the rhetorical structure while at the same time giving it a special nuance.

Unlike Homer, Virgil repeats (e.g. l. 199 repeats 198 in effect; l. 201 repeats 200; note also the repetition in 204, 205–6) in order to achieve a rising tone leading to a climax. Yet the difference of structure and emphasis between the three parts is notable. Parts 1 and 2 each lead up to two conclusions (in 1: *revocate—mittite* and *forsan—iuvabit* and in 2: *sedes ubi, etc.* and *illic fas etc.*) but the two formal conclusions are characteristically different:

> forsan et haec olim meminisse iuvabit
> illic fas regna resurgere Troiae

and bring out the tangible difference between the 'possible' happiness to come and the fateful reason for it.

It is quite evident that Homer has no metrical design of this kind.

[8] *Op. cit.* pp. 353–9.

[9] *What is a Classic?* (1944).

III

Virgil and the Flavian Epic

A. J. GOSSAGE

VIRGIL'S influence on subsequent Latin poetry, and indeed on many prose-writers, was incalculable. He had expressed with profound understanding, and in language ranging from compassion to majesty, so much that was essential in the thought and feeling of the Romans, that his works were studied closely and loved by later generations. Fashions and predilections admittedly changed from one generation to another, so that in the age of Nero, for example, as Persius makes clear in his first *Satire*, sentimental Greek themes, rhetorical grandiloquence and even tendencies towards archaism found favour in various quarters; but generally speaking, apart from an occasional comparison with the Emperor, in which the adulation of a critic set Nero above Virgil as a poet,[1] it was Virgil to whom many writers turned, either as a model for their own poetry, as did Calpurnius Siculus, the bucolic poet, or as an acknowledged example and standard for others, as Persius in his first *Satire*,[2] or as a source of poetic wisdom and philosophic truths happily expressed. Of this last practice Seneca is the best example.[3] In the same period a certain young poet, whose identity is not known, naturally thought of Virgil's greatness, together with that of Horace and the tragic poet Varius, as the finest fruit of Maecenas' patronage; and his words describing Virgil no doubt echo the general opinion of the age:

> ipse per Ausonias Aeneia carmina gentes
> qui sonat, ingenti qui nomine pulsat Olympum
> Maeoniumque senem Romano prouocat ore . . .[4]

It was inevitable that the greatest Roman epic writer should be mentioned in the same breath as Homer.

Virgil's standing in the Flavian era (A.D. 70–96) may be gathered from the many references in Quintilian, who shows a very close familiarity with the poet's works and repeats with approval a remark of the distinguished orator Domitius Afer: 'mihi interroganti quem Homero crederet maxime accedere, Secundus, inquit, est Vergilius, propior tamen primo quam tertio.' In Quintilian's judgment all the other Roman writers of epic fall well behind Virgil.[5] In the eyes of Martial, Virgil was *magnus, summus* and *aeternus,* and although he considered the age of Domitian to be greater in most things than any other in the history of Rome, he realized that this age had no such *ingenium sacri . . . Maronis* to boast of.[6] Similar respect for Virgil is shown by the speakers in the *Dialogus de Oratoribus,* which purports to describe a discussion held among leading critics in A.D. 75. In this work, Maternus, defending the claims of poetry against Aper, the champion of contemporary oratory, observes that 'pluris hodie reperies, qui Ciceronis gloriam quam qui Virgilii detrectent'.[7] This admits that there were adverse opinions of Virgil, but it also suggests that they were few in number. Then Maternus goes on to commend the quiet life which Virgil led. The point of his remarks that follow is that it was possible to enjoy the Emperor's favour and popular esteem, as Virgil did, by writing poetry and at the same time to live in peace and comparative security, which was not possible for an orator caught up in the whirl of public activities.[8] Aper, who prefers the life of an orator with all its strenuous activities to the quiet life described by Maternus, nevertheless holds Virgil in high regard and speaks of him as a poet acceptable to contemporary taste, when he says: 'exigitur enim iam ab oratore etiam poeticus decor, non Accii aut Pacuuii ueterno inquinatus, sed ex Horatii et Virgilii et Lucani sacrario prolatus'.[9] Thus the *decor* of style sought by Flavian orators, as an ingredient of the general *laetitia* and *nitor* at which oratory aimed for the sake of pleasing its hearers, was to be derived from certain poets, among them Virgil, who were generally well-esteemed. A little later, Aper mentions people who preferred Lucilius to Horace and Lucretius to Virgil, but these again appear to have been in a minority.[10]

Among the poets of the Flavian era were two self-confessed admirers and imitators of Virgil. The wealthy Silius Italicus (*c.* A.D. 25–101), a former consul who had earned a bad reputation for informing under Nero and had been a friend and associate of the

Emperor Vitellius, but later redeemed his name by retiring altogether from politics, owned many country residences, especially in Campania, where he spent the later years of his life.[11] His admiration for Virgil is described thus by the younger Pliny:

> multum ubique librorum, multum statuarum, multum imaginum, quas non habebat modo, uerum etiam uenerabatur, Vergili ante omnes, cuius natalem religiosius quam suum celebrabat, Neapoli maxime, ubi monimentum eius adire ut templum solebat.

The *monimentum* mentioned here by Pliny was evidently Virgil's burial-place, as may be inferred from a poem of Martial:

> Silius haec magni celebrat monimenta Maronis,
> iugera facundi qui Ciceronis habet.
> heredem dominumque sui tumuliue larisue
> non alium mallet nec Maro nec Cicero.[12]

A deep respect for Virgil and a sensitive understanding of his poetry inspired a person of far different character and temperament, the Neapolitan poet P. Papinius Statius (*c.* A.D. 45–96), with a similar sense of *religio*. Statius was the son of a *grammaticus* and a man of moderate means. In a poem addressed to Vitorius Marcellus he writes of his poetical activities in Naples, at a time when he had already published his epic poem, the *Thebaid*:

> tenuis ignauo pollice chordas
> pulso Maroneique sedens in margine templi
> sumo animum et magni tumulis accanto magistri . . .[13]

and in the *Thebaid* itself he expresses his own inferiority to Virgil in reverent and humble tones. At the end of an episode describing the nocturnal exploits of two dedicated soldiers, Hopleus and Dymas, which has obvious affinities with the similar episode of Nisus and Euryalus in the *Aeneid*, Statius apostrophizes his heroes thus:

> uos quoque sacrati, quamuis mea carmina surgant
> inferiore lyra, memores superabitis annos.
> forsitan et comites non aspernabitur umbras
> Euryalus Phrygiique admittet gloria Nisi.[14]

The *Thebaid* ends with a passage of ten lines in which Statius speculates on the future fate of his poem; in this passage the following sentiment occurs:

F   69

uiue, precor; nec tu diuinam Aeneida tempta,
sed longe sequere et uestigia semper adora.[15]

Silius' admiration for Virgil, by contrast, is less humble than that
of Statius, but it is no less sincere. Its expression follows naturally
upon the mention of Mantua in the course of a catalogue of troops
from Cisalpine Gaul:

Mantua, Musarum domus atque ad sidera cantu
euecta Aonio et Smyrnaeis aemula plectris.[16]

Besides Statius and Silius, a third epic poet of the Flavian era,
C. Valerius Flaccus (c. A.D. 40–90), was clearly much influenced by
Virgil, but very little is known of his life and he does not mention
Virgil in his poem.

The age in which these poets lived bore certain resemblances to
that of Virgil. Politically, there was civil war in each case, followed
by the establishment of a new régime. But the differences were
more important. Whereas in Virgil's lifetime the civil wars and the
collapse of the Republic led to a new political order under
Augustus, that same political order was unshaken by the civil
wars that followed the death of Nero in A.D. 68, and when Vespasian was acclaimed Emperor most Romans already accepted the
imperial system of rule that Augustus had established nearly a
century earlier but needed to accustom themselves to a new
imperial family. Virgil's generation, after many weary years of
civil war, longed only for peace and a life of security. The *Pax
Romana,* when it came with Augustus, was readily glorified by
Virgil and his contemporaries. In A.D. 68–69, on the other hand,
another generation, which had already witnessed the instability of
Nero and must have begun to fear for its security, experienced a
short but bitter conflict that left a deep impression on men's minds.
Stoic opposition to the imperial system had grown strong under
oppressive emperors and came to a head in the so-called Pisonian
conspiracy against Nero in A.D. 65. Despite executions of men
who were known to be implicated, the opposition lived on and
gathered fresh strength under Vespasian and Domitian. Other
men, who accepted the imperial system, among them Silius Italicus, for example, no doubt retained their partisan feelings of
A.D. 68–69. Vespasian and especially Domitian, with his strong
autocratic tendencies, appear to have lacked the genius of Augustus for conciliation. Although there was civil peace, it was uneasy

for much of the time, and mutual mistrust and fear among the Emperor and his leading subjects, exaggerated by informers under Domitian, grew to an intolerable degree. The explosive atmosphere is reflected by Tacitus, in the *Agricola* and the first chapters of the *Histories* above all, and by the younger Pliny in a number of his letters. Tacitus and Pliny, writing after the death of Domitian, welcomed the new era of Nerva and Trajan, in which there was freedom from fear for men of their class and men could now think what they liked and say what they thought.[17]

Much of the poetry written in the first century A.D., after the grandeur and calm reflection of Virgil and Horace, reveals a deep agitation of spirit. Seneca and Lucan are introspective, bitter and full of turmoil; they are also moralistic and dwell on the evil in human nature. They depict crime and violence in passionate tones and lurid colours, aided by the techniques of a rhetorical training which had otherwise become sterile and found little practical outlet for its concentrated vigour. The aim of the orator and the poet in their public recitations was to please a demanding audience with epigrams, phrases that would delight the ear and a general splendour of expression.[18] No one in the Flavian period could match the intensity of feeling and terseness of expression that characterize Seneca and Lucan, but the influence of these two writers was very strong. They had set new fashions in Roman literature. Quintilian, whose aim was to restore to oratory some of its sobriety and good taste, passes fair judgment on Seneca when he says: 'uelles eum suo ingenio dixisse, alieno iudicio'.[19]

Of the three Flavian epic writers, Statius is perhaps the most clearly influenced by the general trend of fashion. He admired Lucan;[20] the influence of Lucan can be seen especially in the violence, and sometimes the absurdities, of his battle-scenes, and in his complexity of expression and occasional obscurity. Seneca's influence appears in the general treatment of the theme of the *Thebaid*, with its pervading horror. In his treatment of *furor* as a motivating force for men's actions, Statius owes something to both Seneca and Lucan, but on the whole he is less violent and less terse than either. Silius Italicus again resembles Lucan in the realism and exaggeration of some of his episodes and battle-scenes, and in the Stoic flavour of certain passages, and he makes much of *ira* and *furor* as motivating forces in the career and actions of Hamilcar and Hannibal; but his expression is far less complex

71

than that of Lucan. Valerius Flaccus wrote in a lighter but fairly elaborate style, and he sometimes reflects Lucan's exaggeration and extravagance of detail. On the whole, however, there is less intensity of feeling in his poem, and he leaves many motifs and episodes, in the Alexandrian manner, without developing them to their logical conclusion. The outstanding exception is his treatment of Medea, which, with its psychological interest and especially its description of the *furor* which possesses her, is truly typical of the poetical spirit of the age.

The three Flavian epic writers, therefore, were subject to more immediate influences than that of Virgil. Nevertheless, even though they were inevitably removed from him in thought and wrote in a different cultural atmosphere, Virgil's influence on them was greater than that of any other single author. It was Virgil, above all, who had established the pattern for the Roman epic and standardized for his successors many earlier Greek epic conventions.

Although the poems of the Flavian epic writers are widely divergent in scope, outlook and subject-matter, each of them curiously reflects Virgil's influence in a different way. This fact in itself is proof of his universality and of the far-reaching effects that his poetry had on later generations and on poets of varying interests and abilities. In the *Aeneid*, as in no other epic poem, features of the heroic, the romantic, the historical and the national epic are blended into a homogeneous whole and treated with unsurpassed poetical skill and psychological understanding. It is not surprising, therefore, that Valerius Flaccus, Statius and Silius Italicus each found in the *Aeneid* the inspiration and authority for his own type of poem. Valerius' *Argonautica,* for example, although it is based largely on the *Argonautica* of Apollonius Rhodius, owes much to the romantic element in the *Aeneid*. In particular, Virgil's psychological study of Aeneas and Dido and his profound portrayal of their love provided Valerius with a model for his own treatment of Medea and her love for Jason.

The *Thebaid* of Statius has many typical features of the romantic epic, but it shows a closer affinity with Seneca's tragedies and the *de Bello Civili* of Lucan than with the *Aeneid* in its general tone and sombre colouring. The psychological interest is focused mainly upon personalities, like Oedipus, Eteocles and Polynices, perverted by evil passions. At first sight this would appear to have little to do with Virgil; but when it is appreciated that the poem also contains much sympathy and tenderness, expressed in passages of great pathos, for the weak who suffer outrage at the hands of violent characters, it is clear that Virgil's humanity has found a conscious heir. Women and children terrified at the approach of war, families searching for their dead relatives on the battle-field and mothers lamenting for young sons killed in battle are all described with a deep understanding of the sufferings and grief of innocent people who are involved in the conflicts caused by the insane greed and ambitions of their rulers.[21] Much of the pathos associated with the young warriors who die in battle and the subsequent grief of their relatives is expressed by poetical techniques derived ultimately from the *Iliad*, but Statius was clearly influenced in turn by such episodes in the *Aeneid* as the death of Lausus, the death and funeral of Pallas, the lament of Evander for Pallas and the lament of Euryalus' mother. There is occasional pathos in the *Argonautica* and rather more in the *Punica*, but in each of these poems there are many passages in which the opportunity for creating pathos is neglected, so that Statius' preoccupation with such themes and his Virgilian spirit in handling them appear even more striking by contrast.[22]

Again, Statius' interpretation of *pietas* throughout the *Thebaid*, with its particular emphasis on the close ties of duty and affection among members of a family, develops certain aspects of the Augustan *pietas* with which Virgil's Aeneas is imbued. Admittedly, it is the stifling of *pietas* by evil passions within the Theban family on which Statius concentrates for much of the time, but there are remarkable manifestations of *pietas* too, in the expedition of Hopleus and Dymas to recover the bodies of their dead leaders, Tydeus and Parthenopaeus, the self-sacrifice of Menoeceus for the sake of his city and the mission of the Argive women, and in particular Argia, the widow of Polynices, to recover the bodies of their menfolk slain at Thebes and give them burial.[23] The goddess Pietas herself appears at the climax of the action, in a vain attempt to prevent the brothers from engaging in mortal combat.[24] There is *pietas* in Valerius and Silius,[25] but for them it is a more conventional concept and its importance is not emphasized as a leading motif as it is by Virgil and Statius. In these respects, then, the *Thebaid* is Virgilian in spirit at a deeper level than the other Flavian epics.

The *Punica* of Silius Italicus is far different in scope and purpose from either the *Argonautica* or the *Thebaid* and Virgil's influence upon it is mainly of a different kind. It follows to some extent the pattern of historical epic set by Naevius and Ennius in the third and second centuries B.C., a tradition not without influence on Virgil himself.[26] Ennius' *Annals*, however, was little more than a 'chronicle in verse',[27] and this is something which the *Aeneid*, with its dramatic unity and tragic intensity, far surpasses. In this respect, Silius combines Ennius' annalistic approach with a dramatic unity derived partly from Virgil. Like Ennius,[28] he wrote about the great heroes of the Roman Republic serving their country in turn with unselfish courage and devotion. The *Punica* thus differs from the *Aeneid* in its presentation and emphasis. Although from time to time in the *Aeneid* there are intimations of the greatness of individual historical figures, and in the review of national heroes in the sixth book there is a splendid sense of Roman greatness, the poem is essentially the story of a struggle to found a new city:

> tantae molis erat Romanam condere gentem.[29]

Aeneas is far more than a symbol of Augustus, but like Augustus he has a leader's task to perform. This leadership by one man, so important in the *Aeneid* and significantly emphasized in Jupiter's prophecy, in Anchises' speech in the underworld and in the description of Aeneas' shield,[30] cannot be matched in the *Punica*. Unlike Virgil, Silius is unable to achieve dramatic unity through the presentation of a single Roman leader in the mould of Aeneas. The men who serve Rome rise to greatness in their determination to save their country, but the Roman leadership is divided, as it was historically, and not even Q. Fabius Maximus or Scipio dominates the poem from beginning to end. In this respect the *Punica* necessarily bears a greater resemblance to the *Annals* of Ennius than to the *Aeneid*. On the other hand, the poem's dramatic unity is centred round the figure of Hannibal, who is the leader of the invading enemy forces, and the idea of collective Roman courage and stability, against which he strives and by which he is finally overcome. This idea is Augustan and Virgilian in feeling.

Like Virgil, Silius insists on the Trojan origins of Rome. The *Punica* is a poetical anachronism, perhaps partly because Silius himself, after his retirement from politics, could never inwardly

74

accept the new régime which was established after the bitter struggles following the death of Nero. The poem is nostalgic, looking back to a past era of greatness, and although the Trojan legend had ceased to have much political significance after the death of the last Julio-Claudian emperor,[31] Silius' Virgilian heritage causes him to retrace familiar paths. Rome, for example, is described as *Aeneia regna, Troia moenia, fatalia regna Teucrorum* and *cineres Troiae*; the Romans are *Phrygiae stirpis alumni, gens recidiua Phrygum, gens Troiana, Idaeum genus* and *gens Hectorea,* and they are often referred to as *Aeneadae, Troiugenae, Troes, Teucri, Dardanidae, Phrygii* and *Priamidae* and on occasion even *Sigei* and *Idaei.* In the first two lines of the poem Silius speaks of *gloria . . . Aeneadum.* Scipio is *Dardanus . . . ductor* and Laelius *magnum Dardaniae decus.*[32] The Trojan legend enters into a number of important passages, when, for example, Proteus, in prophesying the future greatness of Rome, refers to the judgment of Paris, the fall of Troy and the part played by Aeneas in establishing a new kingdom in Italy, when the Trojan origins of Sulmo, Capua and various places in Sicily are discussed, and when Dasius explains to Hannibal why Rome cannot be taken as Troy was taken.[33] An interesting feature of the legend as recalled by Silius is that the Roman descendants of the Trojans are now reconciled with their ancient enemies, the Greeks. This is symbolized, in the story which Dasius tells to Hannibal, by the meeting and reconciliation of Aeneas and Diomedes, at which Diomedes returns the image of Pallas captured by the Greeks from Troy, and again, in Scipio's *nekyia,* by the mingling of the spirits of Greeks and Trojans and the Sibyl's remark that Homer extolled Troy to the stars:

> atque haec cuncta, prius quam cerneret, ordine terris
> prodidit ac uestram tulit usque ad sidera Troiam.[34]

In this, Silius expresses the Flavian view, and particularly that of Domitian, whose Hellenic sympathies and cult of Athene-Minerva made it necessary to modify the Augustan view, as expressed by Virgil, that the Roman conquest of Greece was vengeance for the Greek sack of Troy.[35]

In writing the *Punica,* Silius must have been constantly aware of the imprecation which Virgil puts into the mouth of Dido when she sees the Trojan fleet sailing away from Carthage:

tum uos, o Tyrii, stirpem et genus omne futurum
exercete odiis, cinerique haec mittite nostro
munera. nullus amor populis nec foedera sunto.
exoriare aliquis nostris ex ossibus ultor
qui face Dardanios ferroque sequare colonos,
nunc, olim, quocumque dabunt se tempore uires.
litora litoribus contraria, fluctibus undas
imprecor, arma armis; pugnent ipsique nepotesque.[36]

The eighth book of the *Punica* contains a passage of more than two hundred lines[37] in which Juno urges the nymph Anna to encourage Hannibal before the battle of Cannae. Anna is introduced as the sister of Dido; she now lives under a new guise as a river-deity in Italy, and her adventures, following the death of Dido, are related by the poet in what appears to be a short sequel to Book IV of the *Aeneid*. In the course of her story there occurs a dream, in which the spirit of Dido appears to her and warns her of the deep enmity between the Carthaginians and the descendants of Aeneas:

ac nondum nostro infaustos generique soloque
Laomedonteae noscis telluris alumnos?
dum caelum rapida stellas uertigine uoluet,
lunaque fraterno lustrabit lumine terras,
pax nulla Aeneadas inter Tyriosque manebit.[38]

This enmity is expressed early in the poem, when Hamilcar forces Hannibal as a boy to swear that he will pursue the Romans with 'fire and the sword' and involve their city in destruction like that of Troy. Hannibal's oath is sworn in a place sacred to the *manes* of Dido, in the presence of Dido's statue—she is now re-united with Sychaeus, and the fatal sword of Aeneas lies at her feet—and by her *manes* and the divinity of the Carthaginian Mars.[39] In another passage Silius describes a shield presented to Hannibal in Spain.[40] Gallician craftsmen had depicted on this shield a series of scenes from Carthaginian 'history', beginning with Dido and the foundation of the city. Among the scenes are the arrival of Aeneas and his men on the shore of Africa, the hunt, the storm and the cave, the departure of the Trojans and Dido's suicide—all important Virgilian themes. Perhaps the most significant detail, and one which is certainly important for its relevance to the poem as a whole, is the description of Dido on her funeral-pyre:

ipsa pyram super ingentem stans saucia Dido
mandabat Tyriis ultricia bella futuris.

This is followed by a brief description of Hannibal, depicted on another part of the shield, swearing his oath of enmity at the altar:

> et primo bella Aeneadum iurabat ab aeuo.

Thus Hannibal's oath, which historians recorded as a historical fact, is given greater poetical force by Silius through the suggestion that it is a perpetuation and a fulfilment of the curse uttered by Dido in the *Aeneid*. Virgil, in making Dido say 'aliquis nostris ex ossibus ultor', had Hannibal in mind; Silius, in making Hannibal the sworn enemy of Rome, had Virgil's Dido particularly in mind. In other ways, too, the Carthaginian heritage from Dido is often suggested, not least by Silius' use of the epithet *Elissaeus,* which he applies to Hannibal, the Carthaginian 'senate', the Carthaginian cause and Carthaginian strength in battle.[41]

Silius' indebtedness and adherence to the Roman epic outlook which Virgil had established can be seen again in his treatment of the gods, particularly Jupiter, Juno and Venus. If Hannibal was made by his father to swear an oath of enmity against Rome, he was also inspired with Juno's anger. In the *Aeneid* Juno is the hostile deity who is ultimately responsible for Aeneas' misfortunes and frustrations; it is the same hostile Juno that tries, in the *Punica,* to prevent the growth of Roman power. In each case her actions are dictated by her special affection for Carthage.[42] In the *Punica* her role is even more prominent than it is in the *Aeneid,* and it is one of the incongruities of Silius' poem that events known as historical facts should be interpreted so simply as the result of divine machinations. Juno's will and intentions and her wrath against the Romans are made clear early in the poem. She is the mainspring of Hannibal's successful invasion of Italy, appearing at various times to pluck a spear from his wound, to encourage, warn or watch over him, to arouse rivers or winds to act against the Romans and to influence Roman action in ways to their disadvantage.[43] Eventually, however, her participation in the events of the war is stopped by Jupiter, but not before Hannibal is at the walls of Rome itself. Then she reveals herself to him and shows him the gods ranged in defence of the city and bids him:

> cede deis tandem et Titania desine bella,

which means that she is powerless to urge him on any further.[44] From this point in the poem Hannibal's fortunes wane and the

Carthaginian forces are weakened. Juno does very little else until the last book of the poem, where she reluctantly accepts the fate of Carthage but pleads with Jupiter for Hannibal's life, which Jupiter promises to spare. She saves Hannibal at the battle of Zama by fashioning a shape to resemble Scipio, which he chases until he is out of danger. This last episode is closely modelled on the similar one in the *Aeneid*, where Juno seeks a reprieve for Turnus and saves him temporarily by making him chase a phantom of Aeneas until he is far away from danger.[45]

By contrast, Juno plays a smaller role in the *Argonautica,* even though, as the protecting deity of Jason, she gives him help from time to time and influences Medea's feelings towards him.[46] She is assisted generally by Pallas, and Venus helps her to influence Medea. This collaboration of Juno and Venus might appear at first sight to be based on their collaboration to unite Aeneas and Dido in the *Aeneid,* but the resemblances in the two situations are only superficial, since in the *Aeneid* Venus, with the help of Cupid, has already influenced Dido's feelings and made her fall in love with Aeneas before Juno becomes aware of the fact, and the compact between Juno and Venus is a temporary compromise without real collaboration. The goddesses are in fact bitterly opposed to each other, because they represent the conflicting interests of Rome and Carthage. In the *Argonautica,* on the other hand, where there are no national issues at stake, Venus readily collaborates with Juno to overcome Medea's resistance to her passion.[47]

As is to be expected, Silius follows Virgil in his treatment of Venus, the patron-goddess of the Romans. He is unable to find —or unwilling to invent—an episode like that of Aeneas and Dido or Jason and Medea in the Punic War, and if he had found or invented one it would probably have been out of place in the *Punica,* but Venus, besides influencing the action of the poem in one or two small particulars, is seen to have the interests of the Romans very much at heart and to be working on their behalf in more ways than one. Her most striking appearance in the poem occurs when Hannibal is in the Alps and threatening to invade Italy. She addresses Jupiter in fear for the fate of the Romans and is answered by him with a prophecy of future Roman greatness. The whole passage, in its construction and content, is modelled closely on the similar interview in Book I of the *Aeneid*, the main variations being that Venus expresses fears for the Romans in a different historical context and Jupiter's prophecy goes about a hundred years further into the future and is adapted to the glories of the Flavian rather than the Augustan era. Venus also assists the Roman cause by enervating the Carthaginians with luxury at Capua and undermining their discipline; and the secret love of Jupiter and Pomponia, whose offspring was Scipio Africanus, is represented as the work of Venus, whose purpose was to provide Rome with a leader who would one day overcome Hannibal![48]

Statius gives Juno and Venus much smaller and less important roles than Silius Italicus or even Valerius Flaccus. At a council of the gods in the *Thebaid*, Juno complains bitterly at Jupiter's decision to destroy Thebes and Argos, but this is a Jupiter whose will no other deity can affect, and consequently Juno must accept his purpose. Her activity is confined to limited aid for the Argives. She intervenes once to save Hippomedon from a dishonourable death by drowning, although she cannot prevent his death in battle, and in answer to the prayers of the Argive women she causes the Theban troops to be overcome by sleep and slaughtered in a night attack by the Argives. Venus champions Thebes against the Argives, but there is no intrigue against Juno; all she can do is to try in vain to prevent Mars from rousing the Argives to war. Otherwise her most important part is as instigator of the Lemnian massacre, in an episode subsidiary to the main action of the poem.[49]

It was inevitable that in any epic poem accepting and employing the traditional divine apparatus Jupiter should occupy the chief role, as indeed he does in the *Aeneid* and the three Flavian epics. In this respect again Silius shows the greatest resemblance to Virgil, in his antiquarian and almost anachronistic adherence to Virgilian conventions. As has been seen above, Jupiter's prophecy of Roman greatness in the *Punica* is closely modelled on that in the *Aeneid*. Although Silius brings his prophecy up to date and speaks of Domitian and the Flavian era in terms acceptable to the Imperial family in his own day, there is no significant point of difference between his Jupiter and that of Virgil. Above all, in the *Punica* Rome's destiny is a matter of the deepest concern to Jupiter, but Rome cannot be a great nation except through experience of danger, toil and suffering. Hannibal is Jupiter's human agent in this trial, but Jupiter will not allow him to attack the sacred city of Rome.[50]

In the *Argonautica* there is a general awareness of the power of Jupiter, but his role is unimportant and he rarely interferes in the action of the poem. Nevertheless, he makes a prophecy in answer to the complaints of the Sun-god and the god of War, who fear lest the Argonauts should in some way diminish their power. This prophecy explains the divine purpose in terms of historical 'cycles': the ascendancy of Asia is nearly over and that of the Greeks is beginning, which in turn will give way to 'other nations' (i.e. the Romans). The object of this shift of power is explained thus:

> ipse locos terrenaque summa mouendo
> experiar, quaenam populis longissima cunctis
> regna uelim linquamque datas ubi certus habenas.

The path to glory is a hard one:

> durum uobis iter et graue caeli
> institui.

This is essentially the same trial as that which Silius makes Jupiter declare for the Romans, but it has a rather more general application in the *Argonautica*; its reference to the Romans, however vague, is irrelevant to the main theme of the poem.[51]

The Jupiter of the *Thebaid*, while owing much to Virgil, is typically adapted by Statius to a new purpose and a new context. This Jupiter is not an anachronism, nor are his prophecies out of keeping with the poem as a whole. His power is much more autocratic, like that of the Flavian emperors and in particular Domitian, so that his will is supreme and cannot be questioned or opposed. Juno's bitter rebuke has no effect on the action of the poem, and as a character she cannot be compared with the Juno of either the *Aeneid* or the *Punica*. The other gods are respectfully subservient to Jupiter. Mars is his chief agent in causing human warfare and when he relaxes his activities he is threatened with a loss of power. Apollo is the interpreter of Jupiter's will. Bacchus and Venus protest at the fate in store for Thebes, but their protests are quickly silenced. At the same time, Jupiter's autocracy, despite his resolution to punish men for their wickedness, is tempered with a mildness and a paternal solicitude for his subjects, human and divine, that bear some resemblance to qualities in the Jupiter of the *Aeneid* but also reflect some of the philosophical and more clearly formulated ideals of kingship that were evolved in the first century of Roman imperial rule, and especially the Stoic concept of the providential ruler of the universe.[52]

Virgil's treatment of Jupiter and Juno provides a good example of his poetical superiority over his two admirers, Statius and Silius Italicus. It has been pointed out[53] that the inner tension of the *Aeneid* is emphasized by the contrast between the serenity of Jupiter and the angry passion of Juno. This contrast, in fact, typifies the victory of Aeneas over Dido and Turnus and, as Virgil saw it, of the Roman genius for organization and order over the forces of destruction, war and civil conflict. The Jupiter of the *Thebaid* who punishes men for their crimes is a moral castigator far removed, despite his basic serenity, from Virgil's Jupiter; moreover, since he too is angry,[54] there is no great contrast with Juno, who, in any case, is not a powerful enough character to make a balance or contrast possible. The inner tension of the *Thebaid* is a more complex matter. Angry passions appear in both Argos and Thebes; the main conflict is between two men who, with their supporters, are both driven on by *furor*. Besides this there is an effective contrast between the uncontrolled violence of men like Polynices, Tydeus and Capaneus and the efforts of Adrastus and Amphiaraus to calm them; this contrast is emphasized and typified by the clash between Tisiphone and Pietas.[55] The pattern of human relationships in the *Thebaid*, therefore, is not, as in the *Aeneid*, simply and clearly reflected in the relationships of the gods. Silius Italicus follows Virgil much more closely in this respect, since the contrast in the *Punica* between Jupiter and Juno reflects and emphasizes the conflict between the orderly and well-disciplined Romans, especially when led by Q. Fabius Maximus, and the treacherous Carthaginians and their general, Hannibal, who is inspired throughout by fury and passion.[56] The contrast is effective, but its effectiveness, like so much else in Silius, is unfortunately anachronistic, and therefore artificial, because it was imitated from Virgil and had no living significance either for Silius himself or for the Flavian era in Rome.

Statius' interest in the psychological condition of his main characters, with its particular emphasis on *furor* as a motivating impetus, owes much to both Seneca, in the tragedies, and Lucan, but his method of exposition is greatly influenced by Virgil. When, in the *Aeneid*, Juno finds that the Trojans are settling in Latium despite her opposition, she determines to delay their work and cause them as much suffering as possible by releasing the demonic forces of the underworld to stir up hatred and enmity against them among the peoples of Italy. She does this by summoning the monstrous 'Allecto, the creatress of grief, from the infernal darkness'. Allecto first assails Queen Amata with one of her poisonous snakes and then thrusts a burning firebrand into the bosom of Turnus, the Rutulian prince, terrifying them both with her appearance and driving them to uncontrollable fury. Finally, she embroils the Trojans and the Latins and creates a pretext for war.[57] The action of the *Thebaid* is motivated partly by a similar demonic force and partly by the anger of Jupiter and his design to punish mankind. The minds of the brothers, Eteocles and Polynices, are predisposed to hatred and enmity as a result of their father's curse, which is answered by the Fury Tisiphone. The work of Tisiphone in the *Thebaid* is like that of Allecto in the *Aeneid*. She is the cause and the embodiment of human frenzy and hatred. She also creates the immediate pretext for hostile action between the Thebans and Argives by maddening the sacred tigers of Bacchus at Thebes, just as Allecto in the *Aeneid* rouses the hunting-hounds of Ascanius against Silvia's pet stag. But the role of Tisiphone is sustained over a much greater part of the *Thebaid* than that of Allecto in the *Aeneid*. She inspires the troops with a savage fury, causes men to commit horrifying acts, drives on Polynices against his brother and overcomes the efforts of Pietas to reconcile the brothers before the final duel takes place.[58] Virgil describes the three phases of Allecto's work with admirable economy, clarity, contrast and power, and the whole episode is most effectively introduced by Juno's tremendous line:

flectere si nequeo superos, Acheronta mouebo.

Statius has something of the power of Virgil in his treatment of Tisiphone and creates a pervading atmosphere of greater horror and gloom, but Virgil's economy, clarity and sense of contrast are missing.

In the *Aeneid* a number of themes, episodes and descriptions traditional to earlier epic are preserved and given a new life and significance. Among these are catalogues of troops, battle-scenes, prophecy by communication with the dead, funeral games, the storm and descriptions of scenes depicted on a shield or in a work of art. These appear again in the Flavian epics with greater or lesser significance and relevance to the purpose of the individual writer. There is a storm, for example, in Book I of the *Argonautica* and again in Book I of the *Thebaid*. There is another in the last book of the *Punica*.[59] Valerius and Silius have their storms at sea, but Statius, whose poem has nothing to do with the sea, sets his in the mountains and forests of the Argolid. This storm, however, is meaningful, like the storm in the *Aeneid*, and bears a similar relation to the rest of its book. It shows an exile in distress and at the lowest ebb of his fortunes; it depicts the 'wildest movement of nature'[60] as a prelude to the wild agitations of human frenzy that follow later in the poem; and it dies down to a mood of deceptive tranquillity in which the book ends.

By contrast, the storm at sea in the last book of the *Punica* reflects and complements Virgil's storm in a curious way. Whereas Aeneas is driven off his course to the Carthaginian coast and delayed in his attempt to found a new kingdom for the Trojan refugees, Hannibal, the enemy of Aeneas' descendants, is driven away from Italy after achieving his greatest successes. Whereas Neptune had calmed the sea after the storm roused at Juno's instigation in the *Aeneid*, it is Neptune who causes the storm in the *Punica*; it is as though Aeneas is finally avenged by the suffering of Hannibal. Apart from these contrasts, the two storms contain many points of similarity in conception, form, sequence of events and even vocabulary. In each case Aeolus is summoned to unleash the winds, the sea is churned up from its depths, the sky is covered with dark clouds, and thunder and lightning follow. Then each hero cries out against his own fate in not having been permitted to die gloriously in battle, and the storm progresses by destroying other ships of the fleet. Even details such as the weapons and treasures from wrecked ships floating on the water are repeated by Silius with remarkable fidelity to his model.[61] In this, as in other respects, Virgil's influence touches Silius more obviously, though less profoundly, than it does Statius.

The communications with the spirits of the dead in both the *Thebaid* and the *Punica* are carried out in a manner more Homeric than Virgilian. Instead of a descent to the underworld there is a *nekyia* in each poem.[62] There would have been little point in making Tiresias, in the *Thebaid*, visit the underworld, since he is not the hero of the poem and his prophecies can be inspired in other ways, and although Scipio becomes a hero for Silius in the last books of the *Punica*, to make him go down to the underworld would have been too incongruous even for this anachronistic poem. As it is, although Scipio's visit to Cumae is possible in a historical sense, his experiences there, as related by Silius, belong only to the realm of fantasy. But apart from its Homeric basis, Silius' *nekyia* is Virgilian in most respects. From Odysseus' meeting with the spirit of the unburied Elpenor[63] Virgil had fashioned a most moving and beautiful passage in which Aeneas and the Sibyl are confronted by the spirit of the unburied Palinurus. Silius has a similar passage, in which Scipio sees the spirit of the unburied Appius Claudius, but all that Silius seems capable of here is bleak imitation, and neither Scipio nor the priestess guiding him has any real comfort to offer Appius Claudius, such as the Sibyl offers Palinurus. Instead, Scipio pronounces a short, irrelevant and un-Virgilian discourse on the burial customs of other nations. After this, there is prophecy from the ghost of the ancient Sibyl and an account of the underworld, which, despite a different eschatology and a revision of topographical details, depends to a great extent for its descriptions on similar passages in the *Aeneid*. For example, the personifications of Grief, Disease, Old Age, Poverty, Discord, etc., at the entrance to the palace of Dis are very similar to those of the *Aeneid*, the mythological inhabitants of the underworld reappear and many of the more deliberately classified groups of the dead, such as warriors, poets, women and those who died young, reflect the groupings of the *Aeneid*. Again, there are glimpses of past heroes and heroines and spirits being prepared for a future life on earth. For all its Virgilian echoes, however, this part of the *Punica* contains nothing comparable either in grandeur or in pathos to the sixth book of the *Aeneid*.[64]

Some of the similarities between episodes in Flavian epics and their Virgilian originals have already been discussed in other connections. A few of the many more may be instanced here. Part of the fifth book of the *Thebaid* is devoted to Hypsipyle's narration of the Lemnian massacre, which she herself witnessed, and of the rescue of her father Thoas from the slaughter in the city. The prelude of her story, addressed to the Argive leader Adrastus, recalls the opening of Aeneas' narration in the *Aeneid*:

ingemit, et paulum fletu cunctata modesto
Lemnias orsa refert: 'immania uulnera, rector,
integrare iubes, Furias et Lemnon et artis
arma inserta toris debellatosque pudendo
ense mares; redit ecce nefas et frigida cordi
Eumenis.[65]

Hypsipyle recoils, like Aeneas, from the horror of her own story. Although the main details of the story are quite different, there are other Virgilian reminiscences, such as the approach of the fleet, the false security before the massacre, Hypsipyle's sudden alarm for the safety of her father, and the escape itself, through the unfrequented places of the city:

> ferimur per deuia uastae
> urbis . . .[66]

There are Virgilian echoes again in Silius' description of the sack of Saguntum, and, like Statius, Silius remembers Aeneas' reference to tears before the narrative of the sack of Troy:

quis diros urbis casus laudandaque monstra
et Fidei poenas ac tristia fata piorum
imperet euoluens lacrimis? uix Punica fletu
cessassent castra ac miserescere nescius hostis.[67]

There is an excellent example of Virgilian adaptation by Valerius Flaccus in the first book of the *Argonautica,* when Aeson and Alcimede bid farewell to Jason before he sets sail for Colchis. This scene is based on Evander's farewell to Pallas in the *Aeneid,* and the parallelisms are so close that a few details must be mentioned here. First of all, the two poets describe the scenes at the partings of the respective expeditions, the tears of other parents, and embraces at leave-taking. Evander is given a single speech, whereas Alcimede and Aeson speak to Jason separately. Evander collapses after his speech and has to be carried into his palace by attendants; Alcimede collapses after Aeson's speech and, together with Aeson, is supported by Jason. This detail is not a significant departure from Virgil. Jason, one assumes, was older and more mature than Pallas, and his physical strength was greater (*cf.* 'magnaque senem ceruice recepit'). But the loneliness of Evander, who has no one to comfort him, is more pathetic. The contents of the speeches in Virgil and Valerius are again similar. Evander's speech falls into two distinct sections. First he reflects on what might have happened if his youth could be restored. Valerius makes Aeson echo this sentiment very closely. But Aeson adds that his prayers have been heard, for he sees Jason as the leader of a company of princes; and he prays further that he will see him return victorious from his mission. The second part of Evander's speech contains a prayer to the gods, begging them to grant him life if Pallas should return safely:

> si numina uestra
> incolumem Pallanta mihi, si fata reseruant,
> si uisurus eum uiuo et uenturus in unum,
> uitam oro, patior quemvis durare laborem.

Similarly, after expressing her fears, Alcimede says to Jason:

> si fata reducunt
> te mihi, si trepidis placabile matribus aequor,
> possum equidem lucemque pati longumque timorem.

But if, Evander continues, some disaster overcomes Pallas, he would wish to die at once:

> sin aliquem infandum casum, Fortuna, minaris,
> nunc, nunc o liceat crudelem abrumpere uitam,
> dum curae ambiguae, dum spes incerta futuri . . .

Similarly, Alcimede:

> sin aliquid Fortuna parat, miserere, parentum,
> Mors bona, dum metus est nec adhuc dolor . . .

There are, of course, differences of detail between the two episodes, but Valerius' adherence to his model is most remarkable, and there are numerous verbal parallels. The main differences are that there is one speech in Virgil and two in Valerius, repeating the two halves of Evander's speech in inverse order; Evander's speech is directed partly to Pallas and partly to the gods, whereas Alcimede and Aeson both address their son; and Evander's pathetic isolation is lost in the scene from the *Argonautica*. This comparison and contrast shows once more Virgil's magnificent economy, clarity and power, none of which Valerius can reproduce.[68]

A Virgilian episode which has its parallel in all three Flavian epics is Evander's story of Cacus and Hercules.[69] The story of Coroebus and the monster in the *Thebaid* and the story of Regulus' battle with the serpent in the *Punica* are introduced in much the same way as Virgil introduces Evander's narration, during the

course of an entertainment, as an explanation of religious observances. In the *Argonautica*, on the other hand, instead of a reported
narrative there is an introductory explanation by a young man
whom the heroes come upon lamenting for the death of his friend,
and then the monstrous Amycus, king of the Bebryces, is killed by
Pollux. There are naturally many differences of detail, but again
there are similarities of construction in these episodes and not a
few verbal echoes.

Some of the characters in the Flavian epics bear resemblances to
characters in the *Aeneid*. The most striking of these is Capaneus in
the *Thebaid*, who is described after the manner of Mezentius but is
more elaborately drawn and plays a more important role. Statius'
concept of Capaneus, the giant who did not fear the gods and
whose avowed intent was to set Thebes on fire, was derived
ultimately from Aeschylus,[70] but in other respects this *superum
contemptor* is another, even more violent Mezentius. The Hannibal
of the *Punica*, who plays a leading part in the poem, is far more
than a Mezentius or a Capaneus, but he too belongs to the same
category. He is inspired by *furor* and *ira* and he has no respect for
the gods—'nullus diuum pudor' and 'armat contemptu pectora
diuum'.[71] On the other hand, king Latinus, a man of far different
character, has his successor in the Adrastus of the *Thebaid*. Latinus
is essentially a god-fearing man and a man of peace, ruler of a
peaceful community before the advent of the Trojans. Although
his people wage war against the Trojans, he takes no active part in
the conflict. He is ready to make peace and he opposes and tries to
calm the passionate ardour and violence of Turnus. Similarly,
Adrastus is unwilling to go to war. He too is a man of peace, ruler
of a peaceful city before the arrival of Polynices and Tydeus in
Argos. He tries without success to restrain the fury and anger of
his two sons-in-law and to prevent the final duel between Polynices and Eteocles; and when he sees that he cannot restrain them
from the fatal combat he flees from Thebes, just as Latinus flees
when the treaty-making is shattered in the *Aeneid*.[72]

Similarities are shown by other characters. Thus, Styrus in the
Argonautica and Tydeus in the *Thebaid* have some affinity with
Turnus, although neither is so finely drawn; Pallas and Lausus
have their counterpart in Statius' Parthenopaeus, who contains
something also of Camilla and is more elaborately developed than
any of the three. None of the Flavian epics, however, has any

character to compare with either Aeneas or Dido. The Medea of the *Argonautica*, like Dido, falls in love with a foreign hero visiting her country, and her passion is aroused and fostered by Juno and Venus; but despite the parallel situation and various details in which Valerius had profited from his study of Book IV of the *Aeneid*, Medea has nothing of Dido's maturity and nobility of character. Similarly, Jason does not develop as Aeneas develops, and in fact he is altogether colourless and uninteresting.[73] In the *Punica* Scipio shows some of the qualities of Aeneas from time to time and is given divine ancestry for good measure, but it is Hannibal, not Scipio, who dominates the poem.

Virgil's influence on the vocabulary, expression, syntax, metre and general poetic technique of the Flavian poets is incalculable, and no analysis of their imitation can be undertaken here.[74] Perhaps the best indication of this influence can be given by noting how Statius, for example, adapts the phrases and rhythms of the well-known line in which Virgil describes a galloping horse:

> quadrupedante putrem sonitu quatit ungula campum.

Not all Statius' horses gallop rhythmically. Their impatience before the chariot-race is described thus:

> stare adeo miserum est, pereunt uestigia mille
> ante fugam, absentemque ferit grauis ungula campum.

When the horse of Hippomedon tries to find a foothold on the river-bed, the motif is varied with skill and sensibility:

> consuetaque campo
> fluctuat et mersas leuis ungula quaerit harenas.

The words 'consuetaque campo' of themselves almost suggest that this is the Virgilian theme in a new setting, and the liquids and sibilants complete the transformation. Elsewhere, the earth is heavily trampled by countless companies of cavalry:

> icta gemit tellus, uiridis graui ungula campos
> mutat, et innumeris peditumque equitumque cateruis
> exspirat protritus ager . . .[75]

Statius and Silius, the self-confessed admirers of Virgil, were much closer to him than Valerius. For Valerius he was a poetical model. Silius seems to have aspired to be Virgil's continuator, but he succeeded only in producing an anachronistic imitation;

Statius was closest to the Virgilian spirit and poetical technique. Many of the general observations made by scholars about the *Aeneid*, for example with regard to its form and composition, its subjective style, its imagery, and the meaningful coherence of details and their integration with the whole, apply equally well to the *Thebaid*.[76] It was no doubt this deeper poetical heritage from Virgil, as well as the Virgilian humanity of the *Thebaid*, that made Dante instinctively think of Statius as a link between Virgil and the poetic culture of the Christian world:

> Al mio ardor fur seme le faville,
>   che mi scaldar, della divina fiamma,
>   onde sono allumati più di mille:
> dell' Eneida dico, la qual mamma
>   fummi, e fummi nutrice poetando;
>   senz' essa non fermai peso di dramma.[77]

NOTES

[1] *Einsiedeln Eclogues* i, 48-9.

[2] Persius, i, 96 ff.

[3] On Seneca and Virgil, see W. S. Maguinness, 'Seneca and the Poets', *Hermathena* 88, 1956, 92-8.

[4] *Laus Pisonis* 230 ff.

[5] Quintilian, *Institutio Oratoria* x, 1, 85-7; cf. xii, 11, 26.

[6] Martial, iv, 14, 14; viii, 55; xi, 48, 1; 52, 18; xii, 4, 1; 67, 5.

[7] *Dialogus de Oratoribus* 12, 6.

[8] *Ibid.* 13, 1 ff. For the *otium* enjoyed by Horace and Virgil, cf. Martial i, 107, 3-4.

[9] *Dialogus* 20, 5.

[10] *Ibid.* 23, 2. Some people appear to have preferred Ennius to Virgil (Martial, v, 10, 7).

[11] Pliny, *Epistles* iii, 7, 3 and 6 ff.

[12] *Ibid.* iii, 7, 8; Martial, xi, 48; cf. also Martial, xi, 50 and xii, 67, 5.

[13] Statius, *Silvae* iv, 4, 53-5. The words 'Maronei . . . templi' have no reference to an actual temple but are rather a poetical description of Virgil's burial-place as it appeared to Statius. One might legitimately ask whether it was in fact Statius to whom Martial contemptuously referred as 'qui coleret pauper et unus' before the site was bought by Silius—Martial, xi, 50 (= xi, 49 in L. Friedlaender's edition). In the same poem Statius exemplifies the Flavian view of the quiet life of poetry, as seen in the *Dialogus de Oratoribus*, when he says (49-51):
> nos otia uitae
> solamur cantu uentosaque gaudia famae
> quaerimus.

The mood of the whole passage is reminiscent of Virgil, *Georgics* iv, 559 ff. For the 'gaudia famae', again with Virgil in mind, cf. *Silvae* iv, 7, 25-8.

[14] Statius, *Thebaid* x, 445-8. These lines are themselves a conscious imitation of Virgil's similar apostrophe to Nisus and Euryalus in *Aeneid* ix, 446-9.

89

[15] *Thebaid* xii, 816-17.

[16] Silius Italicus, *Punica* viii, 593-4. The mention of 'cantu . . . Aonio' is possibly, but not necessarily, a reference to the Boeotian (i.e. Hesiodic) poetry of Virgil, the *Georgics,* in contradistinction to the epic which 'rivalled the poetry of Homer'.

[17] Tacitus, *Histories* i, 1.

[18] The speech of Aper in the *Dialogus de Oratoribus* (16, 4-23, 6) assumes that the orator's aim is to give pleasure (*uoluptas*) to the ear. The *cultus, nitor, laetitia, pulchritudo, decor* and *altitudo* of which he continually speaks appear to have been demanded of orators as much as they were expressed in the architecture of the Flavian period (cf. 20, 7 and 22, 3-4). Poetry, no doubt, was expected to conform to similar ideals.

[19] Quintilian, x, 1, 129. Quintilian's aim (*ib.* 125) is expressed in the words 'corruptum et omnibus uitiis fractum dicendi genus reuocare ad seueriora iudicia contendo'. By doing this, he hoped to counteract the influence of Seneca.

[20] See especially Statius, *Silvae* ii, 7.

[21] *Thebaid* ii, 458-60; iii, 114-68; 578-9; iv, 353-6; vi, 28 ff.; ix, 315-403; 877-907; x, 563-73; xii, 312 ff., 385 ff. etc. Passages in the *Aeneid* are ix, 473-502; x, 505-9, 812-32, 841 ff.; xi, 29 ff., 139-81. In the *Thebaid*, as much as in the *Silvae*, Statius is concerned with a theme that had also appealed to Virgil and is best expressed by the words 'impositique rogis iuuenes ante ora parentum' (*Aeneid* vi, 308).

[22] Pathos in the *Argonautica*: iv, 44 ff.; v, 22 ff.; vi, 563-8; in vi, 690 ff. there is an episode resembling to some extent *Thebaid* vii, 649 ff. in its poetic motifs.

Pathos in the *Punica*: xii, 243 ff.; xiv, 492-515 (a passage in which Silius may well have been imitating Statius).

[23] *Thebaid* x, 347-448, 628-782; xii, 105 ff.

[24] *Ibid.* xi, 457 ff. For Pietas, cf. also x, 780.

[25] e.g. *Argonautica* ii, 310; v, 6; *Punica* iv, 454 ff. (Scipio rescues his father in battle); vi, 100; viii, 328 ff.; ix, 437.

[26] For this, see especially Brooks Otis, *Virgil: A Study in Civilized Poetry* (Oxford, 1963), 20 ff. and 396-8.

[27] M. Grant, *Roman Literature* (Penguin Books, 1958), 180.

[28] Ennius is glorified as a warrior and a poet in *Punica* xii, 390 ff.

[29] *Aeneid* i, 33.

[30] *Ibid.* i, 286 ff.: 'nascetur pulchra Troianus origine Caesar' etc.; vi, 791 ff.: 'hic uir, hic est, tibi quem promitti saepius audis, Augustus Caesar, diui genus, aurea condet saecula' etc.; viii, 679 ff.: 'hinc Augustus agens Italos in proelia Caesar, cum patribus populoque, penatibus et magnis dis' etc.

[31] Silius is fully aware of this fact; but despite his glorification of the Flavian emperors, he sees them as an extension of the power of the Julio-Claudians (*Punica* iii, 593 ff.). Valerius, on the other hand, despite a brief reference in the conventional manner to the 'honours of a better Troy' (*Argonautica* ii, 572-3), appears to regard the 'Phrygian Julii' as inferior to the Flavians (cf. i, 8-9 ,where there is perhaps a conscious improvement, favouring the Flavians, on Virgil, *Aeneid* i, 287). For Juvenal, who so often declaims against the degeneracy of the Roman race, the Trojan legend appears to be only a reminiscence and a joke (*Satire* viii, 42, 56, 181).

[32] The passages are too numerous to be listed here in full, but the following may be noted *exempli gratia*: *Punica* i, 1-2, 14-15, 106, 126, 512-14, 543, 665; ii, 1, 55, 295, 336, 342-3, 351-2; iii, 151, 163-4, 207, 565-6, 710; iv, 670; vi, 106; vii, 16; ix, 348, 530-2; x, 643; xiv, 117; xv, 242, 453; xvi, 129, 239, 655; xvii, 347-8, 363.

[33] *Ibid.* vii, 437-93; ix, 72 ff.; xi, 295 ff.; xiii, 326-7; xiv, 45-6, 205, 220; xiii, 36 ff.

[34] *Ibid.* xiii, 64-78, 790-1, 800.

[35] Virgil, *Aeneid* i, 283-5; vi, 836-40.

[36] *Ibid.* iv, 622-9.

[37] *Punica* viii, 25-241.

[38] Ibid. 171–5.

[39] Ibid. i, 81–122. Similarly (ibid. iii, 81–3), Hannibal bids his wife Imilce, should he die in the war, take their infant son to the altar of Dido and make him swear undying enmity against Rome.

[40] Ibid. ii, 406–31.

[41] Ibid. ii, 239; vi, 346; xiv, 258; xv, 521. cf. the use of the genitive *Elissae*, with general reference to Carthage, in ii, 391; vii, 488; xvi, 614; xvii, 224. From time to time there are other references to Dido as the foundress of Carthage, e.g. iv, 765.

[42] *Aeneid* i, 12–33; *Punica* i, 22–37. Each passage is preceded by a shorter one of four lines, in which the poet states his purpose of examining the *causae* of the events in his poem, and each is immediately followed by an account of how Juno's anger was put into action, beginning with the storm raised by Aeolus in the *Aeneid* and the preparation of Hannibal's enmity against Rome in the *Punica*.

[43] e.g. *Punica* i, 548 ff.; iv, 573 ff.; 725 ff.; v, 206–7; viii, 27 ff.; ix, 491 ff.; x, 45 ff., 83 ff., 337 ff.; xii, 201–2, 701 ff. To modern ways of thought nothing could be more incongruous than the passage in which the famous (and factually authentic) windstorm of the Volturnus during the battle of Cannae is attributed to Juno's intervention ('Iunonis precibus' ix, 494). Traditional Roman opinion did not distinguish so clearly between legend and early history, and scientific explanations of natural phenomena were unnecessary in epic poetry.

[44] Ibid. xii, 691–725.

[45] Ibid. xvii, 341–384, 522–80. Cf. *Aeneid* x, 606–88. The situation of Turnus, who is doomed in any case to die soon, is rather different from that of Hannibal, but Silius was clearly familiar with his model, from which he reproduces a number of details (e.g. 'clipeumque iubasque', *Punica* xvii, 525; *Aeneid* x, 638), besides a general similarity in the construction and development of the episode.

[46] *Argonautica* i, 81 ff., 96 ff.; iv, 543, 682 ff.; v, 182–3, 280 ff., 363–5, 400–1; vi, 427 ff., 477 ff., 575–680 (and esp. 650); vii, 153 ff.; viii, 318 ff.

[47] *Aeneid* i, 657–722; iv, 90–128; *Argonautica* vii, 155–86.

[48] *Punica* iii, 557–69 (Venus' complaint; cf. *Aeneid* i, 227–53), 570–629 (Jupiter's reply and prophecy; cf. *Aeneid* i, 254–96); xi, 385 ff.; xiii, 615 ff. The smaller particulars are in iv, 670 ff. and xvii, 286–9.

[49] Juno: *Thebaid* i, 248 ff.; ix, 510 ff.; x, 49 ff., 282, 912. Venus: ibid. iii, 269–91; v, 58–60, 134 ff., 158, 192–4, 280–3, 445 ff. The work of Venus in bringing together the Lemnian women and the Argonauts (v, 445 ff.) is curiously supplemented by Juno. A detail like this shows how little interest Statius had in either of them as individual deities. In the *Argonautica* the influence of Venus on the Lemnian women is described in ii, 98 ff., 127, 175, 186–7, 196 ff., 209 ff.

[50] *Punica* iii, 163 ff.; vi, 595 ff.; x, 349–50; xii, 603 ff., 691 ff.

[51] *Argonautica* i, 531–67 (esp. 558–60 and 565–6). Cf. *Punica* iii, 163 ff. The idea of trials to be surmounted, in both these prophecies, may well have been inspired by Virgil, *Aeneid* i, 33 and transferred to other contexts.

In the *Argonautica* Jupiter stops the battle at Cyzicus (iii, 249 ff.), rebukes Juno for her maltreatment of Hercules and brings Hercules some relief (iv, 1–17). Otherwise, his participation is limited to events narrated in digressions on Vulcan (ii, 82 ff.) and Io (iv, 351–421).

[52] For Jupiter's power in the *Thebaid*, see i, 201 ff.; iii, 239–52, 304–10; the *reuerentia* of other gods: i, 201 ff., 209, 287–9; iii, 253 ff.; Juno's rebuke: i, 250 ff.; Juno and other gods subservient to Jupiter: i, 287–9; iii, 218 ff., 251–2; vii, 6 ff., 193–221; x, 70–1; Jupiter's mildness: i, 202, 205; vii, 194–5.

[53] By V. Pöschl, *Die Dichtkunst Virgils* (Wiesbaden, 1950), 28–9: 'Auch der Kontrast zwischen der heiteren Ruhe des Gottes (i, 255) und der schmerzvollen Leidenschaft der Juno unterstreicht die innere Spannung.'

[54] For Jupiter as a god of anger and punishment: *Thebaid* i, 215–18, 224, 245–6; iii, 234–5, 244–5, 538; vii, 26; xi, 23, 462. The *ira Iouis* is appropriately the subject of similes in iii, 317 ff.; v, 390–3. Cf. also iii, 26; viii, 409–11.

[55] Adrastus as a restraint on Polynices and Tydeus: *Thebaid* i, 438 ff.; ii, 386–93; in opposition to Polynices and Eteocles: xi, 424 ff. Amphiaraus opposing the violence of Capaneus: iii, 598–677. Tisiphone and Pietas: xi, 457–96.

[56] For the *furor* and *ira* of Hannibal, cf. *Punica* i, 70–1, 443–4, 454, 683; ii, 43, 210, 295; iv, 428; vii, 146; x, 327; xi, 224, 516; xvii, 236, 554. Q. Fabius Maximus, as one of the great heroes of Rome, is 'expers irarum' (vii, 516–17), and he opposes the *irae* and *furores* of others (vii, 217 ff., 564, 575 ff.).

[57] *Aeneid* vii, 323–571. For the demonic forces in the *Aeneid*, cf. Pöschl, *op. cit.* 31, 48 ff.

[58] *Thebaid* i, 89–130; vii, 564 ff.; viii, 65–79, 344 ff. 757 ff.; ix, 147 ff.; xi, 57–112, 197 ff., 208–9, 382, 387, 482 ff., 619.

[59] *Argonautica* i, 608–58; *Thebaid* i, 345–82; *Punica* xvii, 236–90. The storm in the *Argonautica* is modelled fairly closely on that in the *Aeneid* in its composition and vocabulary, but its poetic purpose is far different; see further note 73 below.

[60] cf. Pöschl, *op. cit.* 23: 'Nur das Bild höchster, wildester Bewegung aus der Natur . . . erschien dem Dichter zur Eröffnung des Römerepos genügend wuchtig und gross.'

[61] There is insufficient space here to make a detailed comparison between the two storms, but the following lines should be particularly noted:

Aeneid i	—compare—	*Punica* xvii
84–6		238–9; 242–5
87		255–7
88–91		240–1; 249–54
94–101		260–7
102–3		268–70
106		273
108		274–5
118–19		278 ff.

[62] *Thebaid* iv, 443–645; *Punica* xiii, 395–893. The *Argonautica* contains no *nekyia* or descent by a living person to the underworld, but in the speech of Mopsus explaining the causes of the malaise affecting the Argonauts there is a passage (iii, 377–96) reminiscent of the speech of Anchises (*Aeneid* vi, 724–51) in its doctrine, derived from the Stoics, of the fiery origin of the soul and its assertion that the evils of the body do not immediately pass away at death. The purpose of Mopsus' speech, however, is quite different from that of Anchises'. There is in the *Argonautica* also a passage describing the underworld (i, 833–51) which bears close resemblances to *Aeneid* vi, 893, 660 ff. and 638 ff.

[63] *Odyssey* xi, 51–80.

[64] No attempt can be made here to discuss the many details in which Virgil's influence is to be seen.

[65] *Thebaid* v, 27–33; cf. *Aeneid* ii, 1–13.

[66] *Thebaid* v, 248–9; cf. *Aeneid* ii, 725.

[67] *Punica* ii, 650–3; cf. *Aeneid* ii, 6–8. During the siege of Saguntum a terrifying snake issues from a mound and glides down to the sea. Silius may have had in mind *Aeneid* ii, 203 ff. as the basis of the episode, but the actual description of the snake is much closer to *Aeneid* v, 84 ff. In any case, Virgil's episode of the serpents that attack Laocoön in *Aeneid* ii is far more effective than the snake in *Punica* ii.

[68] *Aeneid* viii, 556–84; *Argonautica* i, 315–49. The speech of Evander (*Aeneid* viii, 560–83) has been minutely analysed and compared with Aeson's speech (*Argonautica* i, 336–47) by F. Mehmel, *Valerius Flaccus* (Diss. Hamburg, 1934), 62–6; but Mehmel's somewhat myopic concentration on these two speeches caused him to overlook the

speech of Alcimede (*Argonautica* i, 320–34) and the introductory and concluding lines of the whole episode in each poem, where the parallels of expression are equally interesting.

[69] *Aeneid* viii, 184–279; *Argonautica* iv 99–343; *Thebaid* i, 557–668; *Punica* vi,137–293.

[70] Aeschylus, *Seven Against Thebes* 423 ff.

[71] *Thebaid* iii, 602; *Punica* i, 58; xii, 91; cf. *Aeneid* vii, 648; viii, 7.

[72] *Aeneid* vii, 45 ff., 194 ('placido . . . ore'), 202–4, 616–19; xii, 18 ff.; 285–6; cf. *Thebaid* i, 390 ff., 438–43; ii, 386 ff., 712 ff.; iii, 38–41; xi, 424–46.

[73] The superiority of Virgil's character-portrayal in the case of Aeneas is a measure of his superiority to Valerius. It is typical of Virgil's mastery of poetic composition that he can employ the epic device of the storm, for example, to further the portrayal of Aeneas in a significant way, whereas the storm in the *Argonautica* leads only to frigid and irrelevant moralisation on man's profanation of the sea by sailing on it. Furthermore, Jason is actually allowed to appear stupid, or at least grossly improvident, in *Argonautica* i, 693 ff.

[74] For Valerius Flaccus and Virgil, see W. C. Summers, *A Study of the Argonautica of Valerius Flaccus* (Cambridge, 1894), esp. 26–33; F. Mehmel, *op. cit.* esp. 55–98. Statius' imitations of Virgil have been collected by a number of scholars from time to time, but the most penetrating analyses are those of H. M. Mulder, *Publii Papinii Statii Thebaidos Liber Secundus* (Groningen, 1954), *passim*.

[75] *Aeneid* viii, 596; *Thebaid* vi, 400–1; ix, 250–1; xii, 656–8.

[76] e.g. R. Heinze, *Virgils epische Technik* (Leipzig, first ed. 1902; fourth ed. 1957); V. Pöschl, *op. cit.*; Brooks Otis, *op. cit.* The treatment of the storm in the *Thebaid* has already been mentioned. Another example of Statius' Virgilian technique is his use of similes depicting Jupiter as an angry god. These harmonize with his general portrayal of Jupiter and suit the mood of the whole poem (cf. above, note 54).

[77] These verses are spoken by Stazio in *Purgatorio* xxi, 94–9.

IV

Virgil into Dante

J. H. WHITFIELD

'VIRGIL loved Naples so much that, being a famous astrologer, he accomplished many notable things there with the help of astrology. For when Naples was cruelly infested by a constant swarm of flies, gnats and gadflies, he made a copper fly under such a constellation that, when it was put on the city wall, looking towards that part where the flies and gadflies came out of a neighbouring swamp, never, for all the time that it was left there, did any fly or gadfly enter Naples. Likewise, he made a horse of bronze, which had the property of curing any horse with pains, or other natural infirmity, when it was led three times around the statue. Beside these he made two heads, carved out of marble, one which wept while the other laughed, and he put them on a gate, which was called the Porta Nolana, one to the left of the gate, the other to the right. And they had this property, that anyone who came on business to Naples, and entered by that gate, if he passed inadvertently on that side where was placed the weeping face, he could never accomplish the matter for which he had come, or if he did, he laboured much, and did it with great pain and trouble. While if he passed upon the other side, where was the laughing face, he soon despatched his business.[1]'

This is Boccaccio, commissioned in 1372 to give the first public exposition of the text of Dante, commenting on *Inferno* I. It is a reminder that Boccaccio, so often hailed as the initiator of the Renascence, is more medieval than Dante. For Dante, to whose knowledge of the *Aeneid* his guide Virgil pays full tribute,

> e coí 'l ca nta
> l'alta mia tragedia in alcun loco:
> ben lo sai tu che la sai tutta quanta,[2]   (*Inf.* XX, 112–4)

gives no heed at any point to the childish legend which had grown up round Virgil the Magician. Or even, we may go further than this, for in the same canto of the Soothsayers, from which this testimony of Virgil to Dante's knowledge of the *Aeneid* is taken, Dante would seem to have defended Virgil to his utmost from any taint of association with this category. When Dante weeps, Virgil upbraids him harshly,

> mi disse: 'Ancor se'tu delli altri sciocchi?
> Qui vive la pietà quand'è ben morta',[3] (*Inf.* XX, 27–8)

and then, when the name of Manto brings Virgil to an account of Mantua, the freedom of his native city from any substantial influence from Manto the soothsayer (a city founded without divination, her empty bones being there, where casually men came) leads Virgil to contradict his own information in the *Aeneid* (cf. X, 198): for here, to assure the absence of the taint of magic, Manto becomes a virgin without issue, so therefore leaves no son Ocnus to survive her, or exercise a taint, in Mantua.

So Dante, with an aristocratic disdain for the crude legend of Virgil, without naming it directly, yet puts it resolutely on one side. And is himself, therefore, repudiating the Middle Ages, and inaugurating the age of Humanism? We must not rush too fast, too far upon this road. Nor does Dante himself advance quickly to that point where Virgil stands waiting for him at the outset of the *Comedy*. In the youthful *Vita Nuova* (c. XXV) those who rhyme in the vernacular do so to make themselves understood of women, and so must rhyme upon no other matter than the amorous. Thus the *Vita Nuova*, and Dante with it, are held apart from Virgil, as far as are the *dicitori per rima* from the *poets*. And ten years later than this, in the *De vulgari eloquentia,* it is a matter for surprise that Dante, while evoking Virgil with Ovid, Statius, Lucan, as a master of *regular poetry* and *bello stile,* yet limits his attention to the *canzone,* the highest form of that love-poetry which is the birthright of the vernacular.[4] It is with the *Convivio* (of *c.* 1306), when Dante is already forty, that Virgil begins to take firm hold of him; and it is significant that it is Virgil as allegorized by the Christian tradition. Here there are two passages in the Fourth Book which signal a complete acceptance of that interpretation of the *Aeneid* which saw in it the figuration of the ages of man:

And Virgil, our greatest poet, shows that Aeneas was thus bridled, in that part of the *Aeneid* where this age is figured; which comprises the IVth, the Vth and the VIth Book of the *Aeneid*. And what a bridle was that, when, having received from Dido as much pleasure as will be told in the seventh treatise, and having so much delight with her, he departed, to follow an honest and praiseworthy way, and a fruitful one, as is written in *Aeneid* IV![5]

Wearing these spectacles Dante sees Virgil as the contemplative poet who depicts the life of man, and Aeneas as one who does what Dante too will do: both change his life to bitter exile, and travel to the underworld. Here are potent reasons why Virgil should become Dante's author in a special sense. And there are others also lurking in the pages of the *Convivio*. Especially in those astonishing chapters where Dante's political vision explodes (*Convivio* IV, iv–v). Here Monarchy becomes the principle to which Dante clings, with one pilot for the human race, and one people divinely appointed for this office. He brushes on one side the suggestion that Rome acquired its power by force (although he will confess that he once held this view himself), to state unequivocally that the 'popolo santo nel quale l'alto sangue troiano era mischiato' was elected by God Himself to the office of empire. If such is the prolusion, no less emphatic is the conclusion: four times in the brief space of half a page Dante asks himself the question, 'E non puose Iddio le mani proprie . . . ?'—Did not God put His own hands to the shaping of the crucial junctures of Roman history? And having answered all of them with an unambiguous, 'Certo sì', he ends the second of these chapters with the statement of Rome as the *santa cittade* imagined and ordained by God. In this divinization of the history of Rome, there are two authors whom Dante cites: the first, St. Luke, the second, Virgil. But here there is no real first and second, for both have equal authority. St. Luke attests the perfect disposition of the world for the birth of Christ. And Virgil shows that it was Providence, and not mere brute force, that brought the Roman power:

And in this Virgil agrees in the Ist Book of the *Aeneid*, when he says, speaking in the person of God: To them—that is to the Romans—I put no limit of time or things; to them I have given empire without end.[6]

So Dante quotes the lines that everybody knows,

> His ego nec metas rerum nec tempora pono,
> Imperium sine fine dedi,

but does so, not with an aesthetic or a historical appreciation: he quotes them as scripture, and as having all the force of an inappellable verdict. In a graphic phrase from *Monarchia* II Dante speaks of St. Luke as *scriba Christi Lucas, qui omnia vera dicit,* and not only is its last clause explicit, but the first word there is technical. And in the second of those political chapters of the *Convivio,* to clinch the point that David and Aeneas were contemporaries (so that the lines to Christ and to Augustus both run parallel) Dante appeals to the witness of the Scriptures, *sì come testimoniano le scritture*: these being here, the Bible and the *Aeneid.* And that this is no solitary instance, proving nothing (as if Dante, at his most solemn moments, could write casually!), the Epistle to Henry VII (*divina providentia Romanorum Regi, semper Augusto*) may assure us. For here also, Scriptum etenim nobis est:

> Nascetur pulchra Troianus origine Caesar,
> Imperium Oceano, famam qui terminet astris.[7]

Now it is well known that during the Middle Ages Virgil had come to be regarded as the highest representation of that pagan culture destined by Heaven as a preparation for the Christian age. In this an element of prophecy was already involved, for Virgil was the author of the fourth Eclogue, universally interpreted since the fourth century as Virgil's prophecy of the Virgin Birth, a Roman sanction to the central mystery of Christianity. Dante, here again, may have been a little less medieval than we might expect, for in a passage of *Monarchia* I he glosses the line

> Jam redit et Virgo, redeunt Saturnia regna

with the statement, 'Virgo namque vocabatur Justitia, quam et Astraeam vocant'; though in a celebrated passage in *Purgatorio,* where he attributes acceptance of this prophecy to Statius, so carrying it back to the first century A.D., he virtually endorses what was then a general belief. But it is plain that Dante, in applying the two former lines of Virgil to the case of Henry VII, has extended Virgil's role as prophet. Nor is there lacking the explicit statement that Virgil is a prophet. It comes in a page of *Monarchia* II which is all constellated with citations of *poeta noster.* Five times he uses this formula, and once he varies it to *noster vates.*

97

But once for Dante is enough, and this once parallels the statement of Dante for himself in *Paradiso* X,

Quella materia ond' io son fatto scriba.

For now we have three writers who are each *scriba Dei*: St. Luke, Virgil, and Dante himself: and what they write must perforce be true. But what did *noster vates* offer us? It was the announcement of Aeneas and Ascanius as prefigurations of Caesar and Augustus. And if we look back again to the Epistle to Henry VII, we shall find there that Virgil's rendering of Curio's advice to Caesar (*Tolle moras; semper nocuit differre paratis*) is proffered to Henry VII, and is linked at the same time with David: 'Eia itaque, rumpe moras, proles altera Isai . . .' 'If you do not think of yourself, think like Aeneas of Ascanius': and once again the words of Virgil, followed by the application of these to Henry, and to Henry's son, 'Iohannes namque, regius primogenitus tuus et rex . . . nobis est alter Ascanius'. And here the lines are filling out, for Aeneas and Ascanius are not only prefigurations of Caesar and Augustus, but too of Henry VII and of Henry's son King John: while alongside these, evoked by the words *proles altera Isai*, there is that other line (which we have seen contemporary with Aeneas in Dante's eyes), of David and his son Solomon, themselves the prefigurations of the perfect monarchy of Christ.

In that same Epistle to Henry VII, Dante addressed his correspondent in, for us, surprising words, 'Tu es qui venturus es, an alium expectamus?' But any doubts (in which, to tell the truth, Dante does not deal) he is ready to cast aside: 'nihilominus in te credimus et speramus, asseverantes te Dei ministrum, et Ecclesiae filium, et Romanae gloriae promotorem'. And in consequence Dante bursts once again into language which had been reserved for Christ: 'Tunc exultavit in te spiritus meus, et tacitus dixi mecum: "Ecce Agnus Dei, ecce qui abstulit peccata mundi".' If Dante can do this, it is not to blasphemy that he proceeds: it is that in the mentality of the Middle Ages the monarch has assumed the typology of Christ. But if he does so, it follows logically enough that his announcer assumes himself the mantle of prophecy. Now this has often been seen, or glimpsed, as true of Dante, but it is only recently that it has been demonstrated as certain. And to what we have seen already we can now add something more. For Dante, as much as for any other medieval, names are the consequences of things. We have only to think of his use of Beatrice (she who blesses) to see this. But what of his own name? In the authorities he found before him there was for Nathan in the Old Testament the accepted explanation, *Natan dedit, sive dantis*. Given by St. John Chrysostom, repeated by Isidore of Seville, then vulgarized by Uguccione in the *Magnae derivationes* as by the *Catholicon* subsequently in the thirteenth century: it was an equation which spoke straight to Dante's heart. For while on the one hand it lit up the Old Testament prophet of David, Solomon and Christ (a providential series), on the other it presupposed a second equally providential series, authenticated by an equally providential mission. For Dante is thus himself the Nathan of his time, and Henry of Luxemburg another David. And his son John, *primogenitus et rex,* have we not seen already that, as well as being by implication another Solomon, he is explicitly another Ascanius,

> Iohannes namque, regius primogenitus tuus et rex . . . nobis est alter Ascanius, qui vestigia magni genitoris observans, in Turnos ubique sicut leo desaeviet, et in Latinos velut agnus mitescet.[8]

So Virgil and Dante stand together as prophets of the same reality, and we know already that the *Monarchia* will not contradict the *Convivio*. Of all Dante's writings the *Monarchia* is the most movable in date, but we may take it as probable that it is not far distant from the year 1311, which is the date of the Epistle to Henry VII. And we know also the kernel, since it is what we found expressed in *Convivio* IV, iv–v. We may put it first in Dante's quotation from the *Golden Legend*: 'Unde recte illud scriptum est: *romanum Imperium de fonte nascitur pietatis*' (II, v). As then again in Dante's own words: 'romanum imperium ad sui perfectionem miraculorum suffragio est adjutum: ergo a Deo volitum; et per consequens, de jure fuit et est' (II, iv). The tenses, past and present, underline the scriptural words of Virgil which Dante had quoted in *Convivio*. To which as pendant in the *Monarchia* Dante now adds the other great pronouncement of Virgil,

> Excudent alii spirantia mollius aera,
> Credo equidem, vivos ducent de marmore vultus;
> Orabunt causas melius, caelique meatus
> Describent radio, et surgentia sidera dicent:
> Tu regere imperio populos, Romane, memento;
> Hae tibi erunt artes, pacique imponere morem,
> Parcere subiectis, et debellare superbos.

99

On the same page he adds, words which the reader will by now endorse, at least with the idea that the topic has been sufficiently pursued: 'Propterea satis persuasum est, quod populus romanus natura ordinatus fuit ad imperandum. Ergo romanus populus, subjiciendo sibi orbem, de jure ad imperium venit.'[9] And certainly we need pursue no further the arguments of the *Monarchia,* in whose three books Dante proposes three doubts (whether monarchy is necessary to the well-being of the world, whether monarchy belongs by right to Rome, whether the power of monarchy derives direct from God, or comes mediate through the papacy). For to those doubts—which are not doubts, of course, in the sense that Dante boggles about the answers to them—we know of certainty what Dante means to say. Or if we hesitate, it may be about the third, where Dante found his own formula, of the two supreme powers, each directly deriving from God, each self-contained and autonomous in its own sphere: with the two beatitudes, of the active and the contemplative life, the two powers that keep mankind, or which should keep mankind, on the right paths. If the authorities go wrong, the world goes wrong; and so Dante, now the contemplator, since he cannot be the actor, joins Virgil on the confines of Hell for the two poets to start their journey through the other world.

It was a commonplace for the chroniclers of medieval times that the birth of Christ had coincided with the pacification of the world.

> Finis consummationis imperii romani fuit tempore Octaviani imperatoris: ante quem et post quem sub nullo imperatore romanum imperium ad tantum culmen pervenit: cuius anno 42 dominus noster Jesus Christus natus fuit, toto orbe sub uno principe pacato; ad significandum quod ille rex coeli et terrae natus esset in mundo qui coelestia et terrestria ad invicem concordaret.[10]

What we have seen Dante doing is to draw the conclusions, and sharpen up the outlines of this process. For if it was a fact that Christ was so born, could the central fact of history (in a world ruled by Providence) be haphazard? 'Dico ergo, quod si romanum imperium de jure non fuit, Christus nascendo persuasit injustum' (*Mon.* II, x). And what would be true of Christ's birth would be true too of his death: for if Tiberius Caesar, whose vicar Pontius Pilate was, had no jurisdiction, the Passion of Christ would have no legality behind it. But the power that rules the world does not work casually, at least in Dante's view.

> Desinant igitur Imperium exprobrare Romanum qui se filios Ecclesiae fingunt, cum videant sponsum Christum illud in utroque termine suae militiae comprobrasse.[11]

Indeed, so far has Dante travelled on this road of sanctifying imperial Rome that Livy also becomes for him *gestorum Romanorum scriba egregius* (*Mon.* II, iii), and in the implications of that solemn *scriba* may there not be that prophecy in Dante's mind which Livy himself ventured, almost at the outset of his History? It was no less a spokesman than the ghost of Romulus to whom Livy lent the claim:

> 'Abi, nuntia,' inquit, 'Romanis, coelestes ita velle, ut mea Roma caput orbis terrarum sit: proinde rem militarem colant: sciantque, et ita posteris tradant, nullas opes humanas armis Romanis resistere posse.' Haec, inquit, locutus, sublimis abiit. (I, xvi)

Echoing this, for medieval thought, we have Aegidius Romanus in the *De regimine principum* (I, 14): 'Romanam urbem Deus praeviderat christiani populi principalem sedem futuram.'

Alongside this view of the Roman Empire, so different from the sentiments of St. Augustine, there had been from the time of Fulgentius at least a privileged place for Virgil amongst pagan writers: the idea that in a time of error with Virgil human reason had advanced as far as it could, without the miracle of revelation, to principles cognate with those of Christianity. And here to the contemporaneity of David and Aeneas, Dante adds another, that of Virgil who writes of the journey of Aeneas to the underworld with the other journey of St. Paul. Here it is significant that in the beginning of his poem Paul and Aeneas are the prototypes for Dante, and are subtly contaminated.

> Andovvi poi lo Vas d'elezione,
> per recarne conforto a quella fede
> ch'è principio alla via di salvazione.[12]   (*Inf.* II, 28–30)

It is a wholly Christian sentiment, but is it an accident that it is stated in Virgilian terms, with the last line a paraphrase from *Aeneid* VI (*via prima salutis*)? In spite of Dante's disclaimer,

> Io non Enea, io non Paolo sono,   (*Inf.* II, 32)

it is clear that it is with these he links himself in setting forth, all medieval visions put on one side. It was Comparetti who first perhaps stated this, long enough ago, and Nardi and others have restated it authoritatively in recent times.[13]

So Dante, convinced that 'at the moment of the Redemption mankind had received almost contemporaneously, by the mouth of Virgil and St. Paul, and by the identical system of a miraculous journey into the otherworld, the double revelation of the providential birth of the Empire and the saving essence of the Redemption',[14] sets out with Virgil on his own providential journey. Nor must we let the apparent modesty of Dante's first disclaimer mislead us. In his Epistle to the Cardinals he tells them proudly, 'Non ergo divitiarum, sed gratia Dei sum id quod sum'; and in *Paradiso*, in the episode of Dante's encounter with his own ancestor Cacciaguida there will come the clear statement of Dante as the equal of both Paul and Aeneas.[15] And what then of Virgil? First, it is clear that the Virgil who stands waiting for Dante's company at the outset of the *Comedy* is the Virgil of medieval tradition, but carried by Dante to a point not known before. It follows too that, though Dante seems to be seizing the historical significance of Virgil and his poem, he is not looking backwards to see who or what Virgil in his lifetime was, but forwards, so that a double authority (his own and Virgil's) supports the statement of Dante's views on Universal Monarchy as God's solution for the world. That this is so is emphasized also by the fact that Dante never sifts the information handed down on Virgil. Some of this goes back via Donatus to Suetonius, and might have proved embarrassing for Dante. For though Virgil is a chaste poet, yet both in his biography and in his *Eclogues* there are things which might have given Dante cause to place him with Brunetto Latini, among those violent against Nature. And there is too the case of Virgil's acceptance of the ideas of Epicurus. Here Dante was not well informed, and since his condemnation of Epicurus rested on the point of the mortality of the soul, and since Virgil obviously did not accept this doctrine (how else could he have written *Aeneid* VI?), no suspicion formed in Dante's mind. But nevertheless the fact remains: Dante who knows all the Aeneid, knows it for his own purposes, and looks forward only, confident with Virgil by his side of the assured nature of their convergent prophecy.[16]

If this is so, is it the true Virgil who acts as Dante's guide? Now in former times there was a tendency to think of Virgil as a symbol only, as Human Reason short of grace. And obviously we cannot pass ever wholly out of earshot of this formula. Does not Dante's Virgil himself suggest it to us?

> Ed elli a me: 'Quanto ragion qui vede
> dir ti poss'io; da indi in là t' aspetta
> pur a Beatrice, ch'è opra di fede.'[17] (*Purg.* XVIII, 46–8)

This is only making plain what Virgil had already said a few cantos earlier:

> E se la mia ragion non ti disfama,
> vedrai Beatrice, ed ella pienamente
> ti torrà questa e ciascun'altra brama.[18] (*Purg.* XV, 76–8)

After all, we know now that Dante works rather with the allegory of the theologians, than with that of the poets: that is, he uses real things as symbols, and does not often invent those masks without a substance which were for Croce the hallmark of allegory. But from this can we jump to Auerbach's glib statement?—'Vergil ist nicht die Allegorie einer Eigenschaft oder Tugend oder Fähigkeit oder Kraft, oder auch einer geschichtlichen Institution. Er ist weder die Vernunft noch die Dichtung noch des Kaisertum. Er ist Vergil selbst.'[19] This is too absolute on both its edges. First, we have seen that Virgil must be a symbol of Human Reason at its highest for Dante. But on the further edge, what does it mean that Virgil is *himself*? He can be only, of course, what Dante thought that Virgil was (and we have seen that Dante did not give much thought to this, except to decide, for strong and obvious reasons, that he was no magician); and what Dante made of him.

Now there is a first clear way in which Virgil's record suffers some distortion as Dante takes him over. The journey which Aeneas had made was not one on which Virgil went, wherever or however he found his knowledge of it. Is it enough to make Virgil a sound guide, through Hell and Purgatory? For Dante it was not sufficient, and he did not hesitate to fake the evidence. In *Inferno* IX Dante and Virgil are halted willy nilly outside the evil city of Dis, and Dante's earlier fears reappear. He asks a sly and covert question, whether any out of Limbo come this way? And means to ask, Do you know what you are doing here? Have you faced this obstacle before? And Virgil admits that few from Limbo do come down, but adds at once that he is of those few:

Ver è ch'altra fiata qua giù fui,
congiurato da quella Eritòn cruda
che richiamava l'ombre a'corpi sui.
  Di poco era di me la carne nuda,
ch'ella mi fece intrar dentr'a quel muro,
per trarne un spirto del cerchio di Giuda.
  Quell'è il piú basso loco e'l piú oscuro,
e'l piú lontan dal ciel che tutto gira:
ben so il cammin; però ti fa sicuro.[20] (*Inf.* IX, 22–30)

We shall look, naturally, in vain in earlier literature for this apocryphal journey of Virgil, down to the bottom pit of Hell, presumably to find the answer on the outcome of the battle of Pharsalia. But in the economy of the *Divine Comedy* it has its uses. It means that Virgil will not be at a loss, at least this side of Lucifer; though possibly, had he been scrupulous enough, Dante should also have invented some pretext to take Virgil previously up the slopes of Purgatory: where it will be evident that Virgil ought not to act as guide. But what a web we have to weave, when once we have begun to invent! Have we not heard Virgil say himself (but not the *himself* that Auerbach said Virgil was) that he went down to the circle where Judas is? Then he is no longer circumscribed within the knowledge of the pagan world? Of course not, what use would he be to Dante as a guide to Hell had he learnt nothing more, and nothing since? That is why, on their first meeting, Virgil assures Dante (and us) of two things. First, there is his maximum connection with the Empire of Rome: born—it is a piece of misinformation on Dante's part, due to a homonym—born under the consulate of Julius Caesar, lived under Augustus.

Nacqui sub Iulio, ancor che fosse tardi,
e vissi a Roma sotto'l buono Augusto.

But while proclaiming the Empire, Virgil adds immediately, to end the same tercet, a disclaimer: he owes no allegiance now to the gods of antiquity.

e vissi a Roma sotto'l buono Augusto
al tempo delli dei falsi e bugiardi. (*Inf.* I, 70–2)

For those who read the *Aeneid* mainly for their ideas on Virgil this last line will come as a surprise. For who but Dante can forget that moment in the *Aeneid* when Venus (she herself *alma parens confessa deam*) reveals to her son Aeneas that it is not men alone who

war against Troy? Rending the mortal veil which prevents
Aeneas's sight, she shows him the gods themselves at work, bent
on the destruction of Troy:

> Non tibi Tyndaridis facies invisa Lacaenae
> Culpatusve Paris. Divum inclementia Divum
> Has evertit opes sternitque a culmine Troiam.

So by Venus's aid Aeneas sees Neptune and Juno, Pallas and
almighty Jove, *Numina magna deum,* completing the efforts of the
Greeks. Nor can we think that Virgil means us at this point to dis-
believe in their reality. But there is another revision made, or taken
for granted, in that first scene of Dante's meeting with his Virgil.
For Virgil understands Dante's (Christian) predicament. On the
edge of the trackless wood of sin, but looking hopefully towards
the sunlit mount, Dante is stopped by the three allegorical beasts
of *Inferno* I. His first appeal, on seeing Virgil in this desert, is for
pity in his plight. And when he knows better whom he has met, in
paying a famous homage to Virgil (*Tu se'lo mio maestro e'lo mio
autore*—the last especially a word which committed a medieval to
an *authority*), he still asks first for help against the beast that made
him turn downhill. And Virgil first twits Dante, asks him why he
descends the slope:

> Ma tu perché ritorni a tanta noia?
> perché non sali il dilettoso monte
> ch'è principio e cagion di tutta gioia?[21]   (*Inf.* 76–8)

And then he states the necessity of *another way*, explains the nature
of the beast, puts forward himself what is Dante's prophecy of the
Hound who will drive the She-Wolf back to hell, and offers himself as guide through hell and purgatory; but not to paradise,

> ché quello imperador che là su regna,
> perch'io fu'ribellante alla sua legge,
> non vuol che'n sua città per me si vegna.
>   In tutte parti impera e quivi regge:
> quivi è la sua città e l'alto seggio:
> oh felice colui cu'ivi elegge.[22]   (*Inf.* I, 124–9)

And here we may well ask ourselves from what experience Virgil
draws this melancholy conviction, and what knowledge he should
have of that 'glad hill which is the fount and cause of every joy'.

The answer was first stated perhaps by Comparetti, and varied a little in one or two places of his classic book on Virgil in the Middle Ages. Dante's Virgil is more Christian than in the preceding medieval tradition, but there is a distinction between what he was while he was living, and what he is now after (long after) death. With death, says Comparetti, the veil dropped from Virgil's eyes, and life beyond the tomb revealed the Truths he had not known, with his involuntary errors, and their just consequence.[23] But though such a formula might well be invoked for the renunciation we have seen, it is not clear that Dante thinks at all bifocally for Virgil. And elsewhere Comparetti unconsciously carries us further on an obvious road. For where another critic had thought to see in Virgil 'a slight pedagogic frown', citing his stern indictment of those who think the normal thoughts on Fortune

o creature sciocche,
quanta ignoranza è quella che v'offende.[24] (*Inf.* VII, 70–1)

Comparetti observes incautiously: 'But here, though Virgil speaks, the scorn for vulgar prejudice is Dante's own, just as the fantastic theory which Virgil expounds for Fortune is purely Dantesque and medieval, and not Virgilian at all'.[25] So Virgil speaks, but Dante's are the words. If we bear these two formulas in mind (and it will already be obvious to which unity they may be reduced), we shall not be at a loss to understand either the supplementary information which Virgil needs to have, to act as an effective guide for Dante through the Christian otherworld; or the closeness of the two poets in their resulting relationship.

If we do not, or if we think of Virgil only as he was within the limits of his life and work, then there are many surprises awaiting us throughout the *Comedy*. For though Virgil, in the repeated utterances that we have seen from *Purgatorio*, professes to leave questions of faith to Beatrice, yet he is perforce ready to give Dante guidance, not only physically upon the way, but also in the sense of Christian instruction. And for once that this is offered to us as a new acquisition of Virgil-shade, there are a score of other times when Dante takes without scruple out of Virgil's mouth Christian information which only he could have lent to him. First, the once in which this is legitimately the experience of Virgil-shade. In Limbo Dante asks eagerly, without reflecting that it may be odd to ask Virgil for certainty about the Christian faith,

> 'Dimmi, maestro mio, dimmi, segnore,'
> comincia'io per volere esser certo
> di quella fede che vince ogni errore:
> 'uscicci mai alcuno, o per suo merto
> o per altrui, che poi fosse beato?'[26] (*Inf.* IV, 46-50)

Once more, it is a covert question, but Virgil sees its drift, and answers readily,

> Io era nuovo in questo stato,
> quando ci vidi venire un possente,
> con segno di vittoria coronato.
>   Trasseci l'ombra del primo parente,
> d'Abel suo figlio e quella di Noè,
> di Moisè legista e obediente;
>   Abraàm patriarca e David re,
> Israèl con lo padre e co'suoi nati
> e con Rachele, per cui tanto fe';
>   e altri molti, e feceli beati;
> e vo'che sappi che, dinanzi ad essi,
> spirti umani non eran salvati.[27]   (*Inf.* IV, 52-63)

So Virgil confirms out of his own post-mortem experience the doctrine of Christ's descent to Limbo (crowned, according to medieval iconography, with the sign of victory), and shows incidentally a new, but well-tried, acquaintance with the personnel of the Old Testament. If we have accepted this without that shock of indignation which an ill-intentioned eighteenth-century critic of Dante expressed for Virgil's *Lombard* birth (*Inf.* I, 68), we shall be ready for Dante's doubts about the scheme of Hell, set forth by Virgil in *Inferno* XI. Here Dante goes astray, first about the Incontinent, and then about the Usurers; and gets reminded sharply by Virgil, first of Aristotle, which may be quite legitimate, but secondly of the Bible, which is less defensible:

> Da queste due, se tu ti rechi a mente
> lo Genesì dal principio, convene
> prender sua vita ed avanzar la gente;
>   e perché l'usuriere altra via tene,
> per sé natura e per la sua seguace
> dispregia, poi ch'in altro pon la spene.[28]
>
>   (*Inf.* XI, 106-11)

And we may note here, that though Virgil speaks of the beginning of *Genesis*, this only makes the reproach, for a Christian, sharper;

while he speaks as one who has acquaintance with the whole. And where else did he derive the knowledge we have seen him to possess of all the patriarchs, from Adam on? Nor shall we find Virgil limited in Scriptural knowledge to the Old Testament. Even in one of those places where Virgil leaves to faith what is too hard for reason, he yet shows that he knows what faith is all about:

> Matto è chi spera che nostra ragione
> possa trascorrer la infinita via
> che tiene una sustanza in tre persone.
>   State contenti, umana gente, al quia;
> chè se possuto aveste veder tutto,
> mestier non era parturir Maria.[29]   (*Purg.* III, 34–9)

So the mystery of the Trinity is outside Reason's, or Virgil's, grasp; but yet he knows as much of its existence, and accepts as much the necessity of the Virgin Birth and the Redemption as any other Christian. For here, of course, all are in Virgil's boat, which is not astonishing, since he is Reason at its best. But what is astonishing, is that Virgil should be in the boat with all the rest. In order not to labour a point which may by now be obvious, I will add only one other case. Dante has heard Marco Lombardo on the cause of human woes, and asks of Virgil for the detail of what he meant. And Virgil stigmatizes the root of envy in the world, the covetousness for merely earthly things, which being limited, can only belong to one because they do not belong to another; while heavenly goods grow by being shared:

> Perché s'appuntano i vostri disiri
> dove per compagnia parte si scema,
> invidia move il mantaco a'sospiri.
>   Ma se l'amor della spera suprema
> torcesse in suso il desiderio vostro,
> non vi sarebbe al petto quella tema;
>   ché, per quanti si dice piú lì 'nostro',
> tanto possiede piú di ben ciascuno,
> e piú di caritate arde in quel chiostro.[30]
>   (*Purg.* XV, 49–57)

It is a purely Christian lesson which Virgil offers to Dante, and he does so, not as one who retrospectively has learnt his ways were wrong; but as one in full and authoritative possession of the Truth.

It was Comparetti's point that Virgil has learnt a lot during his long abode in Limbo. But as we saw he added at another point, on the concept of Fortune in *Inferno* VII, that here Virgil spoke with Dante's voice. I would say that Dante, looking, as we saw, forwards to the accomplishment of both their prophecies, and confident in the journey which he makes on the model of both Aeneas and Paul, never looks back to find a separate reality for Virgil from himself. He has thus not only inherited a medieval Virgil, but his approach to Virgil as an *author* (i.e. as an *authority*) is also medieval. It is Petrarch who will first look back, to Cicero, for instance, with the consciousness of his belonging to another age, to see him as he is, and without involving him in the attitudes of Petrarch's time. Over and again the critics have wished humanism on Dante, because he shows enthusiasm for Virgil. But enthusiasm, in these cases, is not enough. It is a question of the direction in which Dante is going, and we can only note that he is still advancing away from Virgil, using him as a megaphone for his own ideas, and speaking constantly through Virgil with no regard for what Virgil was. For even if we kept to that first formula, of Virgil learning while he waits below, legitimate as this extension-course may be, it is still plain that Virgil plus that learning is not the Virgil whom we read, or whom Maecenas knew. And we can see easily enough that Dante did not think it out like this, and that he lent his voice to Virgil: his voice, and his heart. So much that the Virgil-guide of the *Divine Comedy* is nearer Dante than he is to Virgil; or is Dante under another guise. It does not follow, naturally, that he will seem unanimated, a symbol rather than a person. But it does follow that the more Dante animates a Virgil in his own image the less will he resemble the genuine poet of the *Aeneid*. Indeed, this conclusion seems inescapable, nor can we easily assert its opposite,

> per la contradizion che nol consente. (*Inf.* XXVII, 120)

There remain, however, those points of legitimate contact, where Dante learnt from Virgil what Virgil had to tell; and these may yet be sufficient to make Dante similar to Virgil. First, those particulars from Virgil's (or Aeneas's) journey into the other world. Charon and his boat on Acheron, Cerberus, the Minotaur, the Centaurs and the Harpies, Cacus; the *amoena virecta* of the Elysian Fields which become the *prato di fresca verdura* of Dante's

Limbo; the judges (with Minos) at the entrance to Avernus, the walled city of Dis, with the Furies on the threshold, and the fiery river Phlegethon around it; Phlegyas, and the Giants stuck in the depths of Tartarus. Then categories of sinners: the fraudulent, the violent against God, the avaricious, the traitors. Then there is the straightforward imitation which carries us, nevertheless, into a new context: so that it is the same, and not the same. As when the episode of Dante meeting his ancestor Cacciaguida in *Paradiso* assumes explicitly the semblances of Aeneas and Anchises. And then there are the places, or the place, where Dante acts on Virgil's impulse. As in that startling case by which Rhipeus is found in Paradise among the Blessed, solely upon the strength of Virgil's commendation of Rhipeus as

> iustissimus unus
> Qui fuit in Teucris et servantissimus aequi.

Now it is natural that a wealth of Virgilian particulars should give its own colour to the *Comedy*. Yet it is obvious, in the extent, as in the direction, of Dante's poem that his otherworld is not dominated by that of Virgil. Here it is legitimate to remember the slightness of Virgil's suggestions, his disengaged approach to Hell. Indeed, if Dante had listened properly to Virgil he would not have committed either of them to the descent into the pit of Hell. Was it not explained to Aeneas by the Sibyl, to justify the brevity of her exposition, and to keep him out,

> Nulli fas casto sceleratum insistere limen?

Dante, and Dante's Virgil, behave as though they are unaware of this plain prohibition to gentlemen. But though Aeneas' visit was to the better sort in Hades, Virgil's suggestions as to their status and employment are singularly unenterprising.

> His demum exactis, perfecto munere Divae,
> Devenere locos laetos, et amoena virecta
> Fortunatorum nemorum, sedesque beatas.
> Largior hic campos aether, et lumine vestit
> Purpureo: solemque suum, sua sidera norunt.
> Pars in gramineis exercent membra palaestris;
> Contendunt ludo, et fulva luctantur arena:
> Pars pedibus plaudunt choreas, et carmina dicunt . . .
> Arma procul, currusque virum miratur inanes.

Stant terra defixae hastae, passimque soluti
Per campum pascuntur equi. Quae gratia currum,
Armorumque fuit vivis, quae cura nitentes
Pascere equos; eadem sequitur tellure repostos.

(VI, 637 ff.)

By this economical, and unimaginative, solution the magnanimous
heroes of the Elysian Fields content themselves with the simulac-
rum of their life, wrestling their time away till they are dipped in
Lethe's stream, to be called up once more to the real world they
had left behind, still waiting for them. It is barely enough for
Inferno IV, and it is plain that Dante's poem is organised out of the
theology of the Middle Ages to an enrichment which the mere
episode of *Aeneid* VI could not afford.

It may still be that Dante, even granted the much superior
organization of his afterworld (and its continuation beyond anything contemplated by Virgil, to that *contemplatio Dei* which is the
final goal of Dante), was influenced by Virgil as poet. And there
are places, obvious enough, where Dante has followed Virgil's
lead. One of these is in the Circle of the Suicides (*Inf.* XIII), in that
forbidding wood where Dante hears laments, without knowing
whence they come. Then Dante thinks that Virgil thought he
thought they came from people hid within the wood, and Virgil
bids him pluck a twig to banish all such thoughts:

> Allora porsi la mano un poco avante,
> e colsi un ramicel da un gran pruno:
> e'l tronco suo gridò: 'Perché mi schiante?'
> Da che fatto fu poi di sangue bruno,
> ricominciò a dir: 'Perché mi scerpi?
> non hai tu spirto di pietà alcuno?
> Uomini fummo, e or siam fatti sterpi:
> ben dovrebb'esser la tua man più pia,
> se state fossimo anime di serpi.'
> Come d'un stizzo verde ch'arso sia
> da l'un de' capi, che da l'altro geme
> e cigola per vento che va via;
> sí de la scheggia rotta usciva inseme
> parole e sangue . . .[31]   (*Inf.* XIII, 31–44)

Now very palpably this invention of the imprisoned soul of Pier
della Vigna derives out of the *Aeneid*, copied from that episode in
which Aeneas and the Trojans are warned to flee from Thrace.

Here Aeneas has sacrificed to the gods, and looks for greenery to adorn the altar.

> Forte fuit juxta tumulus, quo cornea summo
> Virgulta, et densis hastilibus horrida myrtus.
> Accessi, viridemque ab humo convellere silvam
> Conatus, ramis tegerem ut frondentibus aras;
> Horrendum, et dictu video mirabile monstrum.
> Nam, quae prima solo ruptis radicibus arbos
> Vellitur, huic atro liquuntur sanguine guttae,
> Et terram tabo maculant. Mihi frigidus horror
> Membra quatit, gelidusque coit formidine sanguis.

Here there is an obvious similarity, but already differences. Aeneas attempts to uproot the myrtle-bush, and blood flows from it on to the ground. But it is Aeneas who is terror-stricken, and so far the imprisoned spirit utters no lament. Again Aeneas strives to tear it out, and kneels to get a better purchase on it:

> Tertia sed postquam majore hastilia nisu
> Aggredior, genibusque adversae obluctor arenae;
> (Eloquar, an sileam?) gemitus lacrimabilis imo
> Auditur tumulo, et vox reddita fertur ad aures:
> Quid miserum, Aenea, laceras? jam parce sepulto,
> Parce pias scelerare manus . . .
> Heu fuge crudeles terras, fuge litus avarum.
> Nam Polydorus ego.

Dante timidly plucked the smallest twig, and raised an outcry of the utmost protest, in which Pier della Vigna talks as if Dante had offended by his plucking all the wood. Aeneas kneels to get the maximum of grip, in order to uproot all the bush, and only at his third attempt does there come forth the moderate request to cease. The situation, though similar, is also different. But then, the circumstances, and the characters, are also different. Pier della Vigna is a suicide, a category for which Dante has necessarily a different judgement from any that could have been understood, formerly at least, by Virgil. For suicide is no longer a hero's action, and, vain and weak, Pier exaggerates most damnably the hurt that Dante causes him. But Polydorus is not a hero, nor is he condemned for any crime. His metamorphosis is compensation, and not punishment.

Hunc Polydorum auri quondam cum pondere magno
Infelix Priamus furtim mandarat alendum
Threicio regi: cum jam diffideret armis
Dardaniae, cingique urbem obsidione videret.
Ille, ut opes fractas Teucrum, et fortuna recessit,
Res Agamemnonias, victriciaque arma secutus,
Fas omne abrumpit, Polydorum obtruncat, et auro
Vi potitur. Quid non mortalia pectora cogis
Auri sacra fames?

This is still a powerful motive force, and Virgil's reflection has remained proverbial. It was, nevertheless, a saying which Dante at one point unaccountably misunderstood. I do not suppose that he could misunderstand the episode of Polydorus from which it springs; but it is clear enough that Dante, though he has stolen the invention of the tree-bound spirit, uses it in a different context, and in a different way. And it is noticeable that the mechanism of speech, under these odd circumstances, as expressed by Dante in the famous simile of the hissing twig, is a necessity felt by the one poet, and quite neglected by the other.

By the side of that unfaithful imitation we may put a simile which plainly comes from Virgil. In *Aeneid* V there are the games with which Aeneas celebrates the anniversary of Anchises' death. Amongst the strong competitors in the ship-race Mnestheus calls on oar and sail as he seeks the open seas; and for him Virgil finds the simile of the dove which rises from some cavern where it nests, with noisy wing-flaps, then sails calmly off towards the fields, with scarce a movement of its wings.

Qualis spelunca subito commota columba,
Cui domus, et dulces latebroso in pumice nidi,
Fertur in arva volans: plausumque exterrita pennis
Dat tecto ingentem: mox aere lapsa quieto
Radit iter liquidum, celeres neque commovet alas:
Sic Mnestheus . . .

It is much better a simile than its context, than the occasion which gives rise to it. And perhaps one would need to be a yachting enthusiast to feel it as not too good for its immediate purpose. But Dante transfers it to a more appropriate place, from the fifth book of the *Aeneid* to the fifth canto of *Inferno*, where the carnal sinners are carried everlastingly in the squall of hell. And Dante, who had listened to Virgil's recital of those famous figures who sinned by love, looks to two only, and desires to speak with them:

> I'cominciai: 'Poeta, volentieri
> parlerei a quei due che'nsieme vanno,
> e paion sí al vento esser leggieri.'
>   Ed elli a me: 'Vedrai quando saranno
> piú presso a noi: e tu allor li prega
> per quello amor che i mena, ed ei verranno.'
>   Sí tosto come il vento a noi li piega,
> mossi la voce: 'O anime affannate,
> venite a noi parlar, s'altri nol niega!'
>   Quali colombe dal disio chiamate,
> con l'ali alzate e ferme al dolce nido
> vegnon per l'aere dal voler portate:
> cotali uscir de la schiera ov'è Dido,
> a noi venendo per l'aere maligno,
> sí forte fu l'affettuoso grido.[32]   (Inf. V, 73–87)

The simile has been captured, and brought by Dante to this most emotive of all contexts, made the fitting prelude to the more than famous tercets which Francesca speaks (Inf. V, 100–108). In the process its direction has been reversed. In Virgil, the dove flies from her nest, and in the silly manner of pigeons makes a startling clatter as she goes, and then the point is of her steady progress down the straight. But in Dante the two doves fly in unison towards their nest, and the simile is not based on speed, but on affection and purpose. Is not the dove the bird of Venus? Dante remembered here what the poet of the *Aeneid* for once forgot (in spite of Aeneas's parentage); and it is for a loving reason that these doves give us the opening note to the episode of Paolo and Francesca, based all on Love. This time no wonder that it is Dante, in spite of his proneness to sound effects, who leaves out the clatter of the pigeons' wings, suggested, though not strongly orchestrated, by Virgil.

Two similes, then, the one most obviously engendered by the other, yet separate in their whole atmosphere, and moving in opposite directions. May we not take them as symbolic of the two authors with whom we are concerned? For we are left now only with that central purpose which drew Dante first to Virgil. An author having the force of Scripture, offering not only the parallel journey of Aeneas (parallel to the rapture of St. Paul), but also the proclamation of the timeless Empire of Rome, to which we have seen Dante giving the stamp of prophecy. Here Dante means what Virgil meant, and should be most Virgilian. But are not Dante and Virgil caught at this point, and looking from it inevitably in opposite directions because they have to stand here, if together, yet only back to back? What is Virgil's poem but the celebration of the plenitude of Rome? a paean in which its origins are given a mythological ennoblement, while Jupiter and all the pagan gods (Juno notwithstanding, or Juno yoked at last to the same chariot) concur in Rome's high destiny. The process is of course one of putting the Royal Arms upon the Royal Train; it gives an ultimate sanction, I mean, to something which exists in its own right, and in its full reality. Hence those accents of full and calm contentment which, despite some old prejudices about the pathos of Virgilian sentiment, swell through Virgil's poem. *Sunt lacrimae rerum*: but these are limited to the fall of Troy, and offset by the rise of Rome. For Virgil is the poet of the Augustan Age, and records for us that moment when the Roman Empire, stretching already to meet the known ends of inhabited space, has been brought to peace. It is an accident that Virgil inherits the combat-epic as the model for his poem, the accident that accounts for its losing interest and direction in the later books. For its real theme is the great accomplishment of Roman power, the settling of the world; and it is this, of course, that echoes in those key passages which we have seen Dante take as gospel.

This is obviously something very different when you are looking back, as Virgil, on achievement, and when you are looking hopefully for a solution in the night of time. For what reality could such a sacred text possess in the world of 1300? In one of the significant texts of the next century, of the Quattrocento, we shall find an admission which Dante would have been well advised to make. 'The dignity of the empire is diminished, till even counts barely nod their heads, where formerly the greatest kings bent to the ground. *Sed est omnium potestatum finis,* nor, what Virgil thought, was the Roman empire given without end, which instead seems now so sick, that it needs think more of the grave than of a doctor.' That is Aeneas Sylvius Piccolomini, Pope Pius II, in the middle of the fifteenth century. But was the Roman Empire in better shape in Dante's time? Dante himself, presenting Virgil first 'as weak through lengthy silence' (*Inf.* I, 63), points to the long gap since Frederick II died in 1250; and in his own lifetime pinned his hopes upon the theory of providential sanction to the rule of Rome, even when its embodiment was given to the slenderest reed, the landless, powerless, Henry VII of Luxemburg. In cold reality the Empire has no further part to play upon the Italian scene, except as a sporadic, and upsetting, element. Politically Dante starts from a vacuum, where Virgil started from its opposite. While Virgil praises and applauds, Dante must condemn. The Roman Tiber is for the first poet, *caelo gratissimus amnis*: his own Arno is for the second 'a damned and wretched ditch', *la maladetta e sventurata fossa*. If Dante and Virgil still stand close together, it is because Dante has cast for himself a new Virgil in his own image, who speaks for Dante, and with Dante's voice. But the first Virgil walks far from Dante's side, and is often opposite in statement, as in poetic tone. Few pairs of poets are in effect in most things so dissimilar as these who have been cast so long, so intimately, together.[33]

[1] Boccaccio, *Comento sopra la Commedia,* Lezione seconda.

[2] 'So my high poem sings it at one point: you know this well, who know the poem all.'

[3] 'He said to me: "And are you still amongst the other fools? Here pity lives when it is truly dead".'

[4] For this, cf. Bruno Nardi, *Sviluppo dell'arte e del pensiero di Dante,* in *Dante* a cura di Umberto Parricchi. Rome 1965, p. 102.

[5] *Il Convivio* (ed. Busnelli & Vandelli), Vol. II Florence 1954, IV, xxiv, 312 and IV, xxvi, 332.

[6] Ibid., IV, iv, 37.

[7] *Epistola* VII, 410 (*Tutte le opere,* ed. Moore). And cf. the important articles of G. R. Barolli, *Dante scriba dei,* in *Convivium* XXXI, 1963.

[8] Epist. VII, ib.

[9] *Monarchia,* II, vii, 338 (in *Opere minori,* ed. Fraticelli).

[10] cf., e.g., Domenico Comparetti, *Virgilio nel medio evo* (ed. G. Pasquali, 1943), I, 214.

[11] *Monarchia* II, xi, 356—and, for this addition to the old text of the *Monarchia,* v. Ettore Paratore, *Dante e il mondo classico,* 111 in the vol. cit., *Dante* (ed. Parricchi).

[12] 'There went there then the Chosen Vessel, to bring back comfort for that faith which is beginning of salvation's way.'

[13] For the *via prima salutis,* v. Paratore *cit.* 115. Comparetti, *cit.,* I, 281; Nardi, *cit.,* 107; Paratore, *cit.,* 114.

[14] Paratore, *cit.,* 114.

[15] cf. *Paradiso* XV, 25–30.

[16] cf. Comparetti I, 268–70.

[17] 'And he to me: "What reason here can see, I can tell you: thence on look but to Beatrice, for that belongs to faith".'

[18] 'And if my reason does not satisfy your hunger, you will see Beatrice, and she will fully take from you both this and any other want.'

[19] 'Virgil is not the allegory of a quality, or a virtue, a faculty, or an art, nor of any historical institution. He is neither reason nor poetry nor the Empire. He is Virgil himself.' cf. Mario Santoro, *Virgilio personaggio della Divina Commedia*, in *Cultura e scuola* IV, 13–14, 1965, 354 (quoting Auerbach, *Figura*, in *Archivum romanicum* 1938, XXII, 4).

[20] 'True is it I have been down here before, conjured by that cruel Erichtho who called shades back into their flesh again. My flesh was scarcely bare of me when she sent me within these walls, to draw from thence a spirit out of Judas' circle. That is the lowest and the darkest place, the furthest from the all-encircling sky: I know the way well: therefore have no fear.'

[21] 'But why do you go back to so much pain? why do you not climb the pleasant hill which is the fount and cause of every joy?'

[22] 'That emperor who reigns up there, since I was rebel to his law, lets me not come into his city. In all parts he holds sway and there he reigns; there is his city and his throne; how happy is the man who is elect!'

[23] Comparetti, *cit.*, I, 270.

[24] 'O foolish things, how great the ignorance besets you here!'

[25] Comparetti, *cit.*, I, 278.

[26] 'Tell me master, tell me, lord,' began I in desire to be made sure about that faith which conquers error: 'Did ever anyone come out, for his own merit's or another's, to be blessed?'

[27] 'New was I in this state when here I saw arrive a powerful One, crowned with the sign of victory. He drew from hence the shade of the first father, of his son Abel, and of Noah; of the law-giver Moses, the obedient; Abraham the patriarch, David the king; Israel with his father and his sons, and Rachel too, for whom he served so long; and many more, and made them blessed; and I would have you know that, before these, there were no human spirits that were saved.'

[28] 'And from these two, if you will keep in mind the first of Genesis, one must take one's life, and aid one's race; and since the usurer takes another way, and puts his hope in something else, both in itself and in its follower he despises Nature.'

[29] 'Foolish is he who hopes our reason can traverse the infinite way which holds one substance in three persons. Content yourselves, o humankind, with *quia . . .*; for if you could have seen the whole, there was no need for Mary to give birth.'

[30] 'Since your desires go to things where part is lost through company, envy moves the bellows to your sighs. But if instead love for the highest sphere twisted your desires aloft, this fear would not be in your breast. For all the more who say there, This is ours, each one possesses so much more of good, and burns the more with charity in that sphere.'

[31] 'And then I stretched my hand a little out, and plucked a twig from a great bush: his trunk cried out: "Why do you rend me?" When it was dark with blood, it said again: "Why do you tear me so? have you no spirit of pity at all? Men were we, now are turned to thorns: your hand should have been indeed more kind if we had been but souls of snakes." As from a green twig that burns one end, which from the other drips and hisses with escaping air; so from the broken branch there issued forth both words and blood.'

[32] 'I began: "Poet, willingly would I speak with those two who go together, and seem so light upon the wind." And he to me: "You shall see when they are near to us, then beg them by that love which carries them, and they will come." Soon as the wind bore them to us I spoke to them: "O souls in your distress, come here and speak with us, if another stops you not!" As doves called by desire, with still poised wings, come through the air carried by their will to their sweet nest, so from the throng where Dido is they came to us through the malignant air, so strong was my affectionate cry.'

I   117

[33] The present discussion of the theme of Dante and Virgil elaborates the conclusions reached in *Dante e Virgilio* (*Le Parole e le Idee* VII, 1-2, 1965) and in *Dante's Virgil* (in *A Homage to Dante*, Norman, Oklahoma, 1965). These complement, but do not replace the extended comparison made in *Dante and Virgil* (Oxford, Blackwell, 1949), to which the reader is referred for a consideration of the poetic essences of Virgil and Dante.

V

Changing Attitudes to Virgil
A study in the history of taste from Dryden to Tennyson

R. D. WILLIAMS

NO Latin poet has had a greater effect on subsequent literature and thought than Virgil; he has been admired, indeed on occasion worshipped, by the great majority of critics and poets for two thousand years. But there has been plenty of hostile criticism too, growing to a crescendo during the Romantic Revival; and the reasons for admiration have been of the most widely diverse kinds. The shifting views of the nature of Virgil's achievement shed light both on the scope and variety of what Virgil offers, and on the strengths and weaknesses of the critics themselves, and this may serve to remind us that our own shifts (in the direction of repeated imagery or psychologically significant symbols or numerical structure or semantic study of key words) are exciting new angles which supplement rather than cancel the approaches and terminology of past generations. My intention here is not to give an account of Virgilian influence on English literature with special reference to the places where it has been most marked (a subject on which indeed much work still remains to be done[1]), but rather to present a fragment in the history of changing taste, an account of what was disliked in Virgil as well as what was liked, of the features which were appreciated by his admirers and the features which were not. I shall be concerned with the period in England from the late seventeenth to the end of the nineteenth century, with Neo-Classical idolatry, Romantic rejection, and Victorian rehabilitation. In order to set the scene and give a basis for comparison, I begin with a brief sketch of Roman attitudes to Virgil.

I

The Romans themselves, both during his lifetime and after his death regarded Virgil as their greatest national poet. Horace, Virgil's close friend, praises his *Eclogues* (*Sat.* 1.10.44 ff.) and echoes his *Aeneid* (e.g. *Odes* 3.3); Propertius (who had little in common with him) says of the *Aeneid* that 'something greater than the *Iliad* is coming to birth' (2.34.65 ff.); Livy's diction and his treatment of some episodes is influenced by the *Aeneid*; the story is told in Tacitus (*Dial.* 13) that when some lines from Virgil were quoted during a theatrical performance at which Virgil was present 'the whole audience rose and showed him veneration as if he were Augustus'. In the century after his death his influence was enormous: Ovid was soaked in him, Seneca quoted him extensively to illustrate his Stoic arguments, Calpurnius Siculus closely imitated his *Eclogues,* Columella took up a suggestion from the *Georgics* and wrote a poem on gardens, while the four Silver Age epic poets, Lucan, Valerius Flaccus, Statius, and Silius Italicus wrote poems based on the versification and techniques of the *Aeneid.* Statius ends his *Thebaid* by urging his poem not to challenge the *Aeneid* but to follow far behind, and we are told that Silius used to make pilgrimage to Virgil's tomb. Lucan, in many ways the most interesting of these four, used Virgilian material and methods for non-Virgilian aims, namely to discredit the Roman Imperial system.

The fame of Virgil in the first century is well illustrated by a passage in Persius (1.96) where bad poetry is dismissed with the semi-proverbial phrase *arma virum*, 'Oh, shades of Virgil'. Juvenal tells us that Virgil was much thumbed in the schools, and that a favourite topic at dinner parties was the relative merit of Homer and Virgil. Juvenal's own brilliant achievement largely arises from his ability to cast into a Virgilian mock epic mould the usually humbler material of satire. The diction of Tacitus, and sometimes the treatment of subject-matter, was greatly indebted to Virgil; finally for Quintilian Virgil was the Roman poet of the greatest value in education.

What were the reasons for such immense admiration in these first 150 years? Two are particularly evident. The first is that the *Aeneid* was regarded as the national poem of the Romans, in the same way as Homer had been for the Greeks. The epic at this time (as for a very long time afterwards) was regarded as the height of literary achievement, and in the *Aeneid* Virgil had expressed the traditions and ideals of the Roman people, deep-rooted in antiquity and inspired and guarded by the powers of Heaven. Here was a repository of the ancient virtues, *constantia, fides, humanitas, religio, pietas,* the national scheme of ethics, a gift from the gods to Rome, and from Rome to all nations. Here was the imperial concept of the mother nation whose family was all the peoples of the world, a concept developed and fostered by patriotic pride and Stoic philosophy, and given noble expression by the last of the Classical Roman poets, Claudian, at the time when the sack of Rome was imminent:

> Haec est in gremium victos quae sola recepit,
> humanumque genus communi nomine fovit
> matris non dominae ritu, civesque vocavit
> quos domuit nexuque pio longinqua revinxit. (24.150 f.)

'Rome it is alone who has taken the conquered to her bosom, and cherished the human race under a common name like a mother, not a tyrant, has called those whom she conquered her citizens, and united distant places in a bond of affection for her.'

The second reason for the admiration of Virgil was his technical mastery of the skills of literary composition. We see this very clearly in the imitation of his phrases and rhythms by other hexameter poets from Ovid onwards; we see it in the discussions about him preserved in Aulus Gellius; and we see it most obviously in the authority afforded to Virgil above all other poets by Quintilian in his treatment of literary devices, figures of speech, rules of diction.

The next phase is the fourth century, the period of the learned commentators, such as Macrobius and Servius. The seven books of Macrobius' *Saturnalia* (end of the fourth century) are full of discussion of Virgil; it is very evident that admiration for him is centred upon his immense learning. Macrobius salutes not only a great poet, but an encyclopedia, a treasure house of ancient language, religion, customs, science, mythology, a compendium of antiquarian lore. Much of course is said about Virgil's correctness of usage and skill in *ars rhetorica*. There is great emphasis on his knowledge of Greek and Latin literature as revealed in his 'borrowings'; this is presented in a somewhat jejune way, without very penetrating conclusions about the use made of the sources.

But the method has had a long pedigree in literary scholarship (its exponents have not always been any more penetrating than Macrobius was), and it is concerned with a most vital aspect of Virgil's art. In some ways we may view the *Aeneid* as a kind of attempted synthesis of human experience as seen in the long chronicles of Greek and Latin poetry. To transplant, with the necessary adaptations, the situations, characters, images, and thought of Homer and the others into the Augustan world, to see what is the same and what different in the many aspects of human activity and vision over a period of a thousand years—this in a sense is what the *Aeneid* is about.

Macrobius' contemporary, Servius, shows in his commentary the same emphasis on learning; he is concerned to expound what he sees as the vast storehouse of knowledge embodied in Virgil's poetry. This he does partly by presenting antiquarian information of all kinds in order to explain and elaborate Virgil's meaning—geography, history, philosophy, religion, myths and fables; and partly by explaining Virgil's art through the medium of the rules of grammar and rhetoric and their labels—acyrologia, tapeinosis, antiptosis, and so on. It was no part of his plan as a commentator to be a literary critic; we find very little in the way of aesthetic appreciation, very little of the warmth and enthusiasm of (say) Longinus.

These then were the enthusiasts for Virgil in ancient Rome; not unnaturally we know much less of his detractors. That they existed is certain; the Suetonius-Donatus Life of Virgil (43 ff.) gives us brief statements about the *obtrectatores* of Virgil, including contemporary criticism such as Agrippa's objection to a new kind of 'cacozelia' (affected writing). Carvilius Pictor, we are told, wrote a book criticizing the *Aeneid*; Herennius made an anthology of faulty passages; Faustus collected his 'thefts', and Avitus had eight volumes under the somewhat kinder title of 'Resemblances'. The *obtrectatores* appear from time to time in Servius' commentary, where they receive short shrift. From the little that we can gather about them their objections seem either to have been on small matters of detail, apparent errors and contradictions, or to have been complaints about excessive imitation (a view destined to be heard again in Virgilian criticism). Donatus gives the well-known story that in reply to them Virgil suggested that they should try it themselves and would soon discover that it was easier to steal his club from Hercules than a line from Homer.

II

We turn now to the English Augustan Age, the Neo-Classical period beginning with Dryden and stretching well on into the eighteenth century. We shall see that in some respects the reasons for Virgil's popularity are basically similar to those of Roman times. The medieval allegorizing approach to Virgil[2] had long since begun to fade, and with it the strange fame of Virgil in folk-lore, the Virgil of the *sortes Virgilianae*, poet of magical powers, talisman of a supernatural wisdom. Under the influence of the Renaissance critics a new veneration arose based on the rules of literary composition, discovered by the Greeks and Romans and codified by their leading critics, Aristotle and Horace. Passing from Italy to seventeenth-century France and then to England, a passion for correctness in accordance with the rules of the ancient tradition became exceedingly powerful. The classical theorizing of such men as Scaliger, Bossu, Boileau, had a most profound effect on Virgilian appreciation which continued on through the eighteenth century.

The English Augustan Age was the high noon of admiration for Horace and Virgil. While Ovid[3] had rivalled in popularity, and often surpassed, all other Latin poets during the previous hundred years, we now find a reaction developing against his ebullient wit, his uninhibited imagination, in favour of the artistic control and judgement, the urbanity and ethical content that was seen in Horace and Virgil. The Roman critics had censured Ovid for lack of artistic control (Seneca complained that he could not leave well alone, Quintilian that he indulged his talent instead of controlling it);[4] Dryden had indeed a high regard for him, but a much higher one for Virgil,[5] whom he regarded as his master. He expresses the outlook of his times (and of his successors) when he says: 'Continence is practised by few writers, and scarcely any of the ancients excepting Virgil and Horace'; and again when he praises Horace for being 'bounded in fancy'. 'All power of fancy over reason', said Johnson much later, still presenting a Neo-Classical position, 'is a degree of insanity'. The English Augustan Age wanted to keep clear of the jungle in which lurked the terrifying creatures of the imagination, to avoid the peculiar, the excessive, the eccentric, the abnormal. There was less interest in the idiosyncratic and personal experience than in the generalized and universal moral lesson. It was a literary climate in which Horace and Virgil would clearly be more congenial than Catullus, Propertius, or Ovid. Here is Waller speaking of Horace, who

> will our superfluous branches prune,
> Give us new rules, and set our harps in tune:
> Direct us how to back the winged horse,
> Favour his flight, and moderate his force.

'Moderate his force'—Pegasus must fly, but on tight rein.[6] Dryden uses a different image to the same effect, maintaining that imagination in a poet can be 'so wild and lawless, that like a high-ranging spaniel, it must have clogs tied to it lest it outrun the judgement'.

This then is the general context in which we may view Dryden's attitude[7] to Virgil, especially as revealed in the long dedication prefixed to his translation of the *Aeneid* (1697). His very high regard for the *Aeneid* is based on aspects of the poem which we may divide into two headings: firstly artistic control, and secondly moral (and political) significance. He has much to say of Virgil's excellence in diction and rhythm, of the 'sweetness of the sound'; the English Augustans had a very special interest in this,[8] and the varied movement, the subtle cadences, the exquisite word-music of the Virgilian hexameter found most receptive ears. How could the elegance, beauty, and harmony of Virgil's language not have been appreciated by the founder of the splendid fluency of the English Augustan Age, to whom Johnson said was owed 'the refinement of our language',[9] for 'he found English poetry brick, and he left it marble'? In a broader sense too Dryden regards Virgil as the master in artistic control: he admires the structural arrangement, the use of similes, the propriety of Virgil's 'imitation'. 'Though he yielded much to Homer in invention, he more excelled him in his admirable judgement': Dryden found Homer 'somewhat too talkative, and more than somewhat too digressive' compared with the precision and correctness of Virgil.

Secondly Dryden emphasized the didactic and ethical content of the *Aeneid*, praising Virgil for having used the epic, 'the greatest work which the soul of man is capable to perform', for its proper purpose: 'to form the mind to heroic virtue by example'. The epic poet for Dryden was one who 'to his natural endowments of a large invention, a ripe judgement, and a strong memory, has joined the knowledge of the liberal arts and sciences, and particularly moral philosophy, the mathematics, geography, and history, and with all these qualifications is born a poet'. And again: 'besides an universal genius is required universal learning'. Like Macrobius and Servius, Dryden was most receptive to the learning which he found in the *Aeneid*, and as an English Augustan he delighted in its ethical application. But there was also a more personal relevance: Dryden was keenly interested and involved in the philosophical, scientific, religious, and poetical currents of his time,[10] and he could read in Virgil's poem reflexions of his own problems and attitudes. The court poet, the supporter of Toryism, the Catholic convert found in the *Aeneid* the public voice of Rome, presenting in a mythological narrative the religious, political and moral behaviour appropriate to a great people.[11] Like Virgil Dryden lived through a period of turbulence and instability, and the fears of further revolution, of new civil war, were very real to him. He saw the dilemma of Virgil with his 'republican principles' under a monarchical system, but lists the advantages of Augustus' rule, and says 'these things, I say, being considered by the poet, he concluded it to be in the interest of his country to be so governed; to infuse an awful respect into the people towards such a prince; by that respect to confirm their obedience to him, and by that obedience to make them happy. This was the moral of his divine poem'. And again, after commenting that the manners of Aeneas were the same as those of Augustus he continues: 'these manners were, piety to the gods and a dutiful affection to his father, love to his relations, care of his people, courage and conduct in the wars, gratitude to those who had obliged him, and justice in general to mankind'. Dryden's concern with these ethical concepts was more specific and particularized (often involving a choice between two schools of thought); Virgil's was universal and general, but both were deeply interested in the processes and problems of political order, and the nature of true authority. Many pages of the dedication are taken up with a defence of the moral virtues of Aeneas against those critics who had detracted from them.[12]

These then were the qualities of the *Aeneid* to which Dryden was particularly receptive: what qualities did he not see or not greatly appreciate? He refers to Virgil's pathos quite often, especially when contrasting him with Homer, but he does not seem to have been very deeply sensitive to it (Johnson thought Dryden too turbulent and violent to be pathetic). He does not see the subtlety of the psychological counterplay between Aeneas'

virtues and his frailties, for he is too concerned to show that they
are not frailties in order to justify the poet. He does not see the
tension in the poem between these virtues and their disastrous
consequences; he is not attuned to the 'balance of discordant
qualities' which Coleridge regarded as fundamental in poetry,
and which is now clearly seen to be a major feature in the greatness
of the *Aeneid*. He has not really penetrated deeply to the implications of the moral substratum of the poem. He does not appreciate
the range of Virgil's imagination, nor (of course) the threads of
recurrent thematic imagery, the pattern of metaphor and symbol;
he does not often respond to the suggestion of the emotive over-
tones. Himself a poet of statement, a master of clarity and precision, who taught Johnson's generation *'sapere et fari*, to think
naturally and express forcibly' he could not respond deeply to the
evocative and half-formed trails of thought, the latent ambiguities,
the unresolved tensions which flicker through the *Aeneid*. His
robust and vigorous mind fed on the formal and intellectual
qualities of the poem.

In a famous passage in the *Temple of Fame* Pope speaks thus of
Virgil:

> A golden column next in rank appear'd,
> On which a shrine of purest gold was rear'd;
> Finish'd the whole, and labour'd every part,
> With patient touches of unwearied art:
> The Mantuan there in sober triumph sat,
> Composed his posture, and his look sedate;
> On Homer still he fix'd a reverent eye,
> Great without pride, in modest majesty. (196 f.)

For all the differences between Pope and Dryden this is basically
the same picture again, a picture of admiration for emotional
restraint, for verbal mastery, for artistic control based on successful imitation of Homer. The point is elaborated in Pope's introduction to his translation of the *Iliad*. Here he awards Homer the
palm for invention, and speaks of his fire, his *vivida vis animi*, the
'wild paradise' as compared with the 'ordered garden'. Homer is
like the Nile in its overflow, Virgil like a river in its banks. Homer
is the greater genius, Virgil the better artist; if Virgil does not vie
in invention with Homer, he does vie in judgement. It is ironic to
reflect that the aspects of Homer defined here were precisely those
which (as Johnson saw) Pope could not reproduce in his trans-

lation, for he 'made him graceful' and 'lost him some of his sublimity'. The qualities attributed to Virgil are much closer to those which Pope possessed.

Not all the Homer-Virgil comparisons[13] of the eighteenth century are as favourable to Homer as Pope's. More than a century earlier Scaliger[14] in his *Poetics* had argued vehemently in favour of Virgil's art to the disparagement of Homer, and there would be some agreement in England at this time (in spite of the general veneration of Homer) with Voltaire's famous dictum 'Homère a fait Virgile, dit-on; si cela est vrai, c'est sans doute son plus bel ouvrage'. What concerns us here of course is not the relative excellence of the two poets, but the nature of what was said about Virgil. He was felt to be more dignified, more ordered; Homer, for all his sublimity and fertile invention had colloquial, 'low' passages, comic or incredible incidents, but Virgil maintained the high style with perfect propriety. Virgil's poetry was more civilized: Homer's had a primitive and barbaric grandeur. The point is illustrated by a passage[15] from Warton's introduction to Pitt's translation of the *Aeneid* (1753): 'He that peruses Homer is like the traveller that surveys Mount Atlas; the vastness and roughness of its rocks, the solemn gloominess of its pines and cedars, the everlasting snows that cover its head, the torrents that rush down its sides, all contribute to strike the imagination with inexpressible astonishment and awe. While reading the *Aeneid* is like beholding the Capitoline hill at Rome,'on which stood many edifices of exquisite architecture, and whose top was covered with the famous temple of Jupiter, adorned with the spoils of conquered Greece.'

Here is a final illustration of the twin concepts on which Virgilian appreciation was based in the English Augustan Age, namely the moral content and the excellence of artistic control; it comes from the introduction to the *Aeneid* in Ruaeus' Delphin edition of Virgil, which was very widely used in the eighteenth century. 'Mores ubique aequabiles, et ad imitationem ac delectationem aptissimi. Sententia autem et Dictio sic absoluta ac perfecta est, ut vel hoc utroque nomine princeps poetarum Virgilius habendus sit.'

Most of what has been said so far has concerned the *Aeneid*: the *Eclogues* and the *Georgics* too had a very special place in the eighteenth century sun. Dryden found the fourth and sixth *Eclogues* of 'a pitch as lofty as ever he was able to reach afterwards', and he called the *Georgics*, in a fine fit of hyperbole, 'the best poem of the best poet'; in another place he says of the *Georgics* 'which I esteem the divinest part of all his writings'. Addison regarded the *Georgics* as the 'most complete, elaborate, and finished piece of all antiquity'. He emphasized Virgil's propriety and pomp of diction in the grand style: there is nothing low and common, but a kind of rustic majesty. 'He delivers the meanest of his precepts with a kind of grandeur: he breaks the clods, tosses the dung about, with an air of gracefulness.' Pope found Virgil much superior to his master Theocritus 'in all points where judgement has the principal part'. He thought the *Eclogues* to be 'the sweetest poems in the world', and closely imitated them in his *Pastorals* and his *Messiah*, as he imitated the *Georgics* in *Windsor Forest*. The *Georgics* was the model for Thomson's *Seasons* and for countless didactic poems on rural themes; the English *Georgic* became a poetic genre in its own right.[16] It is easy to see that the qualities in these poems would commend themselves to eighteenth-century taste: in the *Eclogues* the gentle beauty of cadence, the soft whispering charm of the sound, the delicate elegance of the artificial diction, the elaborate organization and order in accordance with the traditions of the genre, the symmetry of the line and the group of lines and the total poem, the imagination controlled within the clearly defined limits of the convention. In the *Georgics* men responded easily to the underlying moral intention, the ethical precepts, the great sermon on rural and national virtues, the noble patriotic passages interspersed with the interpretation of Nature herself, the absolute control of the medium (Virgil's seven years' work on the *Georgics* averages out at a line a day), the musical brilliance of description, 'excellent images of nature', as Dryden called them. It is of course possible to point to features in these poems not commented on by the eighteenth century (they would have made little of the death-resurrection theme recently discussed by Brooks Otis,[17] or of the various aspects of recurrent imagery, significant symbolism, thematic metaphor in which twentieth-century criticism has a special skill), but very broadly one may say that the *Eclogues* and the *Georgics* must be taken on eighteenth-century terms or not at all; the *Aeneid* may be taken on their terms or quite differently.

III

The second half of the eighteenth century was a transitional

period in which the Neo-Classical position was still briskly maintained in some quarters,[18] but our present concern is with the
beginnings of the new attitude to Virgil which came into full
force with the Romantics in the early nineteenth century. The
doctrine of primitivism, first seen in a moderate form in books like
Blackwell's on Homer (1735), gained great impetus under the
influence of the enthusiasms aroused by the Ossian affair, and
appeared in full flood in writers like Blair and John Brown, fervent
exponents of the purely emotional origin of poetry.[19] Brown
(1763) said of Virgil that he had 'all the secondary qualities of an
Epic poet', but he 'wanted that all-comprehensive genius which
alone can conceive and strike out a great original Epic plan, no
less than that independent greatness of soul which was quenched
by the ruinous policy of the times'. The Scottish antiquary John
Pinkerton (*Letters of Literature*, 1785) was much more wildly out-
spoken: 'Why should I be condemned to follow Virgil thro all his
feeble imitations of Homer, in the plan and conduct of the
Aeneid? . . . Homer hath games: Virgil hath games; his very ships,
which he introduces as a novelty, prove him incapable of originality, for their accidents are from Homer's races. Homer's ships
are on fire, Virgil's are on fire. If Ulysses goes to hell, Aeneas goes
to hell. . . . Wonderful poet! Judicious imitator.' And he adds that
only the style of the *Aeneid* is at all noteworthy, 'the pickle that has
preserved his mummy from corruption'.

In the full flood of the Romantic rejection of Virgil we may take
as our theme the often quoted words of Coleridge: 'If you take
from Virgil his diction and metre, what do you leave him?'
Shelley preferred Lucan to Virgil. Byron saw no reason to go out
of his way in Italy to visit Mantua, the birthplace of that 'harmonious plagiary and miserable flatterer' whose 'cursed hexameters' had been drilled into him at Harrow. Landor called the
Aeneid 'the most mis-shapen of epics', and was never tired of
finding fault with the *Georgics*. Crabbe (*The Village*, 1783) had
expressed the incipient reaction against the *Eclogues*:

> On Mincio's bank, in Caesar's bounteous reign,
> If Tityrus found the Golden Age again,
> Must sleepy bards the flattering dream prolong,
> Mechanic echoes of the Mantuan song?
> From Truth and Nature shall we widely stray,
> Where Virgil, not where Fancy, leads the way?

And Wordsworth found a new kind of nature poetry which dispensed with Phyllis and Amaryllis.

Now clearly it would be nonsense to imagine that Virgil fell immediately and completely from favour at this time. The whole tenor of the educational system made him, along with the other Romans, a familiar part of men's background; he was far more familiarly known than he is today. It would be easy to collect evidence of continuing admiration for him, both in surviving Neo-Classical attitudes, and also in individual Romantics. Wordsworth knew him very well, and translated part of the *Aeneid*, Keats is said to have written a prose translation of the *Aeneid* in his boyhood, Shelley translated part of the tenth *Eclogue*, Landor[20] mingled praise with his blame and imitated the *Aeneid* in his *Gebir* (1798). But it is plain that Virgil's golden sun was temporarily in eclipse, and it is very easy to find reasons for this in the Romantic climate of opinion. In fact there was at this time a quite remarkable convergence of tendencies in outlooks which might in one way or another diminish the appeal of Virgil. I select some of the most important of these.

First, and very simply, he was as a Roman Augustan deeply associated with the English Augustans against whom the new literary movement was in revolt.[21] Secondly he himself had a relationship to Homer such as the English Augustans had to him; that is, he was imitative, and followed the rules of the tradition. Thirdly Virgil was didactic, avowedly so in the *Georgics* and apparently so in the *Aeneid*, and some of the lyricists were in rebellion against this kind of poetry (Keats disliked poetry with a 'palpable design' on the reader, and for Shelley didactic poetry was an 'abhorrence'). Fourthly he was felt to be a poet who supported authority, sometimes in a political sense as the court poet of Imperial Rome (Byron's 'flatterer'), and when voices were raised against authority (as by Shelley) he could hardly be pressed into service as a revolutionary poet (Lucan of course could). Fifthly and finally Virgil was pushed into the shadow by the great resurgence of admiration for Greece,[22] for the fresh vigour and freedom of Greek literature, art, and thought, for the springtime of the world, for

> The isles of Greece, the isles of Greece,
> Where burning Sappho loved and sung.

'We are all Greeks', said Shelley. 'Our laws, our literature, our religion, our arts, all have their roots in Greece'. Rome he thought should have been 'a tributary, not the conqueror of Greece'. For a whole host of reasons—the archaeological discoveries, the beauty of Greek art, the note of political and religious freedom, the philosophy of Plato, the Greek War of Independence—the Hellenic achievement exercised a fascination over men's minds which left Rome very much the lesser partner of antiquity. Here is H. W. Williams (1820) on visiting Athens: 'That city which was for ages the light of the world; where the unfettered energies of man had achieved the noblest deeds recorded in history; where genius, wisdom, and taste had reached their highest perfection.' It was with the Greeks that the Romantics found the pulsating stuff of intense poetry, the clarity of intellectual penetration which they sought; and Roman literature was felt to have been largely like the English Augustan Age—formal and artificial, prosaic, unemotional, unimaginative, without personal involvement. Nearly everything in the *Aeneid*, in Keble's view, 'seems the outcome of a duty and a task rather than the spontaneous flow and impulse of the poet's inmost heart'.

A useful way of defining the nature of the Romantic reaction against Virgil is by considering the relative recession of Horace's popularity compared with that of Catullus (for the Romantics saw the Augustan and Horatian qualities in Virgil far more than the Catullan qualities to which we are now attuned). In the world of *Kubla Khan* or *La Belle Dame Sans Merci* Horace would have been uneasy. A passage from Byron's *Hints from Horace* forcefully expresses the opposition to those very qualities for which Horace had been so admired a century earlier:

> And must the bard his glowing thoughts confine
> Lest censure hover o'er some faulty line?
> Remove whate'er a critic may suspect
> To gain the paltry suffrage of correct?
> Or prune the spirit of each daring phrase
> To fly from error, not to merit praise?

The Metaphysicals had admired and imitated Catullus, but he had not been greatly appreciated in the English Augustan Age. Pope cited him as one who could write agreeably on trifles; Addison had thought it not worth looking for the gems among the dung. For

Johnson the sparrow poem was a lucky trifle, a short-lived flower. It was with Burns that real appreciation of Catullus began again, and a comment which most significantly helps to account for his popularity is Macaulay's 'No Latin writer is so Greek'. Coleridge preferred him to Horace, and Landor said 'Horace has much, Catullus has greatly more than he'. Later, William Morris found in him real imaginative poetry, and for Swinburne he was a literary god.

What appealed to the Romantics about Catullus was the widening of the area of poetry, the liberation of sensibility and emotion from the conventional persona, the search for the unique, the personal involvement in an experience so individual that the glow and colour is still upon it, the exploration of a terrifying vision of desolation such as that of Ariadne on the shores of Dia, or of nightmare images like those of the Attis. The Romantics did not find these things in Horace or Virgil (hence Goethe's *furchtbar Realität* of Horace). They were wrong in the extent to which they denied them to Virgil (though the case of Horace is more arguable).

We can now try to summarise what the Romantics appreciated and what they did not in Virgil. They appreciated his diction and his rhythm (as who has not?); they admired his descriptive passages and sometimes the more intensely written parts of the *Aeneid* (as for instance the portrayal of Dido in Book IV). But they did not respond to the Roman values of the poem, and they were not prepared to generalize them into permanent and universal values; and in particular they were unable to appreciate the 'unheroic' heroism of Aeneas. Henry (on *Aen.* 1.381) quotes the views of Charles James Fox: 'Though the detached parts of the *Aeneid* appear to me to be equal to anything, the story and characters appear more faulty every time I read it. My chief objection (I mean that to the character of Aeneas) is of course not so much felt in the three first books; but afterwards he is always either insipid or odious; sometimes excites interest against him, and never for him.' Charles Butler[23] found him 'worse than insipid:— he disgusts by his fears, his shiverings . . . in his interview with Helen he is below contempt'. Charles Elton says that Aeneas 'alternately excites our contempt and disgust. His piety has the air of cant; of bragging ostentation and hypocrisy . . . it appears nowhere in his actions, except where it is wanted to excuse villainy'. Thomas Green comments: 'Aeneas exhibits few traits which either conciliate our affection or command our respect: and after all the efforts which have been made to interest us in his favour, we dismiss him at last from our recollection with frigid indifference.' Landor thought there was nothing so sublime and impassioned as the last hours of Dido in the *Aeneid*—'omitting, as we must, those verses which drop like icicles from the rigid lips of Aeneas'; and finally he characterises our hero as 'more fitted to invade a hencoop than to win a kingdom or a woman'.

It is not surprising that the Romantics, with their interest in the direct, the simple, the greatly sublime, should react in this way to Aeneas, and their attitude persisted strongly during the nineteenth century,[24] and is not unheard today. Leopardi said of Aeneas that he was 'the opposite of a hero', and so in a way he is. It was Virgil's intention to examine and try to present a new type of heroism which would be appropriate in an age no longer heroic; to move Homer's Achilles and Odysseus into an Augustan milieu and see how they should behave then. In the *Aeneid* we see Aeneas stepping away from the heroic world to which he belonged chronologically, and trying to adapt himself to a more complex world of public responsibilities, complex decisions, conflicting social duties. He cannot therefore cut the figure of an Achilles; his is a less dynamic and direct way of life, with problems to be solved not by the fine gesture or the courting of death, but by steadfastly continuing forward through the long maze of doubt and confusion to the dimly seen goal.

It was this massive Romantic resistance to Augustan ideals which prevented them from appreciating aspects of the *Aeneid* which one would have expected to be congenial. Surprisingly they seem not to have been very responsive (except in patches) to the pathos of the poem, certainly not to the unifying thread of sensitivity to suffering which pervades the *Aeneid* and often focuses on Aeneas himself. Even more surprisingly they do not seem to have responded to the tension of opposites (upon which Coleridge laid such stress as a vital part of poetry), the conflicts and polarities between which the poem moved. They were too concerned to see it as a traditional court panegyric and to dismiss it as tarred with an Augustan brush.

Plainly this very one-sided view could not last, and the time was ripe for a reassessment. The French Romantics had not gone as far in reaction against Virgil[25] as the English or the Germans, and it was in France through the work of Sainte-Beuve that the process of revaluing the achievement of Virgil really began to gather way. In his *Etude sur Virgile* (1857) he showed that Virgil did in fact possess the qualities which the Romantics condemned him for not having. He saw in him a person deeply and personally involved in the emotional issues which the poem explored, a poet whose Roman actors symbolized the human situation in its universal aspects, a poet especially of deep sensitivity and pity, of *humanité, pitié, sensibilité, tendresse profonde*. He gave a new meaning, a new depth to the appreciation of Virgilian pathos, which we can perhaps summarize by saying that the most familiar line of the *Aeneid* during the last century has been not *tantae molis erat Romanam condere gentem,* but *sunt lacrimae rerum et mentem mortalia tangunt.*

The appreciation of Virgil's pathos became very widespread in the second half of the century. Matthew Arnold (*On the Modern Element in Literature*) reflects it, speaking of 'a sweet, a touching sadness', 'the haunting, the irresistible self-dissatisfaction of his heart'. Sellar's book on Virgil (1876)—which has had a tremendous influence on Virgilian criticism—lays strong emphasis on it ('the poem is full of pathetic situations . . . which move our human compassion'), though it must be said that he also restated in terms more acceptable to his times the eighteenth century attitudes, the presence of Roman imperial values and of moral and ethical concepts of abiding importance. Side by side with this sensitivity to pathos came a tendency—which would have been very startling to Dryden and Pope and equally so to Coleridge and Shelley—to find almost medieval qualities of romance and strange colour in the *Aeneid*. William Morris's translation (1875) presents a Virgil of this kind, reminiscent in a way of Chaucer and of the Dido romances in the Middle Ages; and this was one of the facets which captured Tennyson.

Tennyson was pleased, we hear, when Warren called him the 'English Virgil'; so he should have been. Certainly he was receptive to some of the qualities of Virgil, remarkably so.[26] His Arthurian poetry shows Virgilian imitation in a magic world of story: he found in Virgil that 'fancy' which Dryden didn't need and Coleridge couldn't find. And he was of course very deeply sensitive to Virgil's pathos and to the beauty of the Virgilian hexameter. The often quoted phrases of his *To Virgil* (1881) show it as he shows it in the musical yearning of his best poetry:

'Thou majestic in thy sadness at the doubtful doom of human kind'.
'All the charm of all the Muses often flowering in a lonely word'.
'Wielder of the stateliest measure ever moulded by the lips of man'.

Here certainly is the closest approach to Virgil which Victorian English achieved: it saw much which Dryden missed, but it missed much which Dryden saw.

Let us look for a little longer at the Victorian terms. Myers (1879) has phrases such as 'the abiding sadness', 'the indefinable melancholy', 'this obscure homesickness, this infinite desire', and we note in particular an expression which has often and often been used since: 'that accent of brooding sorrow'. This appreciation of Virgilian *mollities,* this emphasis on the inner heart's sadness, can come very near to sentimentality. Fitzgerald tells us that he 'has been visiting dear old Virgil again; Horace never made my eyes as wet as Virgil does'. The twentieth century critic, immersed in this pool of tears, may well look longingly for a dose of the hard and robust Dryden, asking to be allowed to disinvolve himself, to be permitted a little distance. And this surely is what Virgil gives him, provided that he does not substitute for the *Aeneid* an anthology of the most intense parts of the second, fourth, sixth, and twelfth books.

Consider the strong vigour of Jupiter's speech in Book I, poetry of proud and imperial statement; consider the martial swing of Roman history in the pageant of heroes in Book VI or the description of Aeneas' shield in Book VIII. What could be more severe than the stretches of battle narrative in the tenth book, what more 'objective' than the tale of wandering in Book III? There is rhetorical and intellectual exhilaration in the exchanges between Turnus and Drances, still more so in those between Venus and Juno. There is pure descriptive virtuosity in the picture of the harbour in Book I, of Mt. Etna and of Polyphemus in Book III, of the boxing match in Book V, of the Italian towns in the catalogue of Book VII, of Hercules and Cacus in Book VIII. We are not asked to weep for Dares or Cacus.

Virgil's achievement lies in the fusion of two modes: the severe and vigorous mode of Ennius, Cicero, and Lucretius, practical, hard, full of movement and power, direct, intellectually rhetorical;

and the softer emotional mode, introspective, empathetic, which the Alexandrian Greeks and after them Catullus developed. The Roman poets might be divided on these terms into two groups—Ennius, Cicero, Lucretius, Horace in the one group, and Catullus, Propertius, Tibullus, Ovid (the last rather differently) in the other. Virgil stands between the groups. It may be argued that he has not been successful in his attempt to embrace and synthesize these two aspects of experience: many have felt that the battle scenes fail because they need the first mode and are too full of the second; others have considered that the fourth book breaks the back of the poem and denigrates the hero—they would have it either softer or harder; some have felt that the poem has too much of Rome and others that it has too much anti-Rome;[27] some have felt that Turnus is the real hero of the poem because of the emotional sympathy aroused for the man whose role in the intellectual pattern of the poem is to be the anti-hero. What is astonishing about the *Aeneid* is that it contains so many conflicting kinds of expressive modes: direct and oblique, intimate and distanced, sensitive and detached, luxuriant and severe, hyperbolical and real, emotional and intellectual. Virgil lacks the focus, the uniformity of standpoint of a Homer or a Dante; his literary method is diffused over a wider area. What Dryden saw in him is true in part; what Tennyson saw in him is true in part. Our generation can more easily appreciate Virgil's complexity because of the long and varied literary history of his influence.

Virgil's intention was to embrace the themes and modes to which his wide-ranging sensitivity responded into a total poetic world view. In some ways of course the *Aeneid* achieves unity; but perhaps it was a sense of failure in his urge to harmonize the discordant, to reconcile the opposites, that caused Virgil on his deathbed to ask Augustus to see that the *Aeneid* was burned. A lesser poem in a fixed mode could have given a rounded satisfaction on this level or that, could have fulfilled the poet's expectation of the genre, as for example the *Eclogues* and the *Georgics* do; but the inclusive method of the *Aeneid* operates on so many levels that it must remain tentative and questing. 'There is a wavering about the whole poem', T. R. Glover has said: this is because Virgil has presented the human predicament with its triumphs and its failures perplexingly juxtaposed, seeing man as potentially divine but actually confined in the prisons of his own limitations, 'a Being darkly wise and rudely great'. Virgil had no single fixed pattern of moral and spiritual ideas to which he was ready to conform, no single literary mode as a model for what he wanted to do; as he wrote the *Aeneid* he was trying to create both, and this is why it is such an exciting poem.

NOTES

[1] Some general works are: G. Highet, *The Classical Tradition,* 1949; J. A. K. Thomson, *Classical Influences on English Poetry,* 1951; D. Bush, *Mythology and the Romantic Tradition in English Poetry,* 1957; D. M. Foerster, *The Fortunes of Epic Poetry,* 1962; E. Nitchie, *Vergil and the English Poets,* 1919. For detailed bibliography see H. Brown, *The Classical Tradition in English Literature: A Bibliography, Harv. Stud. Phil.,* 18, 1935.

[2] On Virgil in medieval times see D. Comparetti, *Vergil in the Middle Ages,* trans. E. F. M. Benecke, 1895; J. E. Sandys, *A History of Classical Scholarship,* 1903–8; J. W. Spargo, *Virgil the Necromancer,* 1934; R. R. Bolgar, *The Classical Heritage and its Beneficiaries,* 1954.

[3] See R. M. Ogilvie, *Latin and Greek,* 1964, pp. 10 f. (Ovid), and pp. 44 f. (Horace).

[4] Seneca *Controv.* 4.28.17, Quintilian 10.1.98; cf. also Quint. 10.1.88 *nimium amator ingenii sui,* and his use (10.1.88, 93) of the epithet *lascivus* of Ovid.

[5] Dryden had more sympathy for the baroque and was less passionately in love with the 'rules' than many of his successors; nevertheless he cites Seneca's criticism of Ovid with approval in his *Essay of Dramatic Poesy,* and prefers Virgil for his restraint: 'thus Ovid's fancy was not limited by verse, and Virgil needed not verse to have bounded his'. For a detailed list of Virgilian echoes in Dryden see F. Olivero, *Poetry Review,* 1930, pp. 171 f.

[6] cf. Pope on Pegasus (*Essay on Criticism* 86–7): The winged courser, like a generous horse, Shows most true mettle when you check his course.

[7] See L. Proudfoot, *Dryden's Aeneid and its seventeenth century predecessors,* 1960, and R. Fitzgerald, *Arion,* Vol. 2, No. 3, 1963, pp. 17 f.

[8] See M. van Doren, *The Poetry of John Dryden,* 1931, pp. 67 ff., and Douglas Knight, *Pope and the Heroic Tradition,* 1951, pp. 17 ff. Pope had a heading in the index to his *Iliad*: 'Expressing in the sound the thing described'.

[9] In this phrase Johnson had in mind the elimination of metaphysical conceits (see his life of Cowley), and the avoidance of 'low' terms. On both these counts Virgil would give satisfaction.

[10] See Louis I. Bredvold, *The Intellectual Milieu of John Dryden,* 1934, especially pp. 130 ff.

[11] See M. van Doren, *The Poetry of John Dryden,* pp. 10 ff. for the influence on Dryden of 'the tradition of Roman virtue, male virtue, which he found recited so admirably in the ancient histories . . . His dedications are replete with Roman examples'.

[12] Dryden's remarks on Homer's heroes (*Dedic. Third Miscellany*) are such as to indicate his preference for Aeneas: 'He forms and equips those ungodly man-killers whom we poets, when we flatter them, call heroes: a race of men who can never enjoy quiet in themselves until they have taken it from all the world. This is Homer's commendation; and, such as it is, the lovers of peace, or at least of more moderate heroism, will never envy him'. R. J. Kaufmann (Intro. to *All for Love,* 1962) sees Dryden presenting in his drama a critique of the 'unassimilable Achilles' type of hero.

R. D. WILLIAMS

[13] See D. M. Foerster, *Homer in English Criticism,* 1947, with bibliography.

[14] See S. Shephard, *Emerita,* 1961, pp. 313 ff.

[15] I owe the quotation to E. Laughton, *Virgilian Mediaevalism,* Virgil Society Lecture Summaries, No. 37.

[16] See E. Nitchie, *Vergil and the English Poets,* chapter VIII, W. P. Mustard, *A.J.Ph.,* 1908, pp. 1 ff., M. L. Lilly, *The Georgic,* 1917, D. R. Dudley, *Proc. Virgil Soc.* No. 4, 1964–5, pp. 41 ff.

[17] Brooks Otis, *Virgil: A Study in Civilised Poetry,* 1963, chapter V.

[18] See for example Thomas Warton's *History of English Poetry,* 1774–81, discussed by R. Wellek, *The Rise of English Literary History,* pp. 166 ff.: 'A recognition of classical standards and a (tempered) appreciation of Gothic picturesqueness and sublimity went hand in hand' (p. 187).

[19] See D. M. Foerster, *The Fortunes of Epic Poetry,* pp. 15ff. I owe the two following quotations to him.

[20] See E. Nitchie, *Vergil and the English Poets,* pp. 200 ff.

[21] See U. Amarasinghe, *Dryden and Pope in the early nineteenth century,* 1962.

[22] See R. M. Ogilvie, *Latin and Greek,* pp. 78 ff. (I owe to him the quotation from H. W. Williams), T. Spencer, *Fair Greece, Sad Relic,* 1954, E. M. Butler, *The Tyranny of Greece over Germany,* 1935, F. E. Pierce, *The Hellenic Current in English Nineteenth Century Poetry, J. Eng. Germ. Phil.,* 1917, pp. 103 ff.

[23] See D. M. Foerster, *The Fortunes of Epic Poetry,* p. 77; I owe several of the following quotations to him.

[24] Cf. for example James Henry 'the heartless and cold-blooded seduction and desertion of Dido by the hero of the *Aeneid*'; T. E. Page, 'Virgil is unhappy in his hero. Compared with Achilles, his Aeneas is but the shadow of a man'. For arguments against these attitudes in recent times see D. R. Dudley, *Greece and Rome,* 1961, pp. 52 ff., Brooks Otis' *Virgil,* chapters VI and VII, W. Clausen, *Harv. Stud. Class. Phil.,* 1964, pp. 139 ff., and Intro. section IV of my edition of *Aeneid* V.

[25] Hugo had been very enthusiastic over Virgil for a long time before he began to reject him, and Chateaubriand was a fervent admirer.

[26] Cf. W. P. Mustard, *Classical Echoes in Tennyson,* 1904, and D. Bush, *Mythology and the Romantic Tradition in English Poetry,* 1957, pp. 225 ff.

[27] The remarkable article by F. Sforza in *C.R.,* 1935, pp. 97 ff. presents an extreme anti-Roman view.

VI

Virgilian Landscape into Art: Poussin, Claude and Turner

A. G. McKAY

VIRGIL is the acknowledged expert among those landscape painters who have used words instead of pigments. Master of landscape and figures alike, his broad canvas emerges as an organic and harmonious entity. A recent study of Virgil's feeling for landscape and its description has detected more than five hundred references in the *Eclogues, Georgics* and *Aeneid*.[1] Several main groups emerge, those in which the poet's approach is subjective or objective, and those where geographical, historical, and literary associations are evoked. Pastoral or landscape poetry hardly yields to analysis, for the language, charged with ambiguities, may surrender to modern readers only a fragment of the total scene, the impression, or the emotional connotations. But one over-all aspect can surely be charged to Virgil: a peculiarly Roman feeling for *amoenitas,* a sense of the manifold aspects of *otium,* of peace and tranquillity, of mystery and barbaric strengths.

There is little of the English landscape, in feeling or aspect, in Virgil's pastoral settings. The skies of Italy are lacking in the delicate, pastel colourings, the 'season of mists and mellow fruitfulness', the mobile clouds and sudden shifts of temperament in the skies, or the extremes of season. Virgil's environment throughout most of his life was Northern Italy, the territory of Mantua and Cisalpine Gaul, the Roman Campagna, and finally Campania Felix and the Mezzogiorno. Sicily exists, but only in reverie, perhaps as recollections from a circumnavigation of the island, more like views from the deck than actual study or absorption of the terrain.

But throughout the landscape scenery there is a constant clarity of light, the measured beat and immeasurable aspect of the Mediterranean, the evergreen foliage of olive, cypress, and ilex, and the lingering bloom of the oleanders which still enliven the recovered gardens of Pompeii and Herculaneum and spring spontaneously and untrained along the Italian roads.

Pausilypon, the hill of Sans Souci, at Naples, where Virgil ultimately settled to study with Siro the Epicurean and to compose his major *opera*, stands today with its alleged tomb of Virgil as a kind of tumulus memorial to the adopted son of Neapolis. Many have commented on the visual and auditory observations contained in Virgil's seascapes: various, and always precise, they are obviously a personal record of affection. Like Tennyson who loved to watch the sea in storm or calm from the tall cliffs, from the curving shingle bank of Freshwater Bay or from Brook Sands, Virgil must have stood awed by the sights and sounds of the sea timelessly eroding the lava flows, the reefs and cliffs along the Campanian shoreline, working ceaselessly over the sandy shoreline between Palinuro and Anzio.

The sea birds, the migratory birds, dolphins and the like are part of the Mediterranean scene, but so often their entry into the Virgilian text is given a sympathetic turn, from his concern for the smaller, more helpless creatures of nature.[2]

Pastoral, as such, emerges poetically only with the Hellenistic age.[3] Part of a larger context of creativity in a sophisticated time, an age well aware of its isolation from the simpler, more innocent ways of life, it assigns to the poet an incredible role—to pretend that the isolation or separation does not actually exist. And so the pastoral poet in the Hellenistic vein launches a poet-shepherd as spokesman for the poet and his audience, one who may speak for the Golden Age and assume a mask of innocence in a morally bankrupt or depraved era. The setting belies the metropolitan reality where the audience is found. Pastoral poetry by nature is artificial, and we relish the artificiality even today. The genre becomes a metaphor of lost innocence; the work is fiction but the setting is usually close to reality.

Virgil was certainly imbued with a deep, lasting love for the Italian countryside. Wordsworth has often been compared with Virgil—but Wordsworth's descriptions of natural scenery are usually more intense when he speaks of his native Cumberland. Virgil's landscape is a creation—not of observation and record exclusively, but of inspiration. In fact there is in the *Eclogues* very little methodical observation of the countryside; stockbreeding, the normal activity of cowboys, is notable by its absence. Virgil brought into being an Arcadia unlike any hitherto; and thereafter, in his *Georgics,* moved back to the reality with which he had started and treated it in an entirely different spirit.[4] Cochrane and others have sensed the spirit and method of Virgil even in his non-political works: 'The *Georgics* have been described as an epic of mother earth; they are not so much that as of 'wheat and wood-land, tilth and vineyard, hive and horse and herd'; that is to say, a monument to the human effort which transforms the face of the earth and imparts to it, as has been said, something of the warmth and life of an Italian landscape'.[5] This awareness of the impress and the importance of man in the Italian landscape is basic to a realization of 'Virgilian' emphasis in the world of painting. *Saturnia tellus* for Virgil suggests no ideal sentimental rapture but a call to work for the realization of moral values, and an awareness of Italy's finest product, the men she breeds. R. G. Austin has expressed the meaning of the Georgics with skill. In his view the poem 'is a reminder of the Italy that had almost been forgotten, of gods who could still be trusted, or a beauty that could not die; and it is a prophetic vision of peace, begun long before Actium'.[6] Austin has also observed the pictorial grace and skill of the poet: 'The *Georgics* were written about home, and are full of pictures of ordinary men and women in the field and lanes and farms of Italy; it was out of the strength of Italy that Rome became the noblest city in the world. Virgil's method was to construct a great series of word-paintings based on a single unified theme, and arranged with consummate skill in contrast; his domestic pictures are the more significant for their juxtaposition with some foreign scene; and technical descriptions are offset by the contemplation of pure loveliness.'[7] In the *Georgics* Virgil drew forever the beauty of his earthly paradise.

The Odyssey frieze, discovered by chance in 1848 on the Esqui-line and now in the Vatican Library, remains unique in the repertoire of ancient landscape art as the oldest realistic represen-tation of landscape known to us, and besides, the largest and most splendid extant.[8] The fresco offers an uninterrupted panoramic landscape wherein consecutive scenes of the Odyssey are depicted, vista after vista of the 'wanderings of Ulysses over the countryside' as Vitruvius characterized this evidently popular genre in the Augustan Age.[9] Seascape and landscape combine; pastoral scenes, with sheep and cattle along with peaceful shepherd and goatherd, are juxtaposed with the Laestrygonians, gigantic and cannibalistic, at war against the ships and men of Odysseus. Deep inlets, jagged headlands, and arched rocks, reminiscent of Italy's Campanian shores and of Canada's Percé peninsula, provide the momentous settings for the heroic action. Strange architectural forms and remote walled towns frame the scenes and provide additional perspectives. The eighth section, depicting Ulysses' arrival in the Underworld in the misty land of the shadowy Cimmerians, is accorded one of the most memorable settings of all, behind or between towering mountains, with only one access through a vaulted opening in the rocks. The souls stand in an eerie light, thin and unsubstantial. As with Claude and Poussin later, if one were to remove the landscape there would remain an unintelligible congeries of small figures; but with the figures removed there would remain, as eloquent as ever, a vista of bays, rocks, cliffs, trees, etc. Von Blanckenhagen, a recent commentator on the frieze, says rightly that 'the painter has followed the text, but it is not the events, dramatic though they are, which are his main theme; his theme is the setting and the landscape'.[10]

One is constantly reminded of the Odyssey Landscapes in a review of seventeenth century Virgilian landscapes. Both are filled with memories of the classic past, bathed in what approximates a prismatic light, and redolent of the sometimes theatrical, sometimes hypnotic qualities of Southern Italy. There is also the repeated sense that landscape may contribute to an understanding of the scene, the understanding of the hero's destiny.[11]

Nicolas Poussin was to painting what his seventeenth century contemporary, Descartes, was to philosophy: a believer in reason above all. He handled his canvas with an architect's skill and organized his scenes with logic and cool idealism, with a discipline which was almost Phidian, with an organization as calculated as a black- or red-figure vase of the best period. 'My nature forces me to search for well-ordered things,' said Poussin, and he discovered his order in Greco-Roman antiquity. Born in Normandy in 1594, Nicolas Poussin became the master painter of the seventeenth century. He reached Italy, the goal of every enthusiast for the classical past, and proceeded to copy antique remains, to study them and absorb them into his nature. He filled his canvases with superbly modelled figures, reminiscent of classical marbles. The fleshy maenads of his early Bacchanals recall Hellenistic marbles but are alive with the glow of life and the subtlest of flesh tones. His paintings were not an instant success. His austerity and overt solemnity won him few admirers and the French collectors who acquired his paintings were, in his own phrase, 'hérétiques', individuals who set themselves apart from, or perhaps above, the contemporary vogues. Cardinal Mazarin, a celebrated collector, showed little interest in Poussin's output, whereas English collectors, by then thoroughly attuned to classicism, were engaged in a feverish search for his works. The assessment of Poussin, initiated in the nineteenth century, as philosopher and scholar rather than painter, has only lately been revised. The brilliant researches of Sir Anthony Blunt, the publications of Friedländer and others, have produced a more intelligible though, at the same time, a more complicated figure.[12]

The formation of the Classical Landscape painter was a gradual evolution, charged with variety and experiment throughout. The earlier assessment of Poussin as scholar-artist had some basis, for Poussin never shirked study to acquire knowledge. His reading was undoubtedly drawn from a wide range of material. Most notable perhaps for the ultimate design and nature of his landscape paintings was his reading of Philostratus, the Greek sophist, and Duchoul's treatise on ancient Roman religion. Duchoul's plates and those of Blaise de Vigenère's *Images ou Tableaux de platte peinture* by Philostratus, claimed his earnest attention. With Cassiano dal Pozzo, whose palace in Via Chiavari became the intellectual and cultural centre of Rome during the seventeenth century, Poussin and his contemporaries who enjoyed the same patronage found ancient meaning in the present context of Roman monuments and art works. His curiosity and industry were insatiable and tireless. 'He never tired of adding an archaeological detail to a picture, or of driving home some point, of elaborating some allegory. His mythology was the rather over-refined mythology of sixteenth-century humanists, rather than that of the seventeenth century which was simpler.'[13] Marino described the youthful Poussin on his arrival in Rome as 'giovane che ha una furia di diavolo'. And there is evidence of an almost frenetic zeal to put paintings on canvas, and a host of drawings, from this

earliest period (1624–39). We have the superb Windsor drawings
of Ovid's *Metamorphoses* executed for the poet Marino, and
possibly the marvellous *Dido and Aeneas* in the Toledo Museum of
Art. The latter, inspired as much by Ovid as Virgil, and alive with
Hellenistic sentiment and romantic heroism, emerges nonetheless
as something fresh and real almost despite the logical detail and
overall construction, memorable for the way in which the sun
glances off Aeneas' bronze armour, and for the sensitive contrast
of lacy foliage and smooth flesh.[14]

Evident in his earliest paintings was the continuing affection for
Italian landscape, in particular, the Roman Campagna, which he
explored constantly and sketched and painted from nature. Nature
and the antique, rather than the literature, shaped Poussin's vision.
His splendid *Bacchanals,* in the Louvre and in London's National
Gallery, lacking in the later gravity of his style, the Louvre's *Rape
of the Sabines* and the *Finding of Moses* (1638), are all indicative of his
love and formal affection for the Italian pastoral. *The Finding of
Moses,* with its overall classic design and mood, provides a superb
twilight Roman landscape, a view of the Tiber banks close to the
Ponte Molle (the Mulvian Bridge) where Poussin liked to walk and
sketch.

After a disastrous interval in Paris (1640–42), a ghastly error on
the part of the Monarch and his advisers who had designs on
establishing Poussin as a kind of Commissar of the Arts, Poussin
returned to his final period in Rome, and from 1648 until the time
of his death in 1665 devoted himself to panoramic landscape with
small figures. The finest products of his brush come from this
culminating period of his life: the *Funeral of Phocion,* in the collection of the Earl of Plymouth, the *Ashes of Phocion,* in the collection
of the Earl of Derby, the Dulwich *Landscape with the Roman Road,*
the Hermitage Landscape with *Polyphemus,* the Louvre *Orpheus and
Eurydice,* and the *Hercules and Cacus* in the Pushkin Museum, Mos-
cow. The exuberance and excess of the Italian baroque artists who
worked around him failed to impress Poussin who quite literally
stripped his paintings down to cool, hard, brightly coloured
figures, set like stage creatures in the exposition of his ancient
story and setting.

His landscapes in this final period are the last stage in the
rational treatment. Poussin's heroic landscapes, are, as Sir Anthony
Blunt has repeatedly demonstrated, constructed around a Stoical

theme according to a series of calculations, where solid objects recede in well calculated stages, where the classical monuments have a simple, cubistic solidity, justifiable on archaeological grounds, timeless and as manifestly correct as the contemporary knowledge would permit the artist to depict them.[15] Pierre du Colombier has remarked that 'one might describe them as philosophical landscapes. For the most part they are composed in the same manner, in breadth, framed in by two unequal masses of trees (what were known at the time as 'l'arbre fort' and 'l'arbre faible'); in the middle ground, architecture, and in front small figures which provide the subject of the picture.'[16] Behind the often stagelike scenes there lurks an earnest moralistic message: a Stoic contempt for the vanities of the world and its riches. The Hermitage *Polyphemus* has an overpowering design and effect: the Cyclopean figure stands atop the central rock, dominating the canvas, and a lovely seascape emerges through an opening on the right. 'Poussin sometimes seems to consider his figures as mere accessories, and nature herself drives home the lesson of stability, of grandeur, of fertility.'

Wherein lies the Virgilian quality of Poussin's landscapes? The spell and pull of the Roman landscape, particularly the Campagna, is obvious. The intellectual content and inspiration are less so. Certain factors are clear and influential in his artistic formation: his longtime residence in Rome, his sketches of ancient ruins, his reading of Ovid and Philostratus, his observation of nature. Cézanne once claimed that all he wished to do as artist was 'revive Poussin in the contact with nature'. Even Picasso, who approached Poussin as an exercise in technique, found solace as well in copying one of the master's works as gunfire sounded through the streets of Paris in 1944. Jean Seznec has observed with characteristic wisdom and insight that 'with Poussin, meditating in Rome in the silence of the ruins, the gods are surrounded by a different atmosphere, strangely dreamlike and grave. We feel that for this artist the world of Fable represents the Golden Age, gone never to return; everything breathes regret for that lost world and for its serene delights'.[17] This view of the classical past as a lost ideal was perhaps heightened by Poussin's study of the monuments, the decayed memorials of the past in Rome itself and in the Campagna, a grandeur in ruins but an essential ingredient of Classical Nature. Man and the works of his hand and intellect were for Poussin a single entity, an expression and at the same time an extension of Nature. Man could never play a secondary role in Poussin's conception of Nature, could never be subtracted and leave an intelligible or intact landscape or setting. Man and the Landscape are never mutually exclusive or separable; they constitute a unity in his vision, mutually important and meaningful. Unlike Annibale Caracci or Claude, his contemporary, Poussin's classical landscape cannot exist without its figures. Poussin's conception might almost be labelled Greek. Man's rôle and place in Nature is never secondary or subordinate—fleeting shapes of nymphs and shepherds, fauns and satyrs. The myths of Ovid and of Virgil, seen directly or otherwise, were for Poussin a factual statement of man's inextricable relationship with Nature—there was a spiritual reality about the involvement of Narcissus or Echo or others with their natural setting, a timelessness and truthfulness. There is neither *ruinenlust* nor wishful thinking in Poussin's art, no pathetic longing for time past, for the Golden Age. Rome and the Campagna nourished Poussin's vision of the past; the antiquities and the literature were the mainspring of his inspiration and his vision. The Arcadian theme, best exemplified in Virgil's Messianic *Eclogue IV* and *Aeneid VIII*, penetrates such masterpieces as *Et in Arcadia Ego* (1638-40),[18] the *Phocion* Landscapes, and the *Greek and the Roman Road*. The *Wedding of Orpheus and Eurydice,* as Greek as any theme might be, takes place in the context of a Roman prospect, with the Castel Sant' Angelo dominating the whole. *The Roman Road* (Plate I) defies precise topographical identification; but there is an evident concern with topography and archaeology in the composition which awakens specific interest and concern in the viewer.[19] The setting is marked by a bridge, a cistern, a series of tombs a milestone, and a large column surmounted by an urn in the distance. The highways of Roman Italy were numerous and impressive even in their neglect. Specific details, as enumerated, are common to many, but particularly to the great highways, the Via Aurelia, the Via Appia, or the Via Domitiana. The last, enthusiastically described in its construction by the Silver Age poet Statius, has a peculiar affinity with Poussin's painting.[20] Both poet and painter seem to sing the glories of Fertile Campania, *Campania Felix,* the pastoral setting par excellence, and the inspiration to Virgil's poetic counterpart.[21] Peaceful, productive and ancient, Romans fled there to find surcease from the trials of business and government in Rome, to discover *otium* with or without *dignitas* on the shores of Cumae and Baiae, of Puteoli and Neapolis . . . Rome's Tempe, memorialized by Poussin in his *Greek Road*, lay in Campania, where the Muses and the affluent nabobs and wealthier middle class found equal repose and inspiration and Poussin's painting reflects the lonely charm and quiet of the landscape of *Aeneid* VI. Campania provided Virgil and Poussin with Italy's ideal landscape, immoderately beautiful, seductive, and languorous. Poussin's inspiration, in common with Virgil and Horace, lay in the Roman countryside rather than the texts of poets and chroniclers. His vision of the Roman Campagna as the model of Nature exercised what amounted almost to a tyranny over the Landscape artists who followed in his train—until Cézanne and Van Gogh entered upon different terrain.[22]

Memories of the classic past were as vigorous in the canvases of Claude Lorrain as in those of Poussin, but differently. Sir Anthony Blunt has awarded Claude the accolade of having done for Roman and French painting what, in an earlier time, Altdorfer had done for Germany, and Patinir and Brueghel for Flanders; that is, to establish landscape painting as a means of artistic expression as subtle and varied as the older genres of religious and historical painting.[23] Claude's visit to Naples, *c.* 1623, left an ineradicable impression on his mind. The bay of Naples, the glorious coastline from Sorrento to Pozzuoli, and the languorous appeal of Ischia and Capri are frequently mirrored in his classical landscapes, as evocative for him as they were once for Roman artists and writers.

But for Claude, particularly in his later years, the Virgilian associations were uppermost in his recreations of the past; the pastoral life of Virgil's *Eclogues* and *Georgics,* and the noble simplicity of Evander's Pallanteum and the forested glades of Nemi and Avernus, of Tivoli and the Tiber side, are uppermost in his mind and the focus of his creative imagination. Ruins and more stable architectural forms are equally a part of his repertoire with Poussin. But there is a wistfulness about the fragmentary buildings, a less precise, less 'scientific' archaeology about his monuments than in Poussin. Wide open porticoes, shot through with sunlight and veiled with ivy, and picturesque ruins are his recourse, and towers which lose their stark outlines in mist. Light and atmosphere are the hallmarks of his landscapes: idyllic and atmospheric, less heroic, less motivated by moral themes than

Poussin's, perhaps more genuinely bucolic. Though replete with memories of Rome's antiquity, and populated with sylvan gods and nymphs, divinities of the lesser rank and so more congenial, there is practically nothing of Poussin's rational arrangement or didactic point, only an evident longing for the greatness of the lingering, wasting past, a heightened sense of melancholy, an embodiment of Virgil's indefinable but experienced *lacrimae rerum*. There is a mute, poetic beauty to his landscapes, a nostalgia which is quite overpowering, felt within animate and inanimate nature.

The sources or mainsprings of his inspiration are largely different from those of Poussin. Though both artists were flushed with enthusiasm for the Roman countryside and its associations, their literary and intellectual impetus seems to have differed somewhat. Poussin's indebtedness to enlightened patronage and intellectual milieu, to Ovid, Philostratus, and the conversation of the intelligentsia and scholars, is certain. Claude probably found his major inspiration in his own sense of wonder in the Roman setting.[24] Virgil was known to him, likely in an Italian pocket-book translation. He may also have found direction and inspiration in the Vatican Virgil with its miniatures, some of them pastoral in subject matter,[25] and in the earlier efforts of artists, perhaps even in the wall paintings rescued by a haphazard archaeology before and during his residence in Italy. It has been argued recently that Claude's indebtedness to Virgil was profound, that his paintings are saturated with the Virgilian spirit but not recklessly or deliriously.[26] His Virgilian landscapes may lack the logic and the academic heroic quality of Poussin, but there is a comparable care in the composition of his landscapes which bear on a specific literary theme in Virgil. There is an almost embarrassing array of paintings which deal specifically with Virgilian themes and settings. One of the more attractive drawings, *Aeneas and the Sibyl*, (L. V. 183) (1673), now in the British Museum, is simply but sensitively done in pen and brown ink wash, heightened with white, and on blue paper (Plate II). There is a marvellous sense of immediate solitude, a communion between the hero and the prophetess on a gently undulating ground, framed with aged but delicate trees, with a circular temple, recalling the example at Tivoli or in the Forum Boarium at Rome, both falsely ascribed to the Sibyl but sufficiently evocative for Claude's purposes. There are suggestions of the splendid Aragon Castle at Baiae in the middle distance and Capri beyond. Lake Avernus, part of the domain of Deiphobe, priestess of Apollo and Diana, appears on the left and provides access to the Netherworld. The serenity of the landscape and the sense of remoteness of space and time which the artist communicates in this drawing are prophetic of the greater canvases to come. There is nothing cluttered or confused about the setting of 'a poetic solitude conceived in the imagination and made visible in terms of light'. The last decade of Claude's career produced paintings dealing with the adventures of Aeneas, and in almost every instance, save one, they are closely patterned after the Virgilian text. Röthlisberger has called them 'Claude's most personal iconographic and artistic achievement', and it is hard to imagine a finer reproduction of the scenes. Though heavily indebted earlier to Ovid, to Apuleius and Tasso, Claude evidently found in Virgil's *Aeneid* the best spur to his greatest period after 1669. There are six pictures of this period in the artist's life which require notice; his fidelity to the *Aeneid* text is deliberate and remarkable in almost every instance.

I have already examined the drawing of *Aeneas and the Sibyl.* The setting, which is cumulative, is an idealized poetic version of the actual topography, and also a brilliant enlargement of the impressive configurations and ageless nature of the Chalcidic citadel and the associations. Archaeologically there was nothing to be seen in Claude's time, for the significant finds on the Cumaean acropolis date to the twentieth century.[27] But the Virgilian text, explicit on such matters as temples, excavated tunnels, and the grotto itself, the topography of lakes (Avernus and Lucrinus, and Acheron's sluggish overflow), and the massive promontory of Misenum where Aeneas' comrade was to be interred and memorialized, the Cumaean shoreline and the Tyrrhenian Sea, are all included in the descriptive passages which herald the hero's descent into the Underworld.

Coast View of Delos with Aeneas, pride of London's National Gallery, centres on Anius' welcome to his Trojan visitors, Aeneas, Anchises and Ascanius.[28] The early morning light accents the new friendship between the aged Anius and his agemate, Anchises. The most prominent colours are assigned to the three main figures: Anius in light violet, Anchises in blue, and Aeneas in red, but the canvas seems to be a conflation of the accounts in Ovid and Virgil and, by its association with the other five scenes, seems markedly

Virgilian in mood and emphasis. Trees and architecture combine
to frame and enlarge the scene. The round temple, Apolline by
association with the text, derives from the Pantheon in Rome. The
priest's house is decorated with a relief depicting Tityus' attack on
Latona and the vengeance exacted by Apollo and Diana. The two
trees, not mentioned in Virgil's account of the landing, are those
which provided Latona support during her birth throes with
Apollo and Diana. The Trojan ships lie at anchor in the misty blue
sea beyond.

Coast of Libya with Aeneas Hunting, now in Brussels' Musée des
Beaux-Arts, is closely modelled on the Virgilian scene:

> 'There is a haven there, at the end of a long sound, quite land-
> locked by an island in the shape of two breakwaters, which parts
> the waves entering from the open sea and draws them off into long
> channels. On each shore a frightening headland of rock towers
> massively into the sky; and the wide expanse of water which they
> overshadow is noiseless and secure. Beyond the water a curtain of
> trees with quivering leaves reaches downwards, and behind them
> is an overhanging forest-clad mountain side, mysterious and dark.
> There is a cave directly in front at the foot of the cliffs.'[29]

Accompanied by the faithful Achates, and in search of food for his
crews, Aeneas succeeded in felling stags 'with tall antlers like tree
branches', and from the ensuing stampede 'among the green
forest trees' Aeneas was able to bring down seven creatures
enough to feed his seven ships' crews. Claude is almost scrupulous
in his fidelity to the text. There is a fine suggestion of the urgency
of the mission in the agitation and minatory natural setting. The
rock formation at the left and the scene in general seem remarkably similar to the Amalfitan coast or the rocky shoreline of Capri
and the Sorrentine peninsula. The rising sun and the yellowish
white sky are markedly in contrast with the darker hues of the sea
and shoreline. Aeneas wears an orange outfit. The harbour holds
seven ships and four small boats with moving figures. The painting
forms a pair with the drawing of *Aeneas and the Sibyl.*

Virgil's account of Aeneas' landing in Latium is a voyage
through wonderland:

> Greased pine-timbers slid by over shallow water. The very waves
> wondered, and the woods, strangers to such a sight, were surprised
> to see floating in the river the brightly-painted ships with the

warriors' far-gleaming shields. The Trojans rowed tirelessly till a
night and a day were spent. They passed round long bends, and
shaded by trees of many kinds they cut between green forest on
the friendly river-surface. The fiery sun had climbed to the mid-
point of the sky's circle when ahead of them they saw walls, a
citadel, and scattered roof tops; all this Roman might has now
exalted to Heaven, but at that time Evander lived there in poverty.
Quickly they turned their prows shorewards, and drew near to the
city.

It happened on that very day the Arcadian king was paying anniversary honours to Amphitryon's mighty son Hercules and the
other gods in a wood before his city. Together with him his son
Pallas, the leading young Arcadians, and his Senate, all men of
little wealth, were offering incense to the Deities and warm blood
was steaming on the altar. When they first noticed the ships and
saw them gliding between the shady woods with crews silently
bending to the oars, they were alarmed at the sudden sight; and as
one man they arose, leaving their banquet. But Pallas in an
adventurous mood bade them not to interrupt the rite, and then
seizing a weapon dashed off alone to meet the strangers. . . . The
chieftain Aeneas then answered from high on his ship's stern,
stretching out in his hand before him an olive-spray in token of
peace.[30]

Virgil's account retails the arrival of Aeneas at Pallanteum, the
capital of Arcadian Evander's realm, and the ancestor-city to
Rome. Claude in his *Landscape with the Landing of Aeneas in Latium*
(Plate III) pays careful attention to Virgil's description, with only
modest deviations in Aeneas' position at the bow and in the
retinue around Pallas, probably for the sake of structural balance
in the painting.[31] The preparatory drawing for the later canvas has
survived with Claude's notation indicating the true identification
of the topographical features. The Aventine Hill, which Claude
designates incorrectly as Evander's city, may have resulted, as
Kitson has argued,[32] from a false connection between the names
Evander and Aventine. On the far side of the Tiber, Claude has
located the antique Castelli Romani, of Janiculum and Saturnia,
ruins which Evander showed to Aeneas during their city excursion
later the same day. Claude has conflated the topography of the
Hercules-Cacus episode and the guided tour into the scene of
Aeneas' reception by Pallas. Kitson notes wisely that 'it is the
topography as given in the poem which interests Claude, not that

of the actual place. Nor is he attempting an archaeological reconstruction of the scene as it might have looked at the time. His
approach is poetic, not historical; his source is Virgil's text, not
the discoveries of antiquarians or the writings of ancient (or, for
that matter, modern) historians'. Unlike Poussin, who aimed at a
precise and hopefully accurate reconstruction of his settings,
Claude was less research-minded, and more inclined to forfeit
accuracy and even literary detail to gain a wider, poetic perspective
on the incident and its setting. The inclusion of the sea and the
meandering course of the Tiber in the scene is a retrospective
glance to the landing at Lavinium and the start of the voyage at
Ostia. This idea of continuity, before and after the event, and the
imaginative responses gained thereby, is less Virgilian than
sixteenth century in its origin. The hints of grandeur and prophetic
magnificence in the painting, the intimations of heroic achievement to come and magnanimity and understanding on the part of
the actors, the scale of the setting and the essential but diminished
scale of the figures, heighten the mood and the appeal of the
painting. Here, perhaps more than anywhere else, Claude finds
perfect communion with his literary 'model', reacting with keen
understanding and sympathy to the Virgilian scene. In Aeneas'
visit to the future site of Rome, Virgil lays considerable emphasis
on the contrast between then and now (VIII. 98–100), with
patriotic delight in the long and glorious history of his nation's
capital and her monuments. There is the same delightful freshness
in the 'account' of poet and painter. But Claude seems to hint at
another scene which enriched Dante as well as Blake and others.
Rivers and their crossings are strangely associated with great
events and changes in a hero's career in life and in death. The final
crossing, which Aeneas will perform twice, is of course the Styx
where Charon's craft awaits the dead. So here, in a curious kind of
flashback to Virgil's Sixth *Aeneid* and Dante's *Purgatorio* (2, 100 ff.)
where the Tiber mouth is the reunion place for souls destined for
Purgatory, Claude's luminous canvas evokes a strange melancholy
and foreshadowing. Pallas, who greets Aeneas so gallantly and
courageously as his aged father's legate, will one day die and bring
Aeneas and the chivalrous father to intense sorrow. The problem
of pain, omnipresent in the *Georgics*, becomes almost an obsession
in the *Aeneid* and the happiest scenes are soon suffused with the
grey tones of melancholy. Accordingly, in the silvery bluish-green

tints of morning, Claude locates his heroic company: Aeneas clad
in red and yellow, Pallas in yellow. To the delight of his patron, the
Altieri arms are emblazoned on the flag of the second vessel.[33]
*The View of Carthage, with Dido, Aeneas and their Suite leaving for the
Hunt* survives in several drawings, and a painting in the possession
of Col. A. Heywood-Lonsdale at Shavington Hall.[34] The Virgilian passage is once more handsomely illustrated by the artist:

> At last she came, stepping forth with a numerous suite around her
> and clad in a Sidonian mantle with an embroidered hem. Golden
> was her quiver and the clasp which knotted her hair, and golden
> was the brooch which fastened the purple tunic at her neck. Up
> came the Trojan party, too, including the delighted Iulus. As the
> two processions met, Aeneas, by far the most handsome of them
> all, passed across to Dido's side. He was like Apollo . . .[35]

Claude has emphasized the port facilities of Carthage rather than
the woodland setting which Virgil supplies. Aeneas, clad in red
and yellow again, with his son Iulus and Achates (?) as paeda-
gogue, stands rapt while Dido, gesturing towards the sea or the
Temple of Juno (?) in Pantheon guise, attracts the viewer's gaze.
The flagship bears the Arms of the Colonna family to whom
Claude dedicated the drawing. The morning light comes from an
unseen source at the left heralding the day which in Virgil's words
would be the prelude to Dido's suffering and death:

> ille dies primus leti primusque malorum
> causa fuit;
>   (*Aeneid* IV, 169–70)

The last canvas in the series has excited repeated eulogy and extensive argumentation as well, *Ascanius Shooting the Stag of Sylvia*.[36]
(Plate IV). One of the last works of the master artist, the hunting
scene sums up many of the separate virtues and rare insights of the
painter. The story contained within the sylvan scene is marked by
pity and tragic foreshadowing in the Virgilian account:

> Now, as Iulus hunted, his hounds hot on the scent started this
> very stag (of Silvia, daughter of Tyrrhus, master of Latinus' royal
> herds) which chanced, during a lonely ramble, to be floating
> downstream in the river and taking relief from the heat in the
> shadow of its green banks. Iulus joined in the chase, aflame with a
> passion for this special glory. Bending his bow he aimed a pointed
> arrow. His hands, guided by some deity, never lost their aim, and

the arrow, with a loud hiss as it sped, passed through the stag's belly and through his flanks. Wounded, the four-foot creature at once fled back to his familiar home and crept moaning into his stall.[37]

There is of course a close relationship between this hunting scene and the earlier one on Libyan shores. But there is a world of difference between the verdant, idyllic setting in Latium and the portentous, almost inhospitable setting in Libya. The scene is evening. Ascanius has donned a blue-and-red cloak and commands the major notice; his companions, in quieter shades of violet and brown, blue and grey, are a neutral accompaniment to Ascanius' or Iulus' decisive and ill-fated action. The architectural remains, set like a stage-building grandly amid the foliage and neatly graded trees receding into the sea and mountainscape behind, emphasize the human act. There is an almost oppressive weight of land and tree mass on the left side of the canvas, stressing the momentous nature of the act; and nature itself registers its disquietude in the abrupt movement of the tree tops yielding to an unearthly wind which will accentuate the velocity of the shaft. The white stag stands immobile, frozen and fated on the right bank, eyeing the hunter Iulus across the river. Claude has caught a fleeting moment in the order of nature, the rising of a storm, the hunter's aim, guided by a malevolent Juno, and the terror of the stag. Nature's storm will be succeeded by another more terrible one, of warfare between the tribal community and the invading Trojans. Though innocent in the action, and with no malice aforethought, Ascanius will soon unleash the terrors of war and vastly complicate Aeneas' settlement of Latium and the progress of Jove's destiny for Rome. Even while Aeneas negotiates with Evander, Juno and the Fury Allecto generate war and guiltless deaths. Claude's are never idle nature studies: background and human action complement each other. Ellis Waterhouse comments sensibly on this painting with its implications for all the Virgilian landscapes in Claude's last period: 'the mood of his landscapes is dictated by the figure and I would be inclined to bet that he never started a composition without taking thought first of what the figures were to be and what they were to be doing. They were to be the germ round which the most intricate landscapes were built, like that tiny germ of actual incident Henry James used to build his most elaborate stories.'[38]

Joseph Mallord William Turner (1775–1851) is unquestionably

England's greatest painter of the nineteenth century.[39] His chromatic symphonies evolved gradually and with increasing originality until he had completely mastered his colours in evoking the cosmic forces of nature. Though sensitive to the Ideal Landscape as delineated by Poussin and Claude, he transcended their somewhat strict limitations and found new means to express the rôle of man in the midst of fire and storm, the destructive agencies of Nature which Virgil had sensed equally vividly and expressed with comparable brilliance. Turner's repeated triumphs with stormy seas and wrecks are a splendid visualization of Virgil's cruel sea and the upheaval between earth and heaven which the storm scene evokes at the opening of the *Aeneid*.

Turner's affection for Virgil's *Aeneid* and the Virgilian landscape continued to his closing years. His first 'historical' landscape, *Aeneas and the Sibyl* (1798–1800), though indebted to an earlier master of the scene rather than the actual topography, is nonetheless a modestly successful representation of the preliminaries to Aeneas' descent into Avernus.[40] Resplendent in his military garb, Aeneas attends the young prophetess, thereby denying the Virgilian epithet, *longaeva*, as she gesticulates with the Golden Bough towards the shadowy slopes of Lake Avernus. The heavily treed and somewhat precipitous slopes of the volcanic lake provide the major focus of interest. The Neronian thermal establishment beside the lake is accurately portrayed, and the receding landscape is faithful to Lake Lucrinus, the Aragon Castle hill at Baiae, and Cape Misenum beyond. The painting is charged with academic paraphernalia reminiscent of the seventeenth century French masters but is nonetheless a fine indication of Turner's future direction. Turner continued to produce canvases recalling classical subjects and ancient historical themes: *Apullia in search of Apullus learns from the swain the cause of his metamorphosis*, an Ovidian theme (1814); *Dido Building Carthage, or The Rise of the Carthaginian Empire* (1815); and *The Decline of the Carthaginian Empire* (1817). But his visit to Italy in 1819 marked the beginning of a new phase in his career as landscape artist.

Poussin's classical scenes and Claude's Italian idylls had quickened his desire to sense the inspirational force of the Roman Campagna and the Italian landscape in general. His visit coincided marvellously with an eruption of Vesuvius which he hastened to witness with the curiosity of the Elder Pliny. His sketch book,

'Gandolfo to Naples' and two others contain pencil point sketches of Amalfi, Sorrento, Salerno, Paestum, Pompeii and Herculaneum, and this priceless record of his personal and careful observation served him well subsequently. *The Bay of Baiae, with Apollo and the Sibyl* (1823) (Plate V) recalls his *Aeneas and the Sibyl* canvas but only in subject matter and elements of composition.[41] There is a new lightness of tone, a translucent quality which marks the later work as original, even prophetic of his own development. Apollo appears robed and laureate with the half-nude Sibyl, once again young and beautiful, and so evocative of the tragic love-story that brought her to a lingering life-span and increasing sorrow.[42] There is a skilful merging of pastoral and architectural elements in the painting with the shepherd and his flock on the right, the rabbit to the right of the central foreground, and the arched substructures and architrave blocks brought into the foreground with less obvious antiquarian zeal than in the earlier painting. Beyond there rises the so-called Temple of Venus, in reality a Neronian thermal establishment, and the castle hill of Baiae. The sea-scape has the same evanescent quality which is found in the mural counterparts recovered from Pompeii and Stabiae. Unfortunately, the resplendent colours of the original have suffered, particularly in those areas of the canvas where the artist used asphaltum. Comparable canvases testify as vividly to the imaginative excitement which Turner found in the Campanian land and sea-scape, and in the classical associations of the Campagna and the Castelli Romani. In every instance, water colour or oil, there is the same pervasive brilliance, a white-hot atmosphere, or one charged with fiery yellows and reds as varied as the composite volcanic tufa which supports the landscape and many of its monuments and dwellings. *Ulysses Deriding Polyphemus*, (1829), though inspired by Homer's *Odyssey*, finds its setting, as ancient mythographers suggested, along Italian shores, Sicilian or Campanian.[43] *Cicero at his Villa* (1839) is a superb suggestion of the antecedents of the great palazze which crown the Castelli Romani south of Rome, at Palestrina, and elsewhere.[44]

Castel Gandolfo, Lake Nemi and the sacred groves of Aricia, where the Golden Bough grew and supported a twilight cult of superstition and human bloodshed, were a major source of inspiration for Turner. His water colour of *The Lake of Nemi* is bathed in the shimmering heat-laden sunlight of the Campagna, and it is hardly suggestive of the primitive ritual and myth-laden environment at all.[45] *The Golden Bough* (1834) (Plate VI) with its wide perspective, focuses on the sacred grove at Aricia, preserve of Diana and the sanctuary of fugitive slaves in the history—laden environment of Alba Longa.[46] Turner's painting highlights the scene beside the Lake of Nemi, evoking the narrative of Aeneas' quest and successful discovery of the talisman which served as his passport to Hades and to his 'rebirth'. The scene is charged with something of the same potent light which pervades the watercolour, but more colourfully and impressively. Here once more the figures and the mysterious landscape, ancient and indestructible, are perfectly composed to form an organic harmonious unity with the wondrous sky, and the atmosphere is charged with Virgilian atmosphere and perhaps, too, with the inmost beliefs of the artist.

At the close of his life in 1850, Turner produced four oils which illustrated the tragic love story of Dido and Aeneas: *Mercury sent to admonish Aeneas; Aeneas relating his story to Dido; The Visit to the Tomb;* and *The Departure of the Fleet.* These final paintings were, in Finberg's commonly accepted view, 'ghosts of his past triumphs, revenants of bygone ecstasies'.[47] They are, however, tokens of his dogged and emphatic dedication to the dignity, the monumentality, and the pathos attaching to Virgil's melancholy but sustaining vision of man in his potential paradise environment. They testify to the artist's Arcadian vision and to the bitter realities of the human condition, frail in the face of evil but part of a larger and hopefully benevolent pattern.

NOTES

[1] Anna Gesina Blonk, *Vergilius en het Landschap* (Groningen, 1947).

[2] For additional comment and illustration consult Sir Archibald Geikie, *The Love of Nature among the Romans* (London, 1912), G. M. Sargeaunt, *Classical Studies* (London, 1929) pp. 164–86 and 207–25; H. R. Fairclough, *Love of Nature among the Greeks and Romans* (New York, 1930), and F. A. Sullivan, S. J., 'Some Vergilian Seascapes', *Classical Journal* 57 (1961–2) pp. 302–9.

[3] Consult T. B. L. Webster, *Hellenistic Poetry and Art* (London, 1964) pp. 82 ff., and 164 ff.; Adam Parry, 'Landscape in Greek Poetry', *Yale Classical Studies* 15 (1957) pp. 3–29; Bruno Snell, *The Discovery of the Mind* (Cambridge, Mass., 1953) (transl. T. G. Rosenmeyer), s.v. *Arcadia*; Gilbert Highet, *Poets in a Landscape* (London, 1957) pp. 56–82. For the best modern discussion of the implications of pastoral poetry consult William Empson, *Some Versions of Pastoral* (London, 1950), and Frank Kermode (ed.), *English Pastoral Poetry from the Beginnings to Marvell* (London, 1952).

A. G. McKAY

4 Cf. Bruno Snell, *op. cit.*

5 C. N. Cochrane, *Christianity and Classical Culture* (Oxford, 1944) p. 65.

6 R. G. Austin, 'The "Georgics",' *Proceedings of the Classical Association* 46 (1949) p. 23.

7 Ibid.

8 Peter H. von Blanckenhagen, 'The Odyssey Frieze', *Mitteilungen des Deutschen Archäologischen Instituts: Römische Abteilung,* 70 (1963) pp. 100–46, with plates 44–53; A. Gallina, *Le pitture con paesaggi dell'Odissea dall' Esquilino* (Rome, 1964).

9 Vitruvius, *De Architectura* VII, 5: *errationes Ulixis per topia.* The 'Odyssey frieze' originally contained ten or eleven sections: (1) the isle of Aeolus (?); (2) the arrival at Laestrygonia; (3) the fight with the Laestrygonians; (4) the destruction of the ships; (5) the escape of Ulysses; (6) the house of Circe; (7) the Circe episode (?); (8) the arrivals at the Underworld; (9) the Underworld; (10) or (11) the Sirens (fragmentary). The landscape is frequently reminiscent of the same Campanian setting which inspired artists of the Seventeenth and Eighteenth centuries.

10 Op. cit., p. 105.

11 For discussion of Roman innovations in landscape painting consult C. M. Dawson, *Romano-Campanian Mythological Landscape Painting* (Yale Classical Studies IX), New Haven, Conn., 1944; and the exemplary study by Peter H. von Blanckenhagen and Christine Alexander, with an appendix by Georges Papadopoulos, 'The Paintings from Boscotrecase', *Mitteilungen des Deutschen Archäologischen Instituts, Römische Abteilung,* 6. *Ergänzungsheft.* (Heidelberg, 1962).

12 For critical study of Poussin consult: Walter Friedlaender, *Nicolas Poussin* (Munich, 1914); W. Friedlaender, in collaboration with R. Wittkower and A. Blunt, *The Drawings of Nicolas Poussin* (London, 1939–53); A. Blunt, 'The Heroic and the Ideal Landscape in the work of Nicholas Poussin,' *Journal of the Warbourg and Courtauld Institute* 7 (1944) 154–68; Kenneth Clark, *Landscape into Art* (London, 1949) pp. 73–5, 78–82; Pierre du Colombier, 'The Poussin Exhibition', *The Burlington Magazine* 102 (1960) 282–8; W. Friedlaender, *Poussin: A New Approach* (New York 1966). W. Hazlitt, *Criticism on Art,* Series II (1844) p. 191 comments with considerable insight: 'He (Poussin) could give to the scenery of his heroic fables that unimpaired look of original nature, full, solid, large, luxuriant, teeming with life and power; or deck it with all the pomp of art, with temples, towers, and mythological groves. His pictures "denote a foregone conclusion". He applies nature to his own purposes, works out her images according to the standard of his own thoughts, embodies high fictions; and the first conception being given, all the rest seems to grow out of, and be assimilated to it, by the unfailing process of a studious imagination.'

13 Pierre du Colombier, *op. cit.* p. 282.

14 Nicolas Poussin. *Dido and Aeneas,* The Toledo Museum of Art. Oil on canvas; 62 × 74¾ in. Formerly in the collection of the Viscount Scarsdale, England.

15 A. Blunt, *Art and Architecture in France:* 1500–1700 (Penguin Books, 1953; second rearranged impression, 1957) p. 158–71, espec. 165 ff; and Charles G. Dempsey, *Nicolas Poussin and the Natural Order* (Ann Arbor, Mich., 1965), available in *University Microfilms,* 64–6259.

16 Pierre du Colombier, *op. cit.,* p. 287.

17 Jean Seznec, *The Survival of the Pagan Gods* (New York, 1953) p. 322.

18 The mysterious and rather melancholy elegiac painting of Arcadian shepherds exists in two versions, one at Chatsworth, England, and the other in the Louvre. The inscription, ET IN ARCADIA EGO, is the centre of attention in the earlier painting. Four figures examine the inscription and are affected by it in a mood often characteristic of Virgil's *Eclogues* and *Aeneid* and of the Roman elegiac poets. The inscription has been interpreted to mean 'I too (have) lived in Arcadia', thereby

assigning an utterance to the tomb's occupant, or 'Even in Arcadia (am) I', referring to Death. For discussion consult Jerome Klein, 'An Analysis of Poussin's "Et in Arcadia Ego",' *Art Bulletin* 19 (1937) 314–7; A. Blunt, 'Poussin's *Et in Arcadia Ego*', *Art Bulletin* 20 (1938) 96–100; and Erwin Panofsky, *Philosophy and History: Essays Presented to Ernest Cassirer* (Oxford, 1963) 223 ff.

[19] Nicolas Poussin. *Landscape with the Roman Road* (1648–51) Dulwich Gallery. 30¾ × 39 in. *Plate* I.

[20] Statius. *Silvae* IV, 3 (Via Domitiana): 20–37; 124–63; and Pliny, *Natural History* III, 5. The imperial highway began at Sinuessa. At Cumae it passed under an impressive brick-faced arch which buttressed the narrow cutting through Monte Grillo. The arch, which still survives, was called Arco Felice in later times, probably from *Arcus ad Campaniam Felicem* (cf. Pliny, *Nat. Hist.* 3, 60).

[21] A possible source for Poussin's knowledge of Campania was Camillo Pellegrino's *Discorsi della Campania felice* (Naples, 1651; second edition Naples, 1771). The work, which treated many of Campania's assets and attractions, appeared in Joannes Graevius' *Thesaurus Antiquitatum et Historiarum Italiae* (Leyden, 1704–25), Vol. IX, part 2, pp. 1–542, in Latin translation.

[22] For classical details and associations consult T. Ashby, *The Roman Campagna in Classical Times* (New York, 1927).

[23] For critical study of Claude consult: W. Friedlaender, *Claude Lorrain* (Berlin, 1921); U. Christoffel, *Poussin und Claude Lorrain* (Munich, 1942); K. Clark, *Landscape into Art* (London, 1949) pp. 73–83; A. Blunt, *Art and Architecture in France*, etc. cf. note 15 *supra*, pp. 171–7; M. Davies, *National Gallery Catalogues, French School* (London, 1957); Michael Kitson and Marcel Röthlisberger, 'Claude Lorrain and the Liber Veritatis: III', *The Burlington Magazine* 101 (1959) 381–6; M. Kitson, 'The "Altieri Claudes" and Virgil', *The Burlington Magazine* 102 (1960) 312 ff; M. Röthlisberger, 'The Subjects of Claude Lorrain's Paintings', *Gazette des Beaux-Arts* 55 (April, 1960) 209–24; M. Röthlisberger, *Claude Lorrain. The Paintings*. Vol. I, *Critical Catalogue;* Vol. II. *Illustrations* (New Haven, Conn., 1961).

[24] A. Blunt, *Art and Architecture* etc., op. cit. p. 173: 'We know from the artist's early biographers of his constant excursions from Rome, wandering over the whole range of the country, sketching it with the pen, in wash, and even, we are told, in oils. His surviving drawings confirm the extent and the subtlety of his observation'.

[25] For illustrations and details concerning the Vatican Virgil manuscript and the miniatures consult: *Fragmenta et picturae Vergilianae* (Codices e Vaticanis selecti, I) (1899); J. De Wit, *Die Miniaturen des Vergilius Vaticanus* (Amsterdam, 1959); and Kurt Weitzmann, *Ancient Book Illumination* (Martin Classical Lectures, XVI) (Cambridge, Mass., 1959). The miniatures tend to be pastiches, compilations of a selection of heterogeneous elements drawn from several sources, ancient sculpture, mosaics, etc. De Wit argues that the style of the miniatures suits a date ca. 420 A.D. See also A. Blunt, *op. cit.,* p. 174, and note 235.

[26] M. Kitson and M. Röthlisberger, *op. cit.,* p. 385.

[27] For ancient literary *testimonia*, historical and archaeological information, and illustrations see Amedeo Maiuri, *The Phlegraean Fields, from Vergil's Tomb to the Grotto of the Cumaean sibyl* (Rome, 1958); A. G. McKay, *Naples and Campania: Texts and Illustrations* (Hamilton, Canada, 1962); A. Maiuri, *Passeggiate Campane* (Firenze, 1957).

[28] Claude. *Coast View of Delos with Aeneas.* National Gallery, London. 1672. 100 × 134 cm.

[29] Claude. *Coast View of Libya with Aeneas Hunting.* Musée des Beaux Arts, Brussels. 1672. 111 × 158 cm. The translation of *Aeneid* I, 159–66, is by W. F. Jackson Knight, *Virgil: The Aeneid* (Penguin Books, 1956).

[30] *Aeneid* VIII, 91–111, 115–6, transl. by W. F. Jackson Knight, *op. cit.*

[31] Claude. *Landscape with the Landing of Aeneas in Latium*. The Lord Fairhaven. 1675. 175 × 224 cm. *Plate* III.

` [32] Michael Kitson, 'The Altieri Claudes and Virgil', *op. cit.*, p. 316.

[33] The Altieri arms were first noticed by Blunt in *Art and Architecture in France*, p. 274, note 233.

[34] Claude. *View of Carthage with Dido and Aeneas*. Col. A. Heywood-Lonsdale, 1676. 120 × 149.5 cm.

[35] *Aeneid* IV, 136–44, transl. by W. F. Jackson Knight, *op. cit.*

[36] Claude. *Landscape with Ascanius Shooting the Stag of Silvia*. Ashmolean Museum, Oxford. 120 × 150 cm. *Plate* IV.

[37] *Aeneid* VII, 493–501, transl. by W. F. Jackson Knight, *op. cit.*

[38] Ellis Waterhouse, *The Listener*, Feb. 18, 1960, p. 311. Rubens' sketch of the same incident (*Aeneid* VII, 475–508) in the John G. Johnson Collection, Philadelphia Museum of Art, is a baroque version which emphasizes both the fury and the violence of the hunt and also the tender pathos of Silvia's mourning over her suffering pet. See Julius S. Held, 'Rubens and Virgil', *The Art Bulletin* 29 (1947) 125–6, with illustration.

[39] For critical study of Turner consult: Thomas Ashby, *Turner's Vision of Rome* (London & New York, 1925); A. J. Finberg, *The Life of J. M. W. Turner, R.A.* (Oxford, 1939; second edition, 1961); Martin Davies, *National Gallery Catalogues: British School* (London, 1946; revised edition, 1959); John Rothenstein, *Turner* (1775–1851). (London, 1951); Martin Butlin, *Turner Watercolours* (London, Basle, and Baden-Baden, 1962); Jerrold Ziff, 'Turner and Poussin', *The Burlington Magazine* 105 (1963) 315–21; J. Rothenstein and Martin Butlin, *Turner* (New York, 1964), contains colour and monochrome plates.

[40] J. M. W. Turner. *Aeneas and the Sibyl*. Circa 1798–1800. Tate Gallery, London. 30 × 39 in.

[41] J. M. W. Turner. *The Bay of Baiae, with Apollo and the Sibyl*. Exhibited 1823. Tate Gallery, London. 57½ × 93½ in. *Plate* V.

[42] Ovid, *Metamorphoses* XIV, 130–50.

[43] J. M. W. Turner. *Ulysses Deriding Polyphemus*. Exhibited 1829. National Gallery, London. 52¼ × 80½ in.

[44] J. M. W. Turner. *Cicero at his Villa*. Exhibited 1839. Evelyn de Rothschild, Ascot, Buckinghamshire. 35½ × 47½ in.

[45] J. M. W. Turner. *Lake of Nemi*. Watercolour. Painted 1828 (?) National Gallery, London. 23 × 39½ in.

[46] J. M. W. Turner. *The Golden Bough*. Painted c 1834. Tate Gallery, London. 41½ × 64½ in. For details about the custom cf. Strabo V, 3, 12. Plate VI.

[47] A. J. Finberg, *ip. cit.*, p. 427.

For additional examples of Virgilian themes and landscape in art consult H. Bardon, 'L'Énéide et l'art. XVIe–XVIIIe siècle (with English summary), *Gazette des Beaux-Arts* 37 A (1950) 77–98 (published in 1959).

PLATE I
NICOLAS POUSSIN: Landscape with the Roman Road.
(*Dulwich Gallery*)

PLATE II
CLAUDE LORRAIN: Aeneas and the Sibyl. (*British Museum*)

above PLATE III CLAUDE LORRAIN:
Landscape with Landing of Aeneas in Italy: The Lord
Fairhaven. (*Anglesey Abbey*)
below PLATE IV CLAUDE LORRAIN:
Ascanius shooting the Stag of Sylvia. (*Ashmolean
Museum, Oxford*)

above PLATE V J. M. W. TURNER:
    The Bay of Baiae. (*Tate Gallery, London*)
below PLATE VI J. M. W. TURNER:
    The Golden Bough. (*Tate Gallery, London*)

VII

Virgil's Elysium

W. F. JACKSON KNIGHT

THE following essay is part of a work as yet unpublished, entitled *'Elysion'*, on Greek and Roman beliefs regarding life beyond death.

For a more expansive treatment of the esoteric properties of the Sixth *Aeneid* see W. F. Jackson Knight, *Cumaean Gates,* 1936; now re-issued, revised, with other material in *Vergil: Epic and Anthrobology*, ed. John D. Christie, 1967.

The passage entitled Cumaean Gates, with a translation by Jackson Knight, has reference to articles VII and VIII.

CUMAEAN GATES

At pius Aeneas arces quibus altus Apollo
praesidet horrendaeque procul secreta Sibyllae,
antrum immane, petit, magnam cui mentem animumque
Delius inspirat uates aperitque futura.
iam subeunt Triuiae lucos atque aurea tecta.
    Daedalus, ut fama est, fugiens Minoia regna
praepetibus pennis ausus se credere caelo
insuetum per iter gelidas enauit ad Arctos,
Chalcidicaque leuis tandem super adstitit arce.
redditus his primum terris tibi, Phoebe, sacrauit
remigium alarum posuitque immania templa.
in foribus letum Androgeo; tum pendere poenas
Cecropidae iussi (miserum!) septena quotannis
corpora natorum; stat ductis sortibus urna.
contra elata mari respondet Gnosia tellus:
hic crudelis amor tauri suppostaque furto
Pasiphae mixtumque genus prolesque biformis
Minotaurus inest, Veneris monimenta nefandae;
hic labor ille domus et inextricabilis error;
magnum reginae sed enim miseratus amorem
Daedalus ipse dolos tecti ambagesque resoluit,
caeca regens filo uestigia. tu quoque magnam
partem opere in tanto, sineret dolor, Icare, haberes.
bis conatus erat casus effingere in auro,
bis patriae cecidere manus. quin protinus omnia
perlegerent oculis, ni iam praemissus Achates
adforet atque una Phoebi Triuiaeque sacerdos
Deiphobe Glauci, fatur quae talia regi:
'non hoc ista sibi tempus spectacula poscit;
nunc grege de intacto septem mactare iuuencos
praestiterit, totidem lectas de more bidentis.'
talibus adfata Aenean (nec sacra morantur
iussa uiri) Teucros uocat alta in tecta sacerdos.
    Excisum Euboicae latus ingens rupis in antrum
quo lati ducunt aditus centum, ostia centum,
unde ruunt totidem uoces, responsa Sibyllae.
Virgil Aeneid VI, 9–44.

CUMAEAN GATES

Another way went Aeneas the true, to the towering fastness where Apollo reigns, and, near, that monstrous cavern, dread Sibyl's seclusion; where he of Delos, he the prophet, breathes into her spirit's visionary might, revealing things to come. Now they came near the woods of the goddess three-wayed and near that house of gold.

There is a tale of Daedalus, how, in flight from the land where Minos ruled, he took headlong wings and dared his life in the sky; by track unknown right out toward the icy north he swam, till he lightly hovered above that fastness of Chalcidic men. Here, in the first land where he found safety, he hallowed to Phoebus his slant-oar wings, in a monster temple which he founded. There, on the temple doors, Androgeos dying; there next, oh sad, command given to sons of Cecrops to pay annual retribution in seven of their fine sons, the urn visible, the lots just drawn. Opposite, balancing, the land where Knossos is, standing up from the sea. In it, that bull-love, love callous; Pasiphae, bride in secrecy; and there, record how wicked love can be, hybrid procreation, two shapes in one, Minotaur in the midst; and all the old wandering ways of the house that was there, weariness of work inextricable, except the Builder himself pitied the Queen, that her love was strong, and unwinding the craft and the coils, guided sightless footprints with his thread. And Icarus, his share of that picture would have been great indeed, had grief allowed. Hands of an artist twice had tried to mould out his fall in the gold; hands of a father twice had fallen from the trying. . . . Why, straight had they read on, every pictured word, had not Achates, sent ahead before, returned already, and with him she, priestess of Phoebus and of the goddess three-wayed, Deiphobe her name, Glaucus her father. Like this she spake to our king: 'Now is no time that commands staring at sights, as you stare. No: from a herd without spot seven heifers be your sacrifice, seven sheep too, and choose them ritually well. Better so, might it be.' So spake she to Aeneas. They were not slow to do the rite instructed. Then she called the two Trojans into the tall house where she was priestess.

Cleft out is the flank of that Euboeic rock into a cavern terrific. To it a hundred broad accesses lead, a hundred their mouthways. From it a hundred come the streams of sound, the Sibyl's answerings.

Virgil can truly be said to have believed in an after-life if not for every minute of every day at least most often. As Professor T. J. Haarhoff[1] says, he was a peculiarly universal poet. He was also a poet who fully attended to the world of matter and sense, not a mystic with eyes only for the beyond. He probably had some kind of special sensitivity. Virgil both makes death the traditional sombre mystery of epic and also shines a bright light of revelation on to it. But he wrote his poetry by psychological rather than psychic methods. He read immensely, and allowed his poetry and thought to grow out of innumerable reminiscences, combined together to form new expressions carrying new meanings. The new meanings always or nearly always agreed with his judgement in so far as any judgement could be independent of the poetic statement. Thus, if he says that the good go to Heaven, it is because he chose to use words derived from literary sources, which, as he recombined them, came to mean this. It is also because he himself really thought so, whether through direct experience or guess-work or some other means.

Already Virgil, and Horace also, accepted a sky heaven for Augustus when he should be dead and deified. Julius Caesar had been deified, and possibly Virgil's Daphnis in the *Eclogues* represents Julius. Daphnis' elevation to heaven, whoever he may be, is interesting. It is an unusual picture, for the time. The deifications of Julii come unexpectedly, in a Roman context, but not if seen as a continuation of Hellenistic deifications. Virgil soon enough, in the *Georgics*, imagined Augustus as due to be deified. But both the *Eclogues* and the *Georgics* are of this world, and face the hard facts of the reign of Jupiter. At the end of the *Georgics*, Eurydice goes back to Hades, and Orpheus, having saved her once, cannot save her again.[2] It is the world of tragedy, which has to be careful of letting a future life's consolation dilute the intensity. Yet before this in the Fourth *Eclogue*, combining, characteristically, Etruscan prophetic doctrine with an inversion of Hesiod's Five Ages, Virgil imagines a golden age, an earthly heaven to come, in which men, heroes and gods mingle together.[3]

Virgil's language has what has been called an 'apocalyptic majesty'. He, if any one, could surely see the tier on tier of the world's spiritual structure. Certainly, he does not leave us uninformed. His whole universe is instinct with the active Divine.[4] It is, as always with Virgil, interesting to note not only what he does, but also what he does not, say.

He always appears to follow literary tradition; and, with the stupendous learning proper to his epoch and still more to himself, there was no lack of literary tradition to follow. This might seem not worth saying. But it is. Virgil's obvious use of literary sources is often taken to mean that he has little to say himself, and only provides what is second-hand. This view is quite wrong. Virgil profoundly and intricately makes his sources help him to give his own message and nothing else. Such is the simple truth; the full statement of what he does is very complicated, but not essential here. There is another consideration. Virgil says what he himself means, but, helped by his sources, fits it into, or on to, the existing tradition. In the eschatological passages of his poetry he all the time indicates that what he is saying is what Homer, Pythagoras, Pindar, or Plato might have said if they had gone a step forward or had had the opportunity which lapse of time had given to him, Virgil, their inheritor. To be quite exact, this statement too would need elaboration. But it is more urgent to recall that Virgil's own epic successor Lucan, and to some extent Statius, did not do as Virgil had done. Lucan especially, when he mentions the after-life, forgets traditional requirements, and makes allusion to direct experience.[5]

In Virgil's Fifth *Eclogue* Daphnis the shepherd becomes a God and lives after death in the sky. In his Sixth *Aeneid* his hero Aeneas, guided by prophetic advice, goes down into the cave at Cumae near Naples, and finds himself in the world beyond death, where, in some degree, Hell, Purgatory, and Heaven—Elysium—are revealed to him, and he meets his dead father Anchises, as Homer's Odysseus had met his dead mother Anticleia. In the Eighth *Aeneid* the picture is supplemented by a further Vision of those who suffer in the Beyond for their sins.[6] The Sixth *Aeneid* is central, to Virgil's eschatology, to his poem, and perhaps to all non-Christian religious history; it comes near to being central for Catholicism too.

The 'descent' begins by an approach to Apollo, who is allowed full control, and to the Cumaean Sibyl, who is called priestess of both Apollo and Hecate, the Diana of the world below. Virgil might be said here to be reconciling free prophecy with organized, religious prophecy, the contentious issue already at least suspected to be real even for Homer, and already plain in the prehistory of

Delphi. Apollo brings free prophecy, ecstatic, inspired, and mad, as Cicero calls it,[7] 'inside the Church', where it can be watched, and interpreted. Characteristically, Virgil retains the old, and reconciles it with the new.

This is where the labyrinth appears, the maze-like gateway, admissive and exclusive, to the world beyond, reached along a shore, as it still is, among the Malekulans, far away in the New Hebrides. At Cumae, however, it is not a mere maze. It is an elaborate bronze sculptured door, such perhaps as the still existing bronze door to the Baptistry at Florence done by Ghiberti in the fourteenth century, a noble masterpiece. Virgil's door shows the Cretan labyrinth, and indeed a rich précis of the whole myth of the Cretan labyrinth. Athens is shown, and the lot-drawing to decide who is to be among the seven young men who must be sent to Crete to meet the Minotaur, and be sacrificed as reparation to King Minos. Opposite is Crete, with its 'laborious building', the place of 'wandering not to be unravelled'—except that Daedalus himself, who built the edifice, guided the 'blind footsteps' of the intended victims 'with a thread'.[8]

Aeneas was reading the message of the pictured gates. What the message was, we hardly know. Perhaps it was some secret of life and death—how to live, and secure that the transition to the other life will be smooth and felicitous—or even how to know the whole truth of divine justice. However, the Sibyl would not let Aeneas read on. She peremptorily told him that he should not waste time, but sacrifice bulls and sheep. This he did. It is as if the Sibyl had told him not to rely on his own personal explorations and conjectures, but to continue with customary religious observances—'not to neglect his church-going' would be a modern equivalent. She tells him to pray. He prays to Apollo. Only then can the great doors open; and they do, of their own accord. Aeneas remembers to ask the Sibyl not to write her prophecy on leaves, as she often did, for they would blow about, and their message would be lost. It is as if he wanted to retain the full content of free, and not institutional, prophecy. And there is moral cogency also. Aeneas has to find and take as passport a 'golden bough'. This is many things, but it is certainly 'The Golden Bough of the Divine Plato, sparkling all round with every virtue', a conception which he derived from the nearly contemporary Greek poet, Meleager.[9]

When the Sibyl does prophesy, she goes into a trance after signs of great disturbance, and clearly Apollo himself controls her. At least she is, and behaves as, a medium. She seems larger than normal, and her voice 'has not the tone of mortality'[10]—all this in sublime Latin, the only language for 'apocalyptic majesty', and in that language at its best. She is in the tradition of Heraclitus, who centuries before had mentioned a sibyl 'of raving lips'.[11] Ancient mediums, Greek, Roman and Chinese also, and some modern oriental mediums, apparently made and make very heavy weather of going into a trance: modern, western, mediums go off into a trance quite quietly, apart from a little heavy breathing, except when certain less desirable spirits control them.

The Sibyl prophesies the future of Aeneas, or some of it. They then go into Hades, a dark, shadowy world, half-real. They pass the spirits of babies who had died too soon, on the threshold of life, and now surviving on the threshold of death, pathetically.[12] Those, now, who claim experience in these things would say that this is wrong. The babies, even those who were still-born, would have been growing up happily in their world, much as they would, if they had lived, in ours.

So, too, do others suffer, as we might say, unjustly. Among them are suicides, those who died for love, and those not properly buried. They wait, retaining their earth-life's sorrow, debarred from crossing the waters of death, and from reaching rest.[13] All this would be called common, or even normal, pagan belief. In Virgil the unburied have to wait a hundred years; he does not here specify how others are released, but he does not lay it down that they never are, and later in the book he gives a more thorough scheme, of regeneration and reincarnation. Dido is more emphatic in Virgil than most of the other spirits. She has not forgiven Aeneas, but she is happy now with Sychaeus, her former love.

On the way are many symbolic figures and monsters, not solid, and not fully real, such as Centaurs and Scyllas, and there is a great elm tree with dreams clustering under the leaves. Elsewhere, souls cluster, not dreams: there may be here one of Virgil's characteristic light changes. Aeneas and the Sibyl go on in the half-light. The watch dog of Hades, Cerberus, is neutralized: they drug him. A kind of comedy is allowed. There is surely some when they come to the waters of death, a lake or river across which the grotesque ferryman Charon ferries the newly-come souls in his wretched, leaky boat, which sinks lower under the weight of the fully solid

Aeneas, who is certainly no light ghost. Charon will only accept the qualified, who do not include the living. But the Sibyl shows him the Golden Bough. He had seen it before—we have no idea when, certainly not for a long time—and he accepted it as a passport. They crossed; and eventually dedicated the bough, hanging it up in a kind of archway or door or false door, where Proserpine, the Goddess of Hades, could receive it.[14]

To the left[15] a path leads to Hell, and the Sibyl tells Aeneas a little about Hell, through which, at her installation, Hecate had conducted her; as today it is thought that a medium can sometimes come in contact with 'lower spheres'. Virgil believed in eternal punishment for some great mythical sinners, such as Ixion who tried to violate Juno. Many others are punished, and there is a list of sins which earned punishment. It may well be more probable that there is hope for all souls, unless perhaps some who are irreclaimable, very few, who are not punished for ever, but simply dissolved, as in Ibsen's *Peer Gynt*,[16] the material part in them being allocated to new existences. The dissolution seems to be a Chinese thought. Instead of taking an oath, a Chinaman will break a plate and say 'If it is not as I say, may my soul be broken up as this plate is broken up'. That one soul may simply not survive, though other souls survive, is a different conception. The Egyptians thought that the life was in the stomach, and if that was not carefully embalmed the soul would not achieve survival.

Ahead, Aeneas and the Sibyl now saw great ramparts of steel, built by the Cyclopes.[17] They may be part of a very old mythical pattern. The Malekulans believe in a tall fence in the lower world, beyond which is a kind of Elysium.

For Virgil, it is to Elysium that the road to the right leads; and the travellers walk there. They climb up a slope; and see below them a glittering land. The air is bright and fresh, and Elysium has a sun of its own[18]—with a memory of Homer's when he imagined the sun, in a huff, going down to shine among the dead,[19] as of course the Egyptian sun was supposed to do every night. Pindar seems to be trying to say the same as Virgil.[20] It is a problem. The dead live in a different dimension. That is, they should not normally be in a dimension dependent for light on the sun, which, like the rest of the world, is in our dimension, not theirs. They must therefore have their own sun, all the more if they are imagined below the earth, or some other source of light.

Here, at last, Aeneas meets his father Anchises, as is appropriate and indeed inevitable. But it is worth noticing that a father who is to be met fits neatly into the tradition. Gilgamesh meets his grandfather; Homer's Odysseus meets his mother; Aeneas meets his father. This is how great poetry works, by the 'chance which is the friend of art'.

Anchises shows Aeneas souls not yet born but due to be born in their time and to be descendants of Aeneas. The earlier and later parts of Homer's book, the Eleventh *Odyssey*, are different from each other. So they are, but differently different, in the Sixth *Aeneid*. Here the first part is largely elicited from existing myth with mysterious elements of history and anthropology. The later part is based on esoteric material, partly on Pythagorean and Platonic knowledge, the emphasis being on reincarnation, not on the old static Hades and Tartarus. Perhaps Aeneas comes through the delusions of myth to a philosophic and indeed psychic truth.

Aeneas questions Anchises and Anchises answers with a statement of the universal scheme, the rule of spirit throughout, and the purification by fire, by water, or by the winds.[21] Meanwhile the souls of Romans, while on earth, are to build Rome and the Roman Empire. They can be seen, looking as they will look when on earth.[22] This is unusual, to say the least. Prophecy does not often look ahead many centuries and include detail. Perhaps only Nostradamus went so far. The Roman souls are as they might well be as affected by their life on earth. Those claiming second sight often claim also to see very recognizable individuals who have lived on the earth lately or long ago. It is not unlikely that Virgil began with a knowledge of this kind of vision, and simply practised one of his inversions, picturing the souls as they might have appeared to a contemporary of his own who was clairvoyant, but casting the picture dramatically back to the days before Rome was.

Anchises' descriptive prophecy of many individual Romans, in the future to him but of course to Virgil himself in the past, is full of heroic universal values, but it is addressed to Romans. His account of the whole scheme of the universe, his cosmology, is addressed to all.

Anchises presents the universe as matter instinct with spirit in every part of it, mind, *mens,* activating the whole of it. There are also individual living organisms, including humans. They have minds and bodies. Their minds are obstructed by their material bodies, these bodies being the source of feelings and emotions, such as fear, joy, and desire. Therefore the minds or true selves, being imprisoned in windowless matter, cannot 'look with wide eyes at free air'. But they learn and evolve. As they do, they acquire stains of guilt as they live their lives on earth. They die, and undergo a cleaning process, by fire, water or windy air. Then they conceive a desire to live again—strictly, being without bodies now, they should be incapable of desire—and are reborn for a further span of life on earth. After this has happened several times, each soul is left with a purified consciousness: it is 'a spark of elemental fire', and lives, apparently, in bliss for ever. Anchises says 'we few are admitted to Elysium, and have our home in the meadows of delight'.[23]

This class of doctrine is apparently Indian, and pre-Socratic. It gives a descent of spirit into matter, and an ascent again, after experience, purification and enrichment. Heaven is not a place where, says Studdert Kennedy, 'the sheep-faced angels bleat', but rather for those who, as Pindar said, 'have three times dared',[24] or more than three times, according to Empedocles:[25] great heroes and leaders who have done and suffered, for whom the trumpets might well sound on the other side. Plato's scheme is immensely elaborated, but the core is the same. Cicero's *Dream of Scipio* fits.[26] It was left for the Romans to write freely and at length about conditions in their Paradise.

To judge from letters of the rather later Apollonius of Tyana, or of some other author confused with him in the tradition, the Neo-Pythagoreans already had an extremely coherent and progressive doctrine of life and death, in line with Heraclitus, who said that there was no difference between them.[27] Romans of Virgil's time were certainly interested. Probably they believed little in the terrors of Hell; Cicero says no one did.[28] If so, they perhaps regarded the terrors in Virgil as poetry not theology. Virgil adheres to epic tradition, however much more he may provide than just that. He accepted, and indeed required for his poem, the tragic side of the heroic. He could not lament a young, beautiful, warrior, cut off in his prime, if he had just been quoting Heraclitus and saying that death did not matter. Meanwhile the sombre part is only a part. Unlike Homer, Virgil looks forward, to a glorious Roman future, making at least much of the suffering worth while. Many things happen in the rest of the poem. But the

Sixth Book, in the middle, shows the truth behind the phenomena, the activity of a divine mechanism concealed beneath the material world. The adventure of Aeneas can be regarded as a mystical vision, as astral projection, or even as a psycho-analysis, as if, going into the cave, Aeneas went down into his own unconscious mind to become aware of its contents, perhaps 'the Archetypes', as Jung would say.

However, at the end of the 'Descent' and the visions comes the mysterious, equivocal, conclusion. 'There are two Gates of Sleep', one of horn, and one of ivory. The horn gate offers easy exit for 'true shades'. The ivory gate is shining-white: but the spirits of the dead, the '*manes*', the 'good people', 'send false, wakeful, dreams to the sky'.[29] First, Virgil does not say that anything comes through the ivory gate: he says that the spirits send something, itself obscure enough, but he does not say by which way they send it. What they send looks superficially like dreams, *insomnia*. This is a mixed and artificial word, coined by Virgil. He used it in the Fourth *Aeneid* for Dido's fitful, nightmare-ridden sleep and wakefulness[30]—a superb demonstration of sheer poetic might. In the Sixth this same word is used, and nowhere else, till later poets copied it from Virgil. There is the word '*somnium*', dream, and a singular word, '*insomnia*', sleeplessness, both coming from '*somnus*', sleep. But *insomnia* is plural, a mixture between 'dream' and 'sleeplessness'. And this is, or these are, what the spirits send up 'to the sky' either through, or not through, the Ivory Gate of Sleep; and Virgil calls this, or these, false. Finally, Anchises sees Aeneas, and the Sibyl, out through this Gate, and not through the Horn Gate of 'true shadows'.

It is tempting to say that here is the subtlest mind in literary history at its most subtle. Virgil is propounding an eschatological doctrine with reservations. There are many possible suggestions. Perhaps Virgil is saying that Aeneas and the Sibyl, or they and their journey, are just a legend, and not facts. Or perhaps they really made the journey, but what they saw and heard was untrue—hallucinations. Perhaps they and their visions were true, but the spirits also send fitful nightmares besides the true evidence represented by Aeneas and the Sibyl. At least Virgil is not emphatically recommending belief in the system which the Sixth *Aeneid* presents. In the earlier eighteenth century Bishop Warburton published a book, *The Divine Legation of Moses*, in which he firmly stated that 'the masterpiece of the Aeneis, the famous Sixth Book, is nothing else but a description . . . of the Eleusinian Mysteries'.[31] There is truth in this, though probably nothing in Virgil can be called 'nothing but' anything: there are always different layers of meaning. But, if there is a strong reference to the Eleusinian Mysteries, always kept very secret, in Virgil's Sixth Book, it would not be surprising if Virgil subtly indicated, at the end, that, whatever the secret truth of life and death might be, he himself had not revealed it in any guilty sense, or to any guilty degree. At the beginning of the Descent he included—a rarity—a personal prayer, 'sit mihi fas audita loqui', 'may it be allowed to me to speak what I have heard', 'may I be without sin if I speak what has been told to me'.

The *Aeneid* is an epic, and epic like tragedy needs intensity unrelaxed by injudiciously admitted consolation. The thought world in it is of Homeric shape under Homeric deities. But the movement is a linear ascent, divinely aided and foreshadowed, towards a Roman future. There is a strong and sure purpose, reaching farther than any purpose in Homer. There is also a transcendent sanction. The *Aeneid* is not only of this world. The Sixth Book, with its visit to Hades superficially like many others, Orphic, Homeric, or Asiatic, is Platonic rather than Homeric. Aeneas, led by the Sibyl of Cumae, goes down through the cave by Lake Avernus and sees the souls. Some await burial. Some are punished. Some live in bliss. Some await rebirth. The doctrine is elaborate, compressed from many sources, Plato, Pindar, Bacchylides, Cicero in *The Dream of Scipio,* Stoic and Epicurean writers, and no doubt very many more. Aeneas sees the future of Rome, and his own descendants who are to make it. He is strengthened and confirmed by the assurance, and has, on the whole, more confidence after it.

This revelation is important, and meant to indicate truth about the world and its divine government. The best traditions of earlier poetry and thought pointed this way, and Virgil consolidated them with elimination and condensation, and presented a still more profound version. It is not all consistent and the exact experience on which one part or another part may be ultimately based is not explicit. The learning used is, of course, vast. But the result is poetry of incomparable mastery and delicacy, minutely precise in controlling the reader's mood and directing his emo-

tions towards right thinking, a miracle of extreme human attain-
ment. It has not Plato's long elaboration of detail. But it has more
than Pindar tells. And it has the feeling of the Roman, deeper as
some say and more responsible than the feeling of a Greek. It is at
home as far as an earthly heaven, where souls free from rebirth
stay; it does not go with eastern sages, and with Empedocles or
even Pythagoras to the diviner, inexpressible heights; but it asserts
the spiritual government of the universe, and the eternity of souls.

In other parts of the *Aeneid* there is some diversity. Earthly life
is always short, and 'irreparable'; it is succeeded by an existence
among the shades below, or an everlasting darkness, or an iron
sleep. That is all, approximately, Homeric. Intense epic or tragic
action is better ringed with a hard, unshining, boundary; it is
hardly possible, if the characters, like the Getae, are only too glad
to be killed and go to the happy land beyond. But Virgil is above
all comprehensive. Elsewhere, as always partly depending on
sources, this time post-Homeric sources both Greek and Latin, he
gives some interesting and carefully-thought glimpses. Latinus,
King of Latium, consulted the Oracle of Faunus. He slept on skins
of sacrificed sheep, saw the spirits of the dead floating in the air,
and was able to converse with 'gods', who are of course as much
'spirits' as 'gods' in any modern sense.[32] An old Trojan, Nautes,
who advised Aeneas to leave some of his company in Sicily and to
proceed to Italy with the others, has psychic powers, exactly
described, given by Athena, by which he can precisely discern
which events can well start a causal sequence in the future, and
therefore add discrimination to sensitivity.[33] There are in the
Sixth Book itself lines about the Sibyl as she goes under control
which are detailed and express precisely what sometimes, though
not always, happens. There are apparitions. A god or devil
suddenly appears. Or a mist is shed to conceal a character. Much of
this is Homeric, but not less true to fact. Even Homer, when he
lets a god withdraw the veil from a mortal's eyes (*Iliad* V, 127;
Athene to Diomedes, 'I have taken the mist from your eyes'), or
lets him assume or bestow a cloud of concealment (*Iliad,* XVII, 551;
cf. *Aeneid* I, 516: 'nube . . . amicti'), may as Professor T. J.
Haarhoff has suggested reflect some relation to what is known as
'the psychic-mist'. He is not contradicting psychic experience but
using memories of it, and so is Virgil when he, with characteristic
variations, applies such motives.

Often Virgil makes death tragic, sombre, pathetic. Even Jupiter's own son, Sarpedon, as Jupiter himself recalls, had to die. Fate is inexorable—though sometimes it seems to be the instrument of Zeus. 'Cease expecting that the Fates of Gods can be deflected by praying', the Sibyl commands Palinurus, the helmsman of Aeneas who had been drowned.[34] But important results come from prayers, or deeds, elsewhere. Orpheus brings Eurydice back from Hades but loses her again; Hercules stole Cerberus the watch-dog; and Theseus rescued Helen from Hades. It is all traditional, and of course always used with poetic effect. There is some reason for the view that Virgil has two religions and two systems of belief about life and death, the Sixth *Aeneid* evincing one sort and the rest of the *Aeneid* another. The Sixth is Platonic; the rest Homeric. Of course both parts, Homeric and Platonic, are above all Virgilian. But in fact through much of history there have been two strains, the religious and the psychic, the church and the free prophet, the institutional and the spiritual. Usually an individual is mainly on one side or on the other. Characteristically, Virgil includes both sides, respects both, and gives us opportunities to make comparisons, or even achieve some reconciliation, between these opposite poles.

NOTES

[1] T. J. Haarhoff, *Vergil the Universal*, (Oxford, 1949).
[2]   . . . nec portitor Orci
amplius obiectam passus transire paludem.
    Virgil, *Georgics* IV, 502–3
[3] ille deum vitam accipiet divisque videbit
permixtos heroas et ipse videbitur illis
    Virgil, *Eclogues* IV, 15–16
[4] principio caelum ac terram camposque liquentis
lucentemque globum lunae Titaniaque astra
spiritus intus alit, totamque infusa per artus
mens agitat molem et magno se corpore miscet
    Virgil, *Aeneid* VI, 724–727
[5] Lucan, *de Bello Civili* I, 452–62; VI, 569–830.
[6]   hinc procul addit
Tartareas etiam sedes, alta ostia Ditis,
et scelerum poenas, et te, Catilina, minaci
pendentem scopulo Furiarumque ora trementem
    Virgil, *Aeneid* VIII, 666–69
[7] Cicero, *de Divinatione* I, 12; 34
[8] Virgil, *Aeneid* VI, 20–30 (above).
[9] Meleager, *Garland*, 47–8.

[10]   sed pectus anhelum
et rabie fera corda tument, maiorque videri
nec mortale sonans, adflata est numine quando
iam propiore dei.
        Virgil, *Aeneid*, VI. 48–51.
[11] Heraclitus, *ap.* Plutarch, *Pyth. Or.* 6, 397A
[12] Virgil, *Aeneid* VI, 426–9.
[13] Virgil, *Aeneid* VI, 431–44.
[14] Virgil, *Aeneid* VI, 630–6.
[15] respicit Aeneas subito et sub rupe sinistra
moenia lata videt triplici circumdata muro,
quae rapidus flammis ambit torrentibus amnis,
Tartareus Phlegethon, torquetque sonantia saxa.
        Virgil, *Aeneid* VI, 548–51
[16] Ibsen, *Peer Gynt*, V, vii.
[17]   Cyclopum educta caminis
moenia conspicio atque adverso fornice portas.
        Virgil, *Aeneid* VI, 630–1
[18] largior hic campos aether et lumine vestit
purpureo, solemque suum, sua sidera norunt.
        Virgil, *Aeneid* VI, 640–1
[19] Homer, *Odyssey.* XII, 382–3.
[20] Pindar, Fr. 114 in O.C.T.
[21] Virgil, *Aeneid* VI, 724–751.
[22] e.g. *Aeneid* VI, 760, 771, 779, 788, etc., and, especially, the vision of Marcellus, 860 ff.
[23]   exinde per amplum
mittimur Elysium, et pauci laeta arva tenemus
        Virgil, *Aeneid* VI, 743–4
[24] Pindar. *Ol.* II, 68.
[25] Empedocles, Fr. 115 (Diels-Kranz)
[26] Cicero, *De Republica,* VI.
[27] 'The immortal are mortals, mortals are immortal, living the death of the one, dying the life of the other.' Heraclitus, Fr. 62 (Diels-Kranz)
[28] Cicero, *Tusc. disp.* I, 48; *de nat. deor.* II, 5.
[29] Sunt geminae Somni portae, quarum altera fertur
cornea, qua veris facilis datur exitus umbris,
altera candenti perfecta nitens elephanto,
sed falsa ad caelum mittunt insomnia manes.
        Virgil, *Aeneid* VI, 893–6
[30] Anna soror, quae me suspensam insomnia terrent!
        Virgil, *Aeneid* IV, 9
[31] William Warburton, *The Divine Legation of Moses*, (London 1738–41), I, 182.
[32] For the prophecy granted to Latinus see Virgil, *Aeneid* VII, 79–101.
[33] tum senior Nautes, unum Tritonia Pallas
quem docuit multaque insignem reddidit arte
(haec responsa dabat, vel quae portenderet ira
magna deum vel quae fatorum posceret ordo)
        Virgil, *Aeneid* V, 704–7
[34] desine fata deum flecti sperare precando
        Virgil, *Aeneid* VI, 376

VIII

The Path to Daedalus

MICHAEL AYRTON

I DOUBT if any contributor to this volume can have come to the writings of Virgil by a more unlikely or a more circuitous route than mine, yet for ten years a single page from Book VI of the Aeneid has been central to my work in sculpture, painting, drawing and writing. All the major characters who participate in the myth of Daedalus and Icarus occur on that page and it is with them that I have been obsessively concerned since 1956.

I did not read the Aeneid until I was thirty-five and even now my Latin is so rudimentary that I cannot do so comfortably in the original. Furthermore, I must confess that I came to Virgil not through any classical education but through a grand opera by Hector Berlioz. It was his opera *Les Troyens* that first moved me to seek Virgil's Italy, and even then the motive for this quest lay dormant for nearly a decade before I found that I had already begun to pursue it.

I shall describe how I came to shape the concept with which I have been concerned for these ten years because, since I have no scholarship to contribute to the study of Latin literature and its influence in general, I can only record its particular influence on myself, however sporadic, peripheral and even accidental this may appear to have been. As for the specific influence of Virgil himself, I have the feeling that in contrast to his courteous treatment of Dante, he has not so much conducted me through my comedy as given me prods and thrusts from concealment, or come to me disguised by other arts; but then, of course, we do not speak the same language.

In 1947, Sir Thomas Beecham conducted, none too precisely,

two consecutive performances of *Les Troyens* in the BBC studios at Maida Vale. I heard both these performances and therefore heard for the first time the greatest of operas based on Virgil and a work which remains for me the greatest of all nineteenth century music drama. It is a work in two parts, each the length of a normal opera, *Le Prise de Troie* and *Les Troyens à Carthage* and Berlioz contrived his own libretto, adapting the relevant parts of the Aeneid to his purposes. What Virgil scholars would think of this adaptation I cannot judge, but there is no doubt of the passion and reverence in which Berlioz held Virgil. In the second chapter of his Memoirs he describes how, in construing the Aeneid with his father, he could hardly bring himself to stammer out the words *Quaesivit coelo lucem, ingemuitque reperta,* so overcome was he by the terrible vision of Dido's death. His father tactfully closed the book and the young Berlioz 'rushed away to vent (his) Virgilian grief in solitude'. This it seems was in 1810. He completed *Les Troyens* fifty-four years later and in the final entry of those same Memoirs, knowing in his heart perhaps that he would never live to hear his masterpiece properly performed in its entirety, he wrote, 'I must try to console myself . . . as I must console myself for not having known Virgil whom I should have loved so well.' The score of *Les Troyens* bears the votive inscription *Divo Virgilio* and it was Berlioz' votive which bought my entrance into Virgil's world, although curiously enough I still did not read Virgil. Nevertheless, I approached him, for Berlioz' music, so much less filled with romantic hyperbole than his autobiographical prose, is as Virgilian as certain aspects of the Italian landscape are Virgilian. Thus Berlioz' music ran in my head as I wandered for the first time through Italy in 1947.

My own votive, such as it is, cannot be said to be one made to Virgil. Ironically, I might say that my votive of 1956 to 1966 was prophetically described, in passing, by Virgil, a little less than two thousand years before I was aware of it, and he had set the scene when, in 1956, the acropolis of Cumae rose before my startled eyes and started me on my long pursuit of Daedalus.

The Soprintendenza of Naples, or some other official body, has raised in recent years some finely inscribed stone slabs upon the acropolis of Cumae and one, which caught my eye on that first day, quotes a number of these lines, between 9 and 44 from Book VI, which even I was able roughly to construe when I read them cut in

Latin on the stone. Laboriously I translated for myself how Daedalus came to land there and 'hallowed to Phoebus his slant-oar wings'. I read how he came to raise the great temple to Apollo and cast for it the golden doors which depicted the whole story of his sojourn at Knossos, his flight from the city, its cause and its tragedy.

As I sat gazing at the inscription and at the overgrown escarpment shining in the afternoon sun, a fragment of Michelangelo's verse came into my mind. It is a mysterious expostulation and reads: 'This is the way Daedalus rose. This is the way the sun rejects the shadow.' In that to me fateful moment, I was conscious of being possessed and the acropolis of Cumae with its 'hundred mouthways' cut to make audible the subterranean Sibyls mantic utterances, came to haunt me, as it has done ever since.

Between 1947, when I first heard *Les Troyens*, and 1956, when I began at Cumae to make my votive to Daedalus, many influences had come to bear on my life. I had, I felt, been waiting to approach the winding path towards the core of the myth which Virgil's thirty-six lines summarize. I have spent the subsequent ten years in following this labyrinthine track.

In 1947 I made, as I have said, an extended visit to Italy and in subsequent years returned there annually. In the first five of these years I visited only one of the Italies which lie in strata above the Italy of the Greeks where Daedalus landed. This Italy I then inhabited, was the Renaissance and in particular the period between 1400 and 1480 A.D.

Masaccio and Piero della Francesca became my gods, and for the sake of my crafts no less than to gratify an historical curiosity which is one of my greatest appetites, I read all I could acquire and made pilgrimage through the landscape to every relevant church and museum in Lombardy, Tuscany and Umbria. I became fascinated by the forerunners, by Giotto and by the sculpture of the Pisani. I read Plato to understand Marsilio Ficcino and Picc della Mirandola, and recall how in the Greater Hippias, Daedalus finds himself dismissed as outdated by Plato's connoisseurs, much as Vasari patronizes the past when he suggests that in the inevitable progress of the arts, the sixteenth century eclipsed the fifteenth. For myself, perhaps because my taste tends towards a certair archaic severity, I remained faithful to Masaccio and Piero and wa unseduced by the High Renaissance. And still I read no Virgil anc

178

was only remotely concerned with Greeks and Romans. I was them in Renaissance dress, *condottieri* by Mantegna riding out of Mantua, or enrolled to act out the Nativity on the pulpit of the Pisa Baptistery by Niccola Pisano. The Renaissance vision can be totally exclusive to an artist in his twenties, if he succumbs to it.

Gradually I worked my way down through the stratification. Medieval Italy followed the Renaissance, and then the Etruscans took me and held me for a year or more.

It so happens that for me a period is exclusive. I cannot enter the Italy of the Etruscans and yet remain in the Italy of Guelphs and Ghibellines. I cannot trot round and through the centuries in a morning like a tourist, but must move, as it were, through time and shut out the future of an age or its past where that is not clearly germane. Therefore, passing downwards through the strata, I arrived inevitably at the Greeks. I by-passed the Romans and I acknowledge that this eccentric progress, no less improbable perhaps than coming to Virgil by circling out of a nineteenth century grand opera, is probably the result of a lack of formal education. Nevertheless, it seems to me in retrospect that the particular qualities which moved, and still move me, most in painting and sculpture, could be called Virgilian, and perhaps this sympathy with Piero della Francesca's sublime geometry, Masaccio's majestic formality and no less Berlioz' inexhaustibly long melodic line, made my postponed encounter with Virgil the revelation it proved to be.

By 1956 I had reached Greek Italy. Leaving the Etruscans to their entombed picnics, I came to Paestum and finally to Cumae. And somehow pulled by Daedalus, fanciful though that may sound, I arrived at a confrontation with him below the rock upon the isthmus between the sea and the pallid lake, confirmed as to his presence by the carved inscription above the grotto.

The place flung a net over me. Places do. It is invariably a place, a landscape, a building, even a heap of stones marking the site of long habitation which starts in me the need to make the objects in bronze or paint, or even verse and prose, upon which my time is spent. The landscape at Cumae is numinous. It accepts every blemish and every indignity put upon it by twentieth century man. He has made a slum of its setting, but its power is not reduced by the railway lines, tumbledown beach houses and squalid bungalows he has caused to crowd about the isthmus.

At the point below the rock, where Daedalus landed, lies the mouth of the modern *cloacae* from which the sewage of Naples pours into the bay, and even this final 'mouth opening' in its loathsome irony does not diminish the splendour of the place. Perhaps the very fact that Cumae has not been preserved as a beauty spot but continues relentlessly inhabited by breeding, excreting, living and dying humanity contributes by contrast to its potency as a sacred place. The rock alone is protected as an archaeological zone and the rock is sculpture, a carving pierced and honeycombed within by the subterranean labyrinth of the Sibyl's habitation and set with the ruins of the temple to her bridegroom on its surface; a heap of stones marking the site of the long habitation of a god.

I came to Cumae in early summer twelve years ago, moving towards the Greeks. I drew and painted the place in that year (Pl. VII), recording it literally, knowing very little of its implications, knowing the Sibyl only as Michelangelo had shown her to me on the Sistine Chapel ceiling and knowing nothing of the personal significance the place would assume for me. Yet from the moment that I saw the rock in the distance, from the vineyard on Ponte di Procida where first I drew it on the eleventh of May, I knew that I had reached a moment and a place of the greatest importance to my own life.

I began to make sculpture in 1954 after fifteen years of practice as a painter. I did so because my drawings demanded that I make sculpture and because the sculpture of Giovanni Pisano insisted upon my doing so and I came to sculpture as I came to Cumae from the north. The northalpine artist is unavoidably Gothic and no matter how passionate his relationship with the Mediterranean world may become, it is ambivalent. Therefore I came late and uneasily to the Greeks. Furthermore, it is unconventional for a twentieth-century artist to find his sources either in the Greek world or in its renaissance in Italy. Both these periods in art history are beset with academic pitfalls, both represent the climax of an evolution towards 'naturalism' at odds with the most powerful and vital movements in twentieth century art and I, who am as much a child of my time as any, would have found life easier if my inspiration had sprung either from the art of my own time or from periods either earlier or more remote than the sixth century B.C. or the 'quatrocento'. Nevertheless, my allegiance to the Greeks and the Renaissance is also a little unorthodox in that it tends to find its ideals not in the 'high' achievements of these periods but in their 'archaic' phases. It is not the classicism of the age of Pericles nor the world of Raphael that most moves me, but an earlier stage in each development. Thus, what the nineteenth century found most to admire and the twentieth century most to condemn as 'academic' in the arts of the past, finds me differently orientated, for I am not a 'naturalist' even if I find the *Moscophoros* more important to me than African tribal sculpture.

I tend to seek in the art of the past as I tend to find in places long inhabited, a certain intensity, a double life relevant to its own period and to my own which centres upon the interpretation and extension of myth. I do not feel myth to be material for a poetic or aesthetic exercise to be played with as it came to be played with after the fifth century B.C. on the one hand, or during the late fifteenth century A.D. on the other. I must be seized with a belief in the validity of the myth in a sense comparable, however minimally, to Virgil's 'belief' in the myth contained in the Aeneid, or perhaps it would be more accurate to suggest that the reality of my belief is not totally dissimilar to the reality contained in myth for those who, before Herodotus, identified myth with history as being the 'Truth'. I am not being disingenuous when I write this. I am well aware of the distinction between history and myth and I am not advancing the sort of arguments advanced by fundamentalists as to the historical accuracy of the Book of Genesis; I am, however, saying that what I do is driven through me by a force of myth which is nothing to do with aesthetic or allegorical conceit. Therefore I did not choose to spend ten years of my life with Daedalus in order to polish and augment a dramatic fiction, rather I became, on May 11th, 1956, the dedicated chronicler of a myth, the bare bones of which were shown to me on the rock at Cumae, and all the reading of Greek and Latin literature in translation, of archaeology and anthropology and primitive technology, upon which I have spent some part of the subsequent decade, have contributed less to my realization of the fragments of this myth in bronze, paint, drawing, verse and prose than the landscape of Crete, Greece, Italy and Sicily, and in particular, such sacred places as Delos and Cumae.

This digression has been lengthy but is, I hope, meaningful, because it must serve to preface the chronicle of those ten years and also describe my slightly absurd conviction that I have been in receipt of some sort of revealed truth concerning a mythical, archetypal craftsman, his vainglorious son and a cast of subsidiary characters in the drama of their lives. I do not expect the proposition to carry much conviction among most sophisticated scholars, or any at all among art critics. It did, however, seem perfectly satisfactory to W. F. Jackson Knight, on the one occasion we met, for he cheerfully coupled himself with me, on the grounds that he was in frequent personal communication with Virgil, on a similar or even closer basis, for he had the added advantage of speaking Latin with the poet whose use of that language, he informed me, had become a little rusty.

Jackson Knight had the further advantage over me of possessing a profound scholarship and gave me the greatest encouragement by assuring me that work of his which I had not then read, on the labyrinth and on other relevant matters, bore out the accuracy of my imagery and of my first brief version of the narrative which I published in 1961 as *The Testament of Daedalus*. To him and to his writings, especially *The Cumaean Gate*, I owe much and perhaps it would not be out of place to say here that my contribution to this volume is intended in some degree as an inadequate tribute to his memory.

I am a narrative artist, which is an odd thing to be nowadays, when painting and sculpture is mainly concerned, not with narrative or subject matter but with the language—the syntax and vocabulary—of painting and sculpture itself. On the other hand, I am not simply an illustrator. Given a subject, I tend not only to pursue every available aspect of it but I also tend to extend the given narrative and enlarge upon it in what must seem to my audience and the spectators who contemplate my work in visual media, an effort of the imagination. It does not seem to me to work like that. It seems a more inevitable process, as if data were impressed upon me which I have no option but to record. Thus when I first became concerned with the flight of Daedalus and Icarus and Icarus' fall, I came to be informed of more about this event than the bare record of the death of this foolish boy which Ovid and others have set down. The whole ancient legend of Icarus could be written on a postcard. The bald reporting of Icarus' failure to obey his father is, and was to me, no more adequate than the average obituary one might read of a pilot killed in a crash and subsequently blamed by the Air Ministry for careless handling of his aircraft. I therefore found myself making images of what must really have happened if Icarus were to have approached the sun so nearly that his wings melted or burned, and what energy, what transformation of the human frame must have been required to make his epic climb possible. I also found myself seeking a different motive for this gigantic surge of power and what deliberate part Apollo played in the matter, for I was not convinced that the sun's heat at normal altitudes could explain the circumstance.

From any down-to-earth point of view this is fanciful, and I am also well aware of the anthropological explanations advanced for the sources of the legend, but then Icarus was not in a down-to-earth situation and nor perhaps am I. I evolved, or alternatively was given, another explanation which made Daedalus, Icarus and Apollo protagonists in a drama which involved the basic and inevitable misunderstanding between Daedalus the archetypal craftsman and Icarus, an archetypal hero with all the absurdity that posture inevitably creates. Apollo as a god, rather than as a concretion of burning matter, I found to be relating himself to Daedalus and Icarus as personally as the Greeks must originally have conceived him capable. Therefore Icarus' fault was *hubris* and his suicidal passion for the god was at once a sexual one, an heroic one and a gesture made against his father. Those are the bones of the narrative contained in my *Testament of Daedalus* and that conviction, fantasy or folly was the source of my imagery between 1959 and 1962.

Curiously enough, the little volume, when it was published and the images, when they were exhibited, whilst in no way elevating me in the public view to any great heights, passed into a general currency of myth to such an extent that I have frequently been criticized and sometimes praised for my portrayal of an ancient legend three-quarters of which did not exist before I wrote it down, painted it and cast it in bronze. I have found many people who honestly if thoughtlessly believed that it was Homer, or Virgil or Ovid or some other ancient author, who first recorded Icarus in contest with Apollo and that it was in antiquity that the tale of Icarus' lunatic attempt to do battle with the sun was first set down. And if such a comparison may be permitted, there are many people who honestly believe that the legend of Orpheus and

Eurydice, now familiar to us, was first recorded by the Greeks and not by Virgil. I find it amusing to contemplate that given a sufficient passage of time, my *Testament of Daedalus* may come to be read as a late and doubtless corrupt version, badly translated into English, of a lost Greek original. Such is the flexibility, inevitability and immortality of myth.

Before all this occurred and before the 'Testament of Daedalus' was written, before indeed I had been more than impregnated with the seed of the Erechtheids, I went to Greece itself. In 1958 I flew in the opposite direction from that taken by Daedalus and Icarus and arrived in Crete. The ostensible reason for this journey had no direct connection with Daedalus but was the result of my increasing concern with archaic sculpture and especially with bronze sculpture. I was hired to advise on the making of a film about Greece, or rather upon the specialized problem of how best to film sculpture and what sculpture should be selected for the purpose. The end product came to be a film called *Greek Sculpture* and it was my research into this subject which caused me to make a prolonged and continuing study of certain aspects of Greek technology, with special relevance to bronze casting. Again, it was this then separate concern which led me straight to Daedalus, as the archetypal bronzesmith and to Icarus whose waxen wings melted exactly as the 'lost wax' process of casting, which is the most ancient of bronze founding techniques, would have melted them had his wings been intended not to carry him to safety, but to be cast in bronze. This, of course, is the most rational explanation for the legend in that it is thought to be a poetic description of the movement of bronzesmiths from Crete towards Sardinia and the west in general in Minoan times.

One of the strangest by-products of my obsession with the Daedalus myth is that I have often pursued it all unknowing, and for all manner of seemingly disconnected reasons, only to become wise after the event. Thus, in 1959 and 1960 I made a series of reliefs in wax incorporating various natural forms such as seashells, driftwood and bones. One of these represented Icarus falling (Pl. XIII) and I had elected to use the dried spines of two fish I found on the beach at Metala, south of Phaestos, for his wings. Rather earlier, I had made two bronze heads of Talos, the bronze guardian of Crete, also incorporating animal bones into the model. It was not until two years later that I came upon a fragment of the Daedalus legend in which he is reported to have murdered his nephew Talos—another Talos—from jealousy, because, among other inventions, this Talos had found a fish spine on the shore and cast it in bronze, to make the first saw. From these myterious coincidences I received much pleasure and in some sort a feeling that my activity was ordained.

The use of bone forms in sculpture I owe in part to the example of Henry Moore, for if I was anyone's pupil in the art of sculpture, I was his, and owe as much to his encouragement and friendship as I owe to any living human being. For the rest, I have learned from long dead masters. Moore's use of bone differs from mine in that he uses it as a source of his paraphrase of the human figure, whilst I tend to us it metaphorically as a carapace and when, between 1962 and 1964, I became concerned with two other members of the cast of the Daedalus drama, Deiphobe and the Minotaur, bone forms served as part of an image of the Sibyl (Pl. XI) and as the armature of a double image called 'The Minotaur Revealed' (Pl. XII), in which Asterion rises out of the actual skull of a bull cast in bronze.

My involvement with the Minotaur began for me the gradual process of evolving from a particular identification with the legend into a more generalized use of images from the myth as demonstrating my own and the human condition. The process of identification with the subject of one's own work is not easy to describe. It takes place at different coexistent levels. Icarus is remote from me. I have no heroic vein in my nature and can only regard him with wonder and a certain lack of sympathy. The Minotaur is a part of me, as Daedalus is part of me, albeit a different part. Therefore since 1963 the legend has become at once more personal to me and a more general comment on the human condition. Icarus fell and perished, so far as my images are concerned, in 1961. The Minotaur dominated my work during 1962 and 1963, together with an oracular female figure who moves between Delphi and Cumae, being both the Pythia and Deiphobe, both Apollo's brides but also being an aspect of my own relationship with women.

I can best illustrate what I mean by two excerpts from my second book, *The Maze Maker*, for which the 'Testament of Daedalus' must now be regarded as a sketch, a preliminary study for one part of the larger work. *The Maze Maker* is an auto-

N

biography of Daedalus, which has been published as a novel, although I do not myself find that description accurate. The second section of this book is set under the acropolis of Cumae. There, trapped in the rock itself by Apollo, Daedalus seeks the materials and assembles the parts of the temple Virgil describes and here too he models and casts the bronze doors which portray his visual autobiography.

Below the rock of Cumae, deep in the labyrinth of passages in the earth personified as Gaia, Daedalus finds the Minotaur transposed from his own man-made labyrinth at Knossos. The living movement which is perpetual within Gaia's mighty trunk accounts for this transposition, just as the various transpositions of the omphalos are caused by her shifting navel as she breathes. Then too, to me, the Minotaur is immortal and was never killed by the braggart and faithless Theseus. I quote here from the chapter in which Daedalus encounters Asterion long after the flight from Crete.

In the depths below the Foundry Cave, I heard the roaring of a bull. Perhaps Cephalon had guided me to the place: perhaps I had wandered there, brooding on the matrix, on the remodelling of the clay figures of those I had known. I was in some part of the earth I had not seen before. The walls of the passage seemed hand-hewn. They looked familiar. They looked like the walls of the labyrinth of Minos. Yet how could they be? The red thread in my hand pulled tight, like a fishing line taken by a shark.

I was aware of horns but not of who it was who wore them. Minos in his ritual bull-mask rose in my mind, then Zeus, Poseidon, Dionysos, all those gods who assume the bull in violent epiphany, and I was afraid. I knew the place. It lay below the palace of Minos, yet I was not in Crete. I was afraid. I sensed Talos in his bull guise, but it was not Talos. I was near the Minotaur. It could only be the Minotaur. I unwound the red thread further and went towards the sound of the bull despite myself. Cephalon urged me on. I spoke aloud, I think. I said, 'He cannot be here, he is in Crete . . . he cannot be here.' I still could not see him.

The Minotaur did not speak and yet he spoke, he did not think and yet I heard his thought through Cephalon, for this displaced narrator spoke from within the slack trunk or from the horn-heavy skull of this bull-masked thing and yet remained outside him. He spoke in my mind and yet I do not think he inhabited me except when he chose and then he squatted with the ant in my brain and both teased me.

THE PATH TO DAEDALUS

The Minotaur cannot think clearly. He does not know where he is or why. Without Cephalon he would be mute in his anger and misery and Cephalon can couch as easily in his bowels as in my mind. Cephalon is unusually gifted, sharp and cruel. He permits no peace to his involuntary hosts and could be named in a sense the very spirit of the labyrinth, for whether he moves among the intricacies of my cerebral cortex or walks inwards from the anus of the Minotaur he yet wanders in a maze no less entangling than that of Gaia, which I involuntarily inhabited.

Superior to humans and animals Cephalon may think himself, but the poor disembodied thing treads the same path as the rest of us. A small parasite armed with a needle, he is lost in the involuted confusion of a situation which frequently muffles his voice. Cephalon, for all his powers, is uneasily aware that he in turn may be inhabited by some being, even more impalpable than he is, who lies in his invisible gut.

On my behalf he went into the Minotaur as interpreter and thought for the half-bull to express him to me in gusts blown out of the windy and pulsing belly of his unhappy host.

You will know from common talk the general appearance of the Minotaur, this half-man, half-bull, this demigod sprung from the seed of Poseidon in bull form, when that earth-shaking god took Pasiphaë on Crete. His body is part human yet he begins as bull at the loins and he bears a hump of sinews upon his shoulders which carries the great horned skull and the cattle-brute mask of his head. His belly however is human and into this Cephalon, at once contemptuous and alarmed, for a sufficient breaking of wind would catapult him downwards, had burrowed.

The Minotaur moved restlessly and I heard his hoof scrape on the rock floor of his byre. This fissure in the rock, his sanctuary, was scarcely larger than its inmate, a cone-shaped fault set back from a cavern. It was one of many that opened suddenly from the narrow passages of the maze and he, I suppose, had chosen it for stable and found some special comfort there. The cavern itself was circular, like an arena and its circumference was crowded with the great boulders of past rockfalls.

I heard his hoof scrape on the floor and a rough abrasive sound as he rubbed his hide against the wall. I heard the click of horn against stone, an abrupt snort, a whistling breath. These, the sounds of the Minotaur, were ominous because they were such normal cattle sounds. They came to me in the same instant as his alarm. His uncertainty naturally coincided with his instinct to stir. His private darkness, hung like a ragged curtain before his brain, was lit with a quick unease and this caused him, so far as he was able, to think.

187

I felt his fears jolt him and his response was to gather the great mass of muscle on his crest. It was instinct, but perhaps something more.

I stood still in the entrance to the arena, remembering the bull-game and poised to avoid injury. I have watched it many times and marvelled at the spectacle of young men and women with no better way to spend their time than in courting danger. I myself take no such unnecessary risks for sport, or glory, or whatever these rituals involve.

The Minotaur moved suddenly into the light.

You, who have a certain aesthetic interest in him, perhaps because you have seen his picture, will know approximately how he looks. You will not know the details of his structure and should you encounter him, it would be best to know the particular advantages and disadvantages his hybrid shape gives him. He is no taller than a man and his legs are light and sinewy. He is very fast over a short distance, but the weight of his crest and skull are such that his balance is very uncertain. His shoulders are enormously thick and he has hands which can crush stones in their grip. In contest with him it is well to remember that although much of him is bull, his hands and arms are those of a man of superhuman strength. His chest too is deep and he is not quickly winded. He can throw a fully armoured warrior twenty feet with a single toss of his head and his horns will penetrate three inches of seasoned wood.

There are however two flaws in his design which can defeat him because he is neither bull nor man. One is the setting of his eyes in the great shield of bone he wears for forehead. His eyes are set obliquely in his malformed skull. He cannot focus both at once upon an object immediately in front of him. He cannot look straight ahead, but must turn his huge mask and glance sideways at his objective; therefore he hooks to right or left depending upon which eye has his target in vision. Secondly, he is uncertain how to attack and this confusion is central to his condition and gives an opponent the advantage.

A bull is equipped perfectly to fight as a bull and a man may be adept in battle between men, although I am not such a man, but the Minotaur is marvellously made to kill in either capacity except that he cannot decide which. His instincts are double and in perpetual conflict. If he grasps his enemy in his arms he can break him like a twig or tear him apart, but he cannot bring his horns into play and if he seeks to gore his victim his arms and hands are of no use to him. He is not humanly intelligent, but he is also less simple than his animal nature, so that his reflexes are not so certain as a bull's. He is capable of enough thought to frustrate his impulses. His urge to murder is not a lust but his response to the uncertainty by which, so far as his slow brain permits, he is tormented. To understand him is, with luck, to defeat him and I, who am neither athlete nor warrior, did so either because I made quick deductions or because I had entered his mind. I am not sure which.

I stood very still and watched him hunched uncertainly in the entrance to his hide. I saw his crest twitch and his muzzle wrinkle. His spatulate nostrils opened and closed and he blew a spume of saliva which hung in a slender skein from his lolling tongue. Unlike a bull, he bared his teeth. His head swung heavily to right and left and, ox-like, he seemed to look backwards out of the side of each great slab of cheek in turn.

As his spittle dropped I knew his thought to spatter and drip with it. Menaces took shape for him and vanished among the landscape of stains upon the walls of his prison as each eye registered and rolled. To him every crack in the uneven rock face however shallow could become large enough in an instant to hold a potential danger. These shifted and melted into one another under each dull glance. Nothing was secure.

He opened and closed the squat, stub fingers of each hand, opposing the thumb, aware of this approximation to a human gesture. Suddenly he spun round on his heels and, off balance, struck one horn against the wall with a sharp sound like the crack of splitting timber. Shale came away and slid rattling to the floor. He twisted back, moved forward crouching, his head weaving and a little raised so that I saw, swaying and sagging, the great folds of hide which rose from his chest to join his under jaw. He bellowed and the sound was full of doubt and the will to overcome it. Still he had not seen me.

Splay-legged, he moved forward again with the waddling motion of a toad, stopped, spun, fell to his knees groping with both hands, seeming to plead for sight of his enemy. He came springing to his feet like a wrestler and suddenly saw me in his right eye. His head dropped and his shoulders and crest rose. His arms went back and I knew on the instant that he would attack in bull form, favouring the right horn, turn, if he missed his charge, and bring his hands into play on the turn. He came at me fast and I threw myself to his left. His momentum carried him on and when he turned, reaching out, he was ten yards away. He came at me again but uncertainly, trying to be bull and man at once, searching for a hold. I ran straight at him and twisting as I ran, I passed to his right, leaving him stock-still. This unexpected manoeuvre left him rooted and he lost me. I was behind him. He picked up a stone the size of his own head and crumbled it to powder between his hands. He screamed, raised both his arms and gripped his horns, wrenching and pulling at them. Such was the enormous power of his shoul-

ders that it seemed for a moment that he would tear himself in half. He screamed again, lost his footing and fell rolling and jerking. His mouth sprayed foam, his trunk struck the stony floor, thundering against it like a drum. He made a grotesque leap, stood swaying, fell again and remained heaped where he had fallen in a sudden quiet. He had forgotten me.

Step by step I edged back into the comparative safety of the boulders, leaving him at the centre of his bull pen, a mound of sullen muscle and leaden bone. Those few seconds were the extent of the contest and I was in great fear, but that was all there was.

He was the colour of weathered bronze and in the sudden detachment of my relief, I saw him as beautiful in his majestic absurdity. I saw him indomitable and ridiculous in all the grandeur and all the fragility of useless physical strength. Icarus, in his foolishness, had once believed himself half-brother to the Minotaur and believed me the father of both. In that moment I felt I could have been and in that moment I heard the Minotaur begin to weep.

I should perhaps explain the Cephalon is a transposed narrator, an ant lodged in the brain of Daedalus, who acts partly as an alter-ego, partly as an ironic imposition of Apollo's, a symbol of Apollo's, view of Icarus when he flew at the god-head. The ant and his myrmidons play a considerable part in erecting the temple on the rock. I regret, however, that for a lengthier explanation of this curious phenomenon, the reader of this essay must read my whole book.

To understand my intention in setting Daedalus beneath the Cumaean rock for so long a period of time, it is only necessary to recognize the practical problem he had been set, if Virgil is to be believed. Quite apart from the founding of the bronze doors, the temple Virgil describes is a great one—and inevitably a major architectural undertaking even for a man as abundantly skilled as Daedalus. He was called upon to build it in a *terra incognita* utterly remote from the civilized world of Crete and he achieves it, in my narrative, with the help of a troglodite community comparable to the Idaean Dactyls, or the Cyclopes of Etna, a race of metal miners and workers whose lives are spent underground. Daedalus cannot leave the rock until his task is completed. He must live where metals can be mined, ceramics fired, bronze cast and stone quarried. Inevitably, therefore, he meets the Sibyl in her deep sanctuary. This then for me is Deiphobe:

Suddenly in a great rush of wind the door flashed open. The clangour it made was repeated. Other doors, door after door it seemed, opened almost in unison with it, and each crashed back with a brazen shout. The wind that rushed past me from the open door was filled with smoke and sound. When it had passed, the silence was as hard as the bronze door itself. Either that or I was so deafened I could hear nothing.

The chamber beyond the door was not large and its walls were as smooth and faultless as the door had been. It was a room shaped like a cauldron and furnished solely with a hearth, a pitted boulder identical with that which I had imagined I had seen after my contest with the Minotaur, and a bronze tripod-cauldron so shallow as to form a stool. The stone duplicated that upon which the horned god had sat. Upon the tripod sat a woman. She was naked and she held in her right hand a branch of laurel. Smoke from the hearth gushed about her. The light was thick as if it were being filtered through the cast skin of a snake.

The woman did not speak, she changed. She passed through a series of transformations not in any sequence but capriciously as if to demonstrate her variety, so that she bloomed, withered, extended and contracted, rose and subsided, died, disintegrated and took shape again, a curled foetus in a placenta of smoke. Her age passed before me, not logically from youth to senility, but abruptly, in disorder. Her presence seemed to flicker in a broken rhythm. She was a child, huge eyed and slender, a kore with tip-tilted breasts, a woman full of the child kicking in her belly, a matron ripe as autumn, a child again, clutching bay shoots sticky in her hand, a crone twisted and wizened as a dead shrub and again a maiden. Fragments of her persona were shown to me falling as wayward as leaves so that I could not see her whole, nor did she cease to alter.

The woman turned to bronze, each limb flattened and pulled to marry with her tripod. She shaped herself to a fetish, lost her humanity and became an implacable idol. Her features slipped from her face and she was visored. Her arms clove to her and joined into her sides. She became a snake and reared coiling from the bowl of the tripod.

Then again her hands sprang out from her and became a girl's, her arms lifted like greenstick twigs, Daphne athwart the sun, and this metamor-phosis opened to permit the woman to re-emerge from the laurel. She withered so that her skin was rough as bark and wrinkled as dried fruit. She filled with sap and opened her thighs to the smoke licking her belly. She closed them and became again as legless as a serpent. Her disorder was dazzling. If she had gone through a gamut of changes which had any ordered ritual to explain it, I think I should have grasped the meaning, but there was none. Her disintegration and re-integration were totally hap-hazard and continued until I could no longer watch them and hid my head in my hands.

When I looked again the tripod was empty and across it lay the branch of laurel. Standing by the hearth was a middle-aged woman, perhaps more than middle-aged, perhaps elderly. It was difficult to tell her age. She was as ordinary, as utterly unmemorable as a cow in a herd. Furthermore, she was dressed with dowdy modesty and her hair straggled as if she had lacked a mirror to dress it by. This dull housewife addressed me quietly by name. It did not strike me as strange that she knew my name, for she appeared familiar. I felt embarrassed that her name escaped me, but then I am sufficiently celebrated to be known by name to many whom I do not know personally.

I did not identify this unassuming person with the frantic figure on the tripod, indeed I looked anxiously around for fear of some new manifestation.

'You are Daedalus the Athenian, son of Metion of the Erechtheid house,' said the middle-aged woman.

'I am.'

'I know why you are here.'

I asked her who she was and added that I felt we were known to one another, begging her forgiveness for my discourtesy in forgetting her name.

'My name is Deiphobe, daughter of Glaukos.'

This too surprised me; I had grown used to the avoidance of names in this nether world.

'Do you live here?' I asked stupidly.

'I have lived here longer than I can bear.'

'I too look forward to completing my task and seeing the sun again.'

'You will see him sooner than that.'

'You speak as if you know my future.'

'At times I know what will happen.'

'You are an oracle then?'

It embarrasses me even now to think of the foolishness of my part in this conversation. I could not believe that I was in the presence of anyone in the least supernormal and I continually glanced about the cavern seeking the terrible creature I had seen a few moments before and with whom I knew my business lay. I imagined my new acquaintance to be her servant.

She did not reply to me, but smiled. When she smiled I saw at once how beautiful she had been, and again she looked to me familiar. Unsmiling, she looked like a cow and suddenly this train of thought led me to the connection. She resembled Pasiphaë.

PLATE VII
DAEDALUS WINGMAKER
Bronze 1960. (*M. Maurice Druon. Paris*)

above PLATE VIII
THE ACROPOLIS AT CUMAE
Black ink wash drawing. 1956. (*Mr. Hollis S. Baker. Jr.*)
Grand Rapids USA

below PLATE IX
CUMAEAN SECTION
Acrylic Painting. 1965. (*Mr. Leopold de Rothschild. London*)

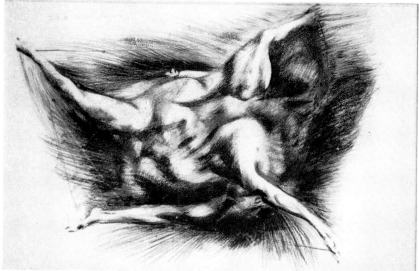

above PLATE X
ICARUS IN FLIGHT
Painted stucco relief 1960. (*The Arts Council of Gt. Britain London*)
below PLATE XI
ICARUS PINWHEEL
Charcoal drawing 1960. (*The Artist*)

Plate XII
ICARUS FALLS
Wax and bone relief 1959. (*Gavin Maxwell, Esq. Scotland*)

PLATE XIII
TALOS, Head
Bronze 1957. (*Nigel Balchin Esq. London*)

PLATE XIV
ORACLE WITH LAUREL LEAVES
Ink wash drawing 1965. (*Dr. Anthony Storr London*)

PLATE XV
ORACLE I
Bronze 1962–63. (*Abe Gottlieb, New York*)

PLATE XVI
MAZED MINOTAUR
Charcoal collage drawing 1961. (*John Wozny Esq. Alberta, Canada*)

PLATE XVII
CROUCHED MINOTAUR
Bronze 1963 (*The Artist*)

PLATE XVIII
MAZE MAKER I.
Acrylic & Collage 1965. (*The Artist*)

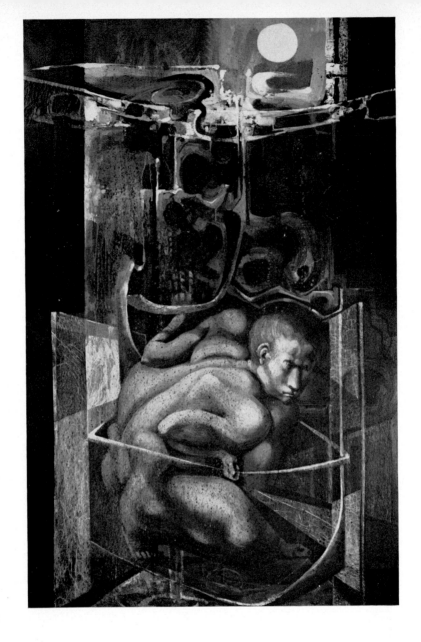

PLATE XX
MAZE MAKER II
Acrylic & Collage painting 1966. (*The Artist*)

'*Pasiphaë.*'

She smiled again and the cow she looked like, unsmiling now, became that most delicate of heifers, Ariadne.

She turned her back on me and that which is bull even in Daedalus rose for her.

'*I am not Pasiphaë,*' *she said,* '*nor are you the Earth Shaker. If you came from the sea it was not as a bull but as a bird.*' *She laughed, walking away, and when she turned to sign me to a seat by the hearth she was once more a housewife whose hair escaped its fillet and straggled about her head. I followed her into the centre of the chamber and crouched near her by the hearth.*

'*Who are you?*' *I asked, again stupidly, but I was much confused.*

'*My father was Glaukos son of Minos and of Pasiphaë. He pursued a mouse when he was a child and, in doing so, fell into a pithos filled with honey. There he drowned. Apollo restored him to life by means of an oracle so that, surviving, he sired me. My own life therefore is Apollo's.*'

'*Then you are Pasiphaë's granddaughter.*' *This, to me, new-minted, genealogy left me baffled. Here was a woman clearly older than Pasiphaë, who had lived here a long time, or so she inferred. Either she was mad or I had misheard her.*

'*How can this be?*' *I asked her.*

'*You yourself have said that time is a liquid,*' *she replied.* '*How do you know when these things took place or even if they have yet taken place, for how do you know which way up you float?*'

She must have been mocking me.

'*Pasiphaë as I knew her was not old and she was beautiful,*' *I said.*

'*Pasiphaë is all manner of women, all phases of the moon are Pasiphaë and she is much distributed about. In Laconia she is already an ancient oracle and near Menina, where she inhabits a shrine, she is a girl. It is a family name and you know how confused Greeks become about family names.* "*Giver of light*", *as I am sure you know, is the family name.*'

'*The most improbable people are called that.*'

'*You mean the Minotaur? What would you expect? He is a member of the family.*'

I found myself floundering in this catalogue, not so much because of the names but because the time span made no sense. Deiphobe was clearly speaking the symbolic language of priests who contrive to make proper names flicker backwards and forwards in time and everyone can be shown to be someone else. I have never been able to make out the age of sacred persons at any specific moment.

I thought suddenly of the Pasiphaë I had known to my cost. She was indeed like the moon and as remote.

'*The moon is at once old and a young woman,*' *said Deiphobe, cutting through my thought,* '*and as for me, although I have lived here so long, do I look so old?*'

She did not. She looked middle-aged and I assured her at once that she looked young.

'*I was first mounted in the year the Bull calved.*'

I cannot work out this sort of thing. I began again.

'*I came to ask . . .*'

'*I know why you have come.*'

'*Then will she, do you think, speak to the earth for me? I come at the sun's instigation.*'

'*I am she who will speak.*'

I stared at her.

'*You should know,*' *she said,* '*who I am, and I shall tell you first what I am, for when I come to speak to the goddess from the god, I shall not be as you see me now, nor shall I know you.*'

I was silent.

'*I shall even tell you about the mouse,*' *she said and smiled her sweet cow's smile so that I, who had had no woman for so long, looked away for fear she would see me roused.*

'*You know well that Minos is the name of a line of kings each one called Minos and each Minos is the bull-god on earth who represents the sun. Who therefore is Minos? I am the granddaughter of Minos. Pasiphaë is his queen and represents the moon. Who therefore in all that line of queens is my grandmother?*'

'*I have no notion,*' *I said with some irritation. I hate conundrums.*

Deiphobe smiled at me again.

'*In order to know who I am you must accept that everything is duplicated, everything elides, everything has its reverse, nothing is clear cut.*'

I said nothing. Deiphobe touched the great pitted boulder in the centre of her cavern.

'*This stone, the omphalos, is the earth's navel, yet the navel of the world is at Delphi. This stone you saw elsewhere when you contested with the Minotaur, yet it is here. There is also an omphalos at Eleusis. Does it surprise you that so multitudinous a being as Gaia should sport a clutch of navels, all of them at the centre of the world? Each one is joined to her centre, since she is a sphere, and each has its cord spun out to join the belly of one of her children. Each is also a pillar which props the sky.*'

I said nothing. My own navel is concave. I pushed my forefinger into it through my tunic.

'I too am more than one. Here I am Deiphobe, at Delphi, Pythia, who once was male Pytho and female Delphyne, two serpents coiled about the navel stone. Your snake, Erechtheid, is a relative of mine.'

At this moment there sprang up beneath the tripod two green snakes closely interwrapped. Tightly coiled, they rose out of the earth until their heads touched the cauldron base which they then cradled with their necks. They were so green they looked vegetable, aping the quick tendrils of the vine. And there they remained motionless.

'As this tripod is supported, so the omphalos supports the sky, and when Apollo couches in the tripod he remains in the sky. I, his woman, am straddled open to him here in the earth and yet he never leaves his ordained circling of the world. He wears me round his sex as you wear your serpent emblem round your wrist.'

'You are of the earth?' *I asked, to gain time, for I am slow to digest this kind of information.*

'I am also Themis. Apollo breeds heat through me to fertilize my mother.'

Laden with paradox piled on improbability, I felt like an overburdened mule.

'Patience,' *said Deiphobe, variously called Pythia and Themis.*

'Are you mortal?' *I asked lamely.*

'To be that would be my release. Then I could die.'

She said this with such a weariness that I was moved to touch her hand. It burned me. When I looked later at my fingers they were blistered, although I did not feel any pain at the time.

'Gaia is very old and as she ages she grows cold. Apollo's fire passes through me to warm her. My menstrual blood is oil and feeds her dying fires. My pregnancy is earth's. What I conceive she bears.'

However complicated Deiphobe's relationships might be with the divinities, her power was not in question. She was the one person who could intercede for me with Gaia on Apollo's behalf and enable me to release the earthbound tools of my trade from Gaia's pull. Without Deiphobe, Apollo would get no temple and I should be buried in the Mother all my life. I tried to relax.

'I shall tell you the rest,' *said Deiphobe,* 'for I seldom find anyone to talk to. Those who visit me, and they are rare enough, want only my oracles, but heat is your medium too and your use of it, although so different from mine, has its value. We are in sympathy, I think.'

195

I was much flattered by this remark. Praise is never unwelcome to a craftsman and one is pleased to be accepted by immortals.

'See how my room is furnished. This hearth is cleft and from it runs a channel to Gaia's centre below the omphalos. Into this cleft I flow. This tripod and its cauldron are my marriage bed. Here the god takes me and when he does I speak, if I do speak, not as I speak now but in orgasm. What I say then I do not know, for it is not my voice but Apollo's and I am charged with his divinity. His semen jets through me and his ejaculation makes me cry to his rhythm. In this cauldron my apotheosis manifests. In its boiling bowl my flesh is consumed and flows downwards. In the steam lies whatever prophecy may be found and when that steam condenses into words you will learn what you already know and be confirmed in it. The condensation takes a little time. All will be over before you hear words.'

I could not see how I could tell her that prophecy was not what I had come for. Prophecy as to one's personal future is hard to resist, but my primary need was not reassurance as to my future career but rather an intercession of a practical nature which would permit me to enjoy a future career of any sort. I changed the subject as politely as I could.

'What,' I asked, 'is your reward for these terrible labours?'

'My reward will be mortality.'

'Death.'

'Death.'

'Why?'

She laughed at me.

'When will that be? I mean, how long must you suffer?'

'You misunderstand. I am a woman, immortal, but a woman. The penetration of the god is an ecstasy no mortal knows and in its train it carries an exhaustion no woman ever knew. I am tired with eons of bearing the brunt of the randy sun, tired beyond death and now want only death.'

'Will you be granted death?'

'I pray for it and I believe a time will come when I shall be given it.'

She fell silent and I too could think of nothing more to ask. This woman who looked so ordinary in her drab chiton, who seemed newly risen from bending over cooking pots and pushed her hair back from her damp forehead with so familiar a gesture, was herself continually cooked and on such a fire that molten metal would dissolve in steam at its lightest touch.

In the silence my thoughts wandered to practical matters. I began covertly to examine the tripod and cauldron in which this blaze of coupling took place. The melting point of any alloy known to me could be achieved in any furnace capable of containing a reducing rather than an oxidising heat. Normal cooking took place on fires so mild they could not even bake clay adequately. Any metal cauldron would naturally be undamaged by normal fires. But given bellows and a tightly enclosed kiln, such heat could be generated as to melt and fuse rocks, for ores are parts of rock in one sense. The tripod and cauldron looked normal enough bronze to me. I was intrigued and puzzled.

'You are a man so absurdly practical,' said Deiphobe, 'that even in the presence of divine mysteries you can only mind your own business. Now you would like to know why the tripod can withstand the heat of Apollo's orgasm?'

I nodded. Really there was so easy a communion with her that I had no need to speak at all.

'Your friend the Greek Speaker, as you call him, has described to you how the four forces act and how each particle of matter is a sum of dancers joined in a dance around a centre. All things are thus particular and each visible thing is a concordance of dances.

'Metals you know are fused in a liquid dance in the furnace, yet when they cool and harden those invisible particles dance still. Only their measure is altered. Conceive then how a god, by choosing a different chain of steps can so change the structure of any creation as to make its dance as impervious to heat or cold as to time. Even Gaia herself, with all her crushing pull, could not crumple up those slender tripod legs nor dent the cauldron and when the sun himself sits in the bowl it does not even glow with his heat.'

'And you, spread beneath him?'

'I too am made in a different measure and when I come to die that measure will change its pace and I shall be consumed utterly. I shall no longer know the music of the round but go into a quiet. Only my voice will stay here, only my voice.'

I did not question this.

I began to feel a warmth, a choking warmth envelop me and the sweat started from me. I looked up from where I was crouched by the hearth and saw Deiphobe rise. She seemed taller and to be growing before my eyes. Her own eyes were wide open and glazed.

'Go now,' she said, 'and wait beyond the door.'

I knelt before her and then got to my feet. The walls of her room were wet. No longer at rest they were contracting, moving like gripping flesh towards the tripod. The cleft in the hearth opened and the pitted stone swelled, turning red.

I backed towards the door and saw for the first time that there were other doors, uncountable doors all opening in the flesh of the chamber.

The lights changed. Golden, yellow as midday, it increased and heat blazed through the ceiling of the place.

At the door, at one of the doors, I looked back. The twin snakes uncurling from below the cauldron had twined about Deiphobe's arms and legs. Lifting her, they spread her in the cauldron bowl, her thighs extended, and she was naked and beautiful. Her mouth opened and her head fell back as the door closed, cutting me off from her, and I was outside. I stood sweating, facing the shining surface of the great bronze door which had closed so silently that I had not known it had moved. From behind it a sound rose, cry after cry, each one greater than the last and added to these cries was a sharp but vast breathing like the panting rush of air one never hears but somehow expects to hear in the moment before a great storm breaks. It was as if a mighty silence was shaken behind sound.

I do not know how long it lasted, this coupling, but the earth rose and shook and threw me from wall to wall of the passage. I could see nothing but whiteness and as the sound went beyond human hearing I could hear nothing but the beating of my own blood behind my eyes. I clung to the ground, trying to hold myself down on the heaving floor and I felt blackness swimming up through the white sheeting my senses. Then the doors crashed open, not in unison but in rapid and uneven sequence like a rockfall spraying boulders, a broken clattering of dented gongs, and I looked up.

In the basin of the cauldron there was no woman. There was a brazen, extended throat rising from a drum which had become part of the tripod cauldron. It was an entity, boneless as a snake but rigid as metal standing upright on tripod tangs. This image, topped by a head as featureless as an axeblade, spoke in words condensed from scalding steam. Each word came sybillant. The pythoness was whispering. Then her speech thickened and the words stuck mollusc in the mass of sound. Words came from her that rang, others that fell plummeting like stones, and through it all the serpent hissing breathed through the sense.

I do not to this day know exactly what she meant, for I think she spoke of my future in your time and of another coming of Icarus and of great peril to man, but I do not know this for certain. What she meant I must leave to you, but this is what she said:

> '*My speech is split, suck at my thistle speech*
> *My spittle swells to sweeten surety*
> *See where my mouth is eyed and sees in smoke*
> *Your summit sky in sallow solstice sleep.*

Wax in that summit sky burns out to bronze
This wax, your waxing lost, you are not lost
But molten propagate the eagle's clutch
In bronze out-bronzed blatant to blot out blood.

Know that the fish shall fully hatch the hawk,
Who in the egg fed on the ram's rod yolk,
In water springs the pinions to take wing,
And wingless wheels above the crawling gull.

At such a time your son is multiplied
And burning, bristles at his burning god.
The fish sign's season sinks into the dark
And he who carries water carries light.'

Oracles make it their business to be obscure, or else they cannot help it.
In any case, it would have been stranger still if the strange configuration of
humanity, divinity, metal and serpent, which I saw in that brief span
while the door stood open, had said anything readily comprehensible. If, in
her voice, the god spoke through her, then it is even less surprising that I did
not understand what was meant. There was no priest there to interpret for
me. There was no one there but Deiphobe daughter of Glaukos, who was
the granddaughter of one Pasiphaë or another and who was also Themis,
Pythia and the mistress of the god. The door now shut upon her with such
finality that I knew I should not see her again.

The Maze Maker's narrative ends in Sicily at the point where
Daedalus is about to make his last journey, which will take him to
Sardinia. Diodorus Siculus leaves him there and it was from there
that the Shardana—if they can be identified with the Sardinians—
went with other 'Sea Peoples' to confront the Pharaoh Meremptah.

In Sardinia they built stone fortresses and began to work in
bronze sometime before 1200 B.C. and who could have taught
them these techniques but Daedalus?

Where my narrative ends Daedalus speaks:

'I have called myself Maze Maker with a certain irony because although I
believe myself pre-eminent in many crafts, I have been, as Minos described
me, first and last a maker of labyrinths. I have made them as simple as a
dancing-floor for partridges and as complex as the deep tomb for Minos
which was also a prison for the Minotaur. I have inhabited labyrinths I did
not make, of which one was the sky, Apollo's web, which I penetrated and

from which I escaped, but which drew Icarus into its blazing heart to destroy him. Into another I was driven and that was the earth maze of Gaia where she confined me until I could placate the sky-god. Then there was the fortress maze I built at Kamikos to exclude Tauros and within that bastion another maze to frustrate those who might come to rob his grave. Nor am I finished, for I shall build one more and that will be my last. It will be in Sardinia and there I shall dig a twisting path back into Gaia so that the sun will no longer persecute me, for he will have no further cause.

All this long burrowing and building, to protect or to imprison, this flight through the sky and tunnelling in the earth, seems to me now to add up to no more than the parts of a single great maze which is my life. This maze for the Maze Maker I made from experience and from circumstance. Its shape identifies me. It has been my gaol and my sanctuary, my journey and its destination. In it I have lived continually, ceaselessly enlarging it and turning it to and fro from ambition, hope and fear. Toy, trial and torment, the topology of my labyrinth remains ambiguous. Its materials are at once dense, impenetrable, translucent and illusory. Such a total maze each man makes round himself and each is different from every other, for each contains the length, breadth, height and depth of his own life.

I, Daedalus, maze maker, shall take this that I have written with me to Sardinia and dedicate it at the entrance to the maze which leads to death. Then you, before you follow me down into Gaia, who is the Mother, will know what is to be known of my journey and the fate of my son, Icarus. Before you follow me, look into the sky-maze and acknowledge Apollo who is the god.

The book from which I have quoted at such length, I wrote between 1964 and 1966. It was published in 1967. During those two years my work in sculpture and painting has centred on a series of images called Maze Maker, all of them variations on the theme implied in this last speech of Daedalus, all of them show a man in one kind of maze or another and they seem to me to express in metaphor my view of the human condition and of my own life (Pls. XVI–XVII).

If then, in all the foregoing I have contrived to show the influence of Virgil on my life and work, it must be clear that it is not the master's verse, nor any aspect of his style which has compelled me, but rather a sense of his presence at my elbow as if, like some diminutive Dante, I have been led by him into the rock at Cumae and through the labyrinth of Gaia.

It would be idle for me to pretend that the beauty of Virgil's verse is something I can truly appreciate. What I am concerned with is neither an aesthetic nor a scholarly view of his achievement. He has influenced me simply because, at the level from which my own art stems, such as it is, what the man said is true.

Index of Names

I

Ibsen, Henrik Johan, 168, 175
Icarus, 162 f., 176, 182–5, 190,
198, 200, 202
Idaean Dactyls, 190
Idas, 52
Ilioneus, 51
Ilium, 44 f.
Iopas, 46
Isai (= Jesse), 98
Ischia, 147
Isidore of Seville, 99
Israel, 107, 117
Italicus, [see Silius]
Italy (-ian), 9, 18, 29, 38 f., 41,
75–8, 82 f., 90, 116, 123, 129,
135, 139–42, 144, 146 ff., 155 f,
173, 176–81
Ithaca, 30, 32
Iulus, 153 f.
Ixion, 168

J

James, Henry, 154
Janiculum, 151
Jason, 30, 34 f., 52, 57, 66, 72,
78, 85 f., 88, 93
Jesse (Isai), 98
Jesus, 100
John (son of Emp. Henry VII),
98 f.
John, Saint, 99 [see Chrysostom]
Johnson, John G., 160
Johnson, Samuel, 4, 123–6, 137
Judas (Giuda), 104, 117
Julians, 164
Julio-Claudians, 75, 90
Julius, 15, 104, 164 [see Caesar]
Jung, Carl, 171
Juno, 34 f., 39 f., 49, 51, 75, 77–
83, 88, 91, 105, 115, 135, 153,
168

Jupiter (Jove), 30–4, 37–40, 46,
49, 51, 61 f., 74, 77–82, 91 ff.,
105, 115, 127, 135, 153, 164,
174
Juturna, 41, 63
Juvenal, 90, 120

K

Kamikos, 200
Kaufmann, R. J., 137
Keats, John, 9, 130
Keble, John, 131
Kermode, Frank, 157
Kitson, Michael, 151, 159 f.
Klein, Jerome, 159
Klingner, F., 25 f.
Knauer, Georg, 28, 41, 58, 61
Knight, Douglas, 137
Knight, W. F. Jackson, 159 f.,
182
Knossos, 163, 178, 186

L

Lacaena (Spartan), 105
Laconia, 193
Laelius, 75
Laertes, 31, 33
Laestrygonia(n), 142, 158
Landor, Walter Savage, 129 f.,
132 f.
Laocoön, 92
Laomedon, 76
Latin (lang., lit.), 6, 10 f., 19, 22,
59, 67, 119, 121 ff., 132, 167,
173, 176, 181 f.
Latini, Brunetto, 102
Latinus, (King), 87, 153, 173,
175
Latium (Latin), 38 f., 54 ff., 64 ff.,
81 f., 99, 150 f., 154, 173
Latona, 150
Laughton, E., 138
Lausus, 62, 73, 87

Index of Passages

AENEID

AENEID (continued)

ECLOGUES

GEORGICS

AUTHORS OTHER THAN VIRGIL

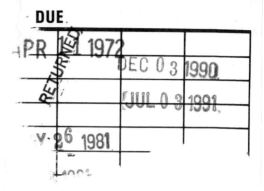